Increasing Productivity with pfs®

by Kevin R. Burton

TAB BOOKS Inc.
BLUE RIDGE SUMMIT PA 17214

This book is dedicated to people who serve people,
and who want to do their very best at it.

FIRST EDITION

FIRST PRINTING

Printed in the United States of America

Library of Congress Cataloging in Publication Data

Burton, Kevin R.
Increasing productivity with PFS.
Includes index.
1. Microcomputers—Programming. 2. Computer programs.
I. Title. II. Title: Increasing productivity with P.F.S.
QA76.6.B874 1984 001.64'2 84-8793
ISBN 0-8306-0789-7
ISBN 0-8306-1789-2 (pbk.)

Contents

Introduction

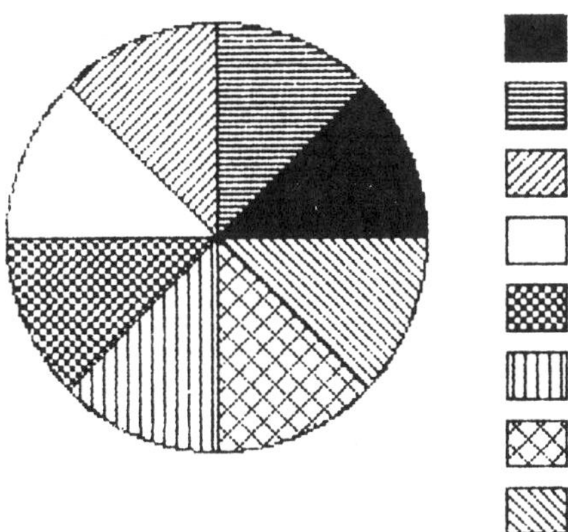

Many of us see and hear about computers and feel strangely left out. For them to be so popular, there must be something to them, but where should we begin? It all seems so overwhelming. We know that computers can handle large quantities of information, do complicated math, and send bills, but we don't know if they are for us. If we think they might be, we must try to figure out the differences between the $87 model and the $3000 one. As soon as we hear about bytes of RAM *(Random-Access Memory),* ROM *(Read-Only Memory),* and storage capacity, we want to run away.

Still we press on. We want to do the best job we can. We want to improve our efficiency. We want a machine to do our repetitive, boring, and mechanical tasks and leave us more time for creative work. We are determined to learn enough about computers to find out what it will take for a microcomputer to do some of the things we want it to do.

Walking into a computer store and listening to a litany on the salesman's microcomputer compared to the competition's model is *not* the best way to begin. That would be like walking into a car dealership and listening to a comparison of horsepower, torque, and performance specifications. Sure, they are important, but only after you have decided the purpose of your vehicle.

This book is designed to serve as a "how-to" for those who want to have access to the most up-to-date productivity tools without knowing the ins and outs of computers or computer languages. It is for people or organizations who write a significant quantity of letters, keep track of a large number of files and records, manipulate numbers, or prepare reports, charts, and graphs. It is about a set of programs from Software Publishing Corporation called PFS (Personal Filing System) that can help you do any or all of these tasks more efficiently.

Any microcomputer that will operate PFS will allow you to use the tools described herein. Currently, the entire PFS series will operate on the Apple *II*e and *II*c, and on IBM PC and its compatibles, such as Columbia, COMPAQ, Cornona PC, Eagle PC, and Panasonic Sr. Partner. It also runs on the hard disk version of the IBM PC—the IBM PC/XT. Several other microcomputers will operate only some of the PFS program modules. Those PFS program modules always include *PFS:File* and *PFS:Report*. The computers that currently operate at least two, although not all, of the modules are the Apple Macintosh, Texas Instruments Professional Computer, Tandy Model 2000, TRS-80 Models III and 4, Apple III, Digital Rainbow, HP 150, Gavilan Mobile, Chameleon, Hyperion, and IBM PCjr. As other computer systems with sufficient power become popular and as the program conversions are completed by the staff at Software Publishing Corporation, the series will also be made available for them.

This book is also applicable for the IBM Assistant™ series of programs. IBM has contracted with Software Publishing Corporation, and both companies hold the copyright for the programs distributed as IBM Filing Assistant, Reporting Assistant, Writing Assistant, and Graphing Assistant. The Planning Assistant will be IBM's version of the expected spreadsheet program.

Some very minor modifications have been made in converting the PFS series into the IBM Assistant series. For example, to maintain consistency with other IBM programs, the ENTER key is used to continue operations in addition to the F10 key. Provisions have also been made to support IBM's multicolor printer. Finally, the IBM Writing Assistant combines the *PFS:Write* and *PFS:Proof* programs in one package.

All of the techniques, procedures, templates (forms), and descriptions of the programs shown in this book will work equally well for the IBM Assistant Series and for the PFS programs. Since Software Publishing Corporation's versions of PFS were available first, and for simplicity's sake, all of the programs will be referred to by their original names throughout the text of this book.

Personal Filing System is currently comprised of six modules, each of which can be purchased separately: *PFS:File*, *PFS:Report*, *PFS:Graph*, *PFS:Write*, *PFS:Proof*, and *PFS:Access*. At least one more program, a spreadsheet program *PFS:Plan*, will be released in the fall of 1984. Each program is supplied on a disk that looks like a small record and supplies the computer with the instruction code that allows you to turn a microcomputer into a powerful productivity tool. All the user has to do is insert the disk into the disk drive and follow the excellent user's manuals that accompany the program. Once the disk has been inserted into the computer and has spun for several seconds, the program is loaded into the computer's memory. You can use it for many applications. The information that you create, such as letters and filing forms, are then stored on data disks that you supply. There is no limit to the number of data disks that the programs can use. All os the programs have similar methods of operation, so much of what you learn for one program will transfer to other programs in the series, helping you master them even more quickly. The six program modules of PFS are as follows:

PFS:Write. A word processor.

A word processor allows words to be displayed on the video screen before being printed on paper. Its advantage is that it allows the user to bring together a final version before committing it to paper. Corrections are easily made—paragraphs and sentences and words can be moved, and documents may be stored on disk for future use.

PFS:File. A database manager.

A database manager may be thought of as a sophisticated filing system. It is unlike a traditional card index, which may be referenced in only one manner. Usually, entries are filed alphabetically, and it is up to us to determine the category we filed the desired material under. Questions like, "Did I file that under 'automobile,' 'car,' or 'transportation'?" are humorous reminders of the inefficiency of traditional filing systems. Typically, too, we must remember a person's last name in order to find his address or telephone number. Remembering a person's first name does us little good. *PFS:File* allows the user to create his/her own forms that can be cross referenced in any number of ways. With PFS you can search for all of the people named "Connie," or people who live in Kansas, or salesmen from the XYZ Company. Recently, Software Publishing Corporation has even begun to sell their "Solutions" packages, which are forms for frequently used applications such as inventory, payroll, and tickler files. Purchasing a "Solutions" package, usually for less than $25, makes the process of setting up a system even less painful by removing most of the planning phase. However, if you rely on "prepackaged" forms, you may not get exactly what you want or the versatility you need. To utilize the program to its full potential, you must know how to use it, and you must plan adequately.

PFS:Report. A report generator.

A report generator turns out reports using your data. *PFS:Report* manipulates data from *PFS:File*. For example, if you used *PFS:File* to enter all bills received (a kind of accounts payable system), you might want a listing of all bills by date, and want to know your total liability. *PFS:Report* could summarize that information. It could alphabetize by payee or group information numerically, sorting by zip code or telephone area code and exchange.

PFS:Graph. A business graphics package.

PFS:Graph allows the user to graph reports and charts from *PFS:File* and from spreadsheet programs such as *PFS:Plan, VisiCalc*, and *SuperCalc*. We all know the impact a chart or graph can have in a report or presentation. *PFS:Graph* can create pie charts, bar graphs, and line graphs to give that professional look to your presentations. Different kinds of printouts are possible on different kinds of printers and plotters, and all can be integrated with *PFS:Write* to produce a completed document that does not have to be pasted together or submitted in separate stacks of text and graphics.

PFS:Proof. A proofreading program.

PFS:Proof checks the spelling of the documents created by *PFS:Write*, or any other ASCII files. It is a "single pass" proofer that corrects misspellings once they are identified. The program uses its 100,000-word dictionary to suggest correct spellings and allows the user to update the dictionary with words he/she uses often. *PFS:Proof* also identifies irregular capitalizations and repeated words. It is very thorough, yet also very fast.

PFS:Access. A link to telecommunications services.

PFS:Access allows the user to painlessly hook up with electronic mail services such as MCI and others. The program will dial, enter passwords, and provide all of the proper *handshaking* that enables effective use of many of the telecommunications services commercially available. It is able to send documents previously prepared by *PFS:Write* and *PFS:Report*, keeping connection time (and cost) to a minimum. There is also a feature that allows for the *encryption*, or scrambling, of messages so that only those with the correct password can view them.

Software Publishing Corporation has scheduled a seventh PFS program module for release in September of 1984. This final package is:

PFS:Plan. An electronic spreadsheet.

PFS:Plan provides a means of manipulating numbers. It is a spreadsheet consisting of rows and columns. Mathematical manipulations can be carried out on the rows, columns, or any *cell* block designated by a row and column. *PFS:Plan* is useful for setting up accounting applications. You can also set up various "what if" scenarios, where the program can quickly recalculate a projection to take into account, for example, inflation rising 1 percent more. One of its chief selling points will be the ease with which graphics displays of the calculations can be shown by interacting with *PFS:Graph*.

Each of the PFS modules works nicely by itself and is competitive with similar programs on the market. Each is designed to be *user-friendly*, which means there are menus to choose from; there are help messages available, and the user does not need to know programming or have special knowledge about computers in order to successfully use the programs. User-friendliness also means that the program is forgiving, so pressing one wrong key will not *break* (stop) it or cause data to be lost.

The real advantage of the Personal Filing System set of programs, however, is how they work together. Individually, each program will satisfactorily complete the task it was intended to perform. Together, they are almost all of the software you will ever need to bring computer age efficiency into your office. I say *almost* in recognition of the modern office's financial/accounting needs. It is my recommendation that you discuss your accounting system with your accountant and together create a system that will avoid any future incompatibilities. In all probability, a "spreadsheet" program such as *VisiCalc*, *SuperCalc*, or the new PFS spreadsheet, *PFS:Plan*, that allows individual financial modeling can be set up to provide ease of use and good accountability, and double as your financial statement. *PFS:Graph*, as mentioned earlier, will be able to give pictorial summaries of all of your statistics, including income and expense reports. Chapter 8 provides an overview of how the program modules can work together, plus some hands-on tips for using them.

Using the PFS series of programs is not the only way to organize and streamline office work. Some will argue, and quite correctly, that they are not the most powerful programs available. Others may say (although I have never heard it) that there are simpler programs to operate. PFS provides a very workable balance between power and ease of use. Few compromises have to be made in either area. No, using PFS is not the only way to computerize an office. But is is one good way to bring effective productivity to the office.

In order to adequately illustrate the applications of these PFS productivity tools, we will apply them to an imaginary nonprofit organization. Agencies typically have a wide variety of needs that are quite similar to the needs of businesses in general. If you are a member of a social service agency, look into the operations of your organization to see if a computer and these programs could be of use. If you run a small business, you will find that many of the solutions in this book will be directly applicable to a business setting. Even if you are a single employee within a large company, you will surely have many ideas of how Personal Filing System will turn your desk into a more efficient and productive work station.

What You Can Do with a Computer and PFS

Chapter 1

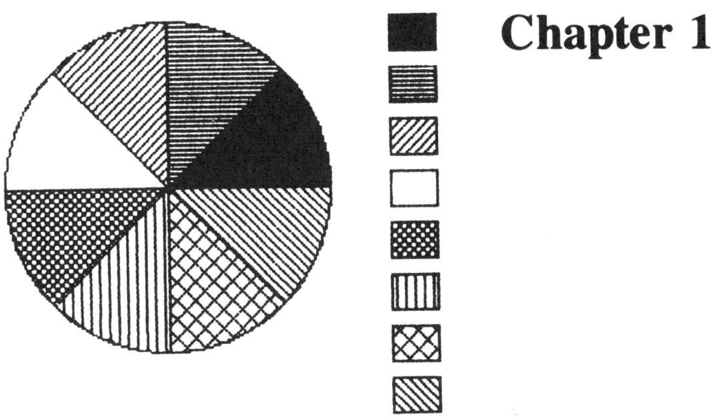

Many people approach the concept of computerizing an organization asking "What can a computer do for me?" As easy as it would be to recite numerous examples of successful office computerizations, one must step back and realize that the question is essentially an inappropriate one. First of all, it assumes a passive stance, one of having a computer come in and take over a lot of work, which will *not* come to pass. The process is really much more of an active one. The whole process is better conceptualized in this question—"What can *I* do with a computer?"

The things that you do now are mainly the things that you will do with a computer. A computer is a tool that provides the opportunity to do many of those things faster and more efficiently. It may even provide extra time for you to do some new things, because of the speed at which it operates. Probably many of the new things you will start will also be done in cooperation with a computer and further increase your efficiency. For example, if you have analyzed numbers for years, you will continue to analyze; however because of the lightning speed of the computer, after you have used the computer to organize and calculate, you may also have time to branch out and display those numerical relationships with graphs and charts. So the computer will not simply generate charts for you. You will continue to analyze numbers, but with more efficiency, because you'll have additional tools, in this case charts, that quickly put all those numbers in perspective.

Another question that frequently follows "What can a computer do for me?" is "Which computer should I buy?" That question is an appropriate, even necessary one. However, it should not be the first or second question you ask. First, you must determine what you are going to do with a computer. After assessing your needs, you need to identify the *software* (programs) that will allow you to reach those goals. Finally, you must identify the *hardware* (equipment) that will operate the programs you need; then you can balance the cost/effectiveness issues and come to an informed decision.

There are many issues to consider, and few of

them are black and white. The procedures I will describe and solutions to many of the common business problems I will provide are not the only ones that exist. But they provide one approach, and one that many others have tested. There are approximately 650,000 owners of PFS program modules. There would certainly not be so many people buying these programs if they did not provide solutions to problems. Nor would there be so many people buying them if they were not fairly easy to operate. You may already own one or more of the modules and be wondering what you can do with the other program modules. Or you may be wondering how to maximize your effectiveness with the program that you own. Whatever your point of access, I hope that this book will be another tool for your toolbox; a tool that gets you out of a jam or two and helps improve your effectiveness on the job.

Some of the most common ways in which offices can utilize the tools of a microcomputer and productivity are listed here.

INFORMATION MANAGEMENT

Every organization must determine how it is going to manage mailing lists. One way is to have staff or volunteers type them with typewriters. Besides being potentially inaccurate, typing on a typewriter is an activity that will take people and time that could be spent on more creative tasks. Another solution to the mailing list problem is to purchase some kind of addressing machine from an office supply company. The cost of such a machine can easily be as much as a personal computer would cost, while the continued costs of metal or plastic plates could soon create a white elephant. Additionally, the way tray after tray must be fed into such a machine severely limits its flexibility. Duplicate name plates must often be made for addresses that appear on more than one mailing list. Also, all but the most expensive plates eventually wear out.

PFS:File will handle your mailing lists as just one part of its repertoire. All of the information that you will ever need to recall (up to 3000 different storage fields) can be stored on a form that you design. A *field*, described more thoroughly in Chapter 3, is an item that can be sorted, such as City or State. A single entry into the data base can be used in a number of ways. If Jerry Cole is a member of the organization, a member of the Board of Directors, and a member of the finance committee, his name need only be entered once, not three times. The computer will automatically select and print the members of the lists that you specify. If you want to send a mailing to members who have not yet contributed to this year's fundraising drive, it is as easy as specifying the criteria for selection (contribution = 0). Self adhesive labels are one of the easiest and most common ways of getting the printed name and address to the envelope. These labels come on continuous sheets of paper, usually have six lines available, and are quite inexpensive. You can also have the printer print directly onto the envelopes, one at a time. Letter quality type put directly onto an envelope creates a more personal image, but the amount of paper handling required to feed each envelope into the printer reduces the speed of throughput.

Other information you might want to include on the general membership form besides name, address, and committee membership would be contribution history, general interests, other organization memberships, and interest in/time available for volunteering.

Any number of different forms can be developed using the *PFS:File* program. You might want to keep a "Do-Doing-Done" file in order to track your current and future projects as well as to catalog your accomplishments. Such a file would normally include milestones for completion of tasks and could be used to notify you when a project is behind schedule. When funding time comes around, you will have an accurate record of the events that were held and the number of people who benefitted from each activity without searching through old calendars, notebooks, and brochures. If your organization schedules films or speaker's bureaus, a file can be developed to schedule those dates, search for materials that are overdue, and remind participants before they are scheduled to make an appearance. Chapter 2, *PFS:File*—Organizing Creativity, provides a thorough description of the uses of *PFS:File* and hints for its efficient use.

WORD PROCESSING

Word processing is the process of typing words on a computer keyboard, having them displayed on the video screen, modifying them, and, finally, printing them. Words may be changed, paragraphs may be moved and thoughts may be inserted or deleted until the document is ready for printing. When you are satisfied with what you have written, a command is given to have the printer print the document. The document can then be saved on disk as a record of your correspondence, or for use and modification at a later time. If you send a number of letters that are similar in nature, such as "Thank you for your inquiry about our organization . . ." or "This is to confirm your reservation for the film . . . " the benefits of word processing can really start to pay off. The shell of the stored letter can be recalled, displayed on screen, and then adapted for that particular use. Sometimes that use will be no more than inserting the name and address of the recipient and time and place of the reservation.

If you use individualized form letters, the information needed to fill in the blanks can actually be provided by *PFS:File*. A letter that looks personal but human hands touched only to sign can be routinely generated. Letters in the following format can save large amounts of time and not offend the recipient. Figure 1-1 shows how an individualized form letter looks when it is saved on a disk.

The same letter, with the "blanks" filled in will actually look like the display in Fig. 1-2 when it has been printed and sent to the recipient. In this example, "Ext." allows for the handling of name extensions such as "Jr." or "III." The "T" in parentheses (T) tells the word processor to treat the provided information as "text" and to adjust the length of the spaces used so as to fit it properly into the body of the letter. More hints about the formation of *PFS:File* forms and *PFS:Write* letters will be presented in the final chapter, Bringing It All Together—Creatively.

In addition to saving time, the information stored on the disk may pay benefits at a later time. All of the people who borrowed films could be sent a letter like the one in Fig. 1-3. With a computer,

```
May 30, 1984

*Fname* *Lname**Ext(, Jr.)*
*L2 (T)*
*L3*
*L4 (T)* *Zip*

Dear *Title (Dr.,Ms.)* *Lname (T)*:

     This letter is to confirm your reservation to use the
film *Film name(T)* on *Date(T)* at *Time(T)*.  If you are
unable to meet this commitment, please notify us at the
earliest possible time.

Sincerely,



David J. Wagner
Executive Assistant
```

Fig. 1-1. Form letter "shell" with spaces for name, address, and other information.

```
May 30, 1984

Raymond A. Collins
73 Top of the Hill Drive
Cascade, MD 17214

Dear Mr. Collins:

     This letter is to confirm your reservation to use the
film ONLY HUMAN on June 15,1984 at 2:00 p.m.  If you are
unable to meet this commitment, please notify us at the
earliest possible time.

Sincerely,



David J. Wagner
Executive Assistant
```

Fig. 1-2. Individualized form letter with information inserted.

such routine follow-up is extremely easy. In fact, the addition of a microcomputer and use of the strategies suggested in this book will probably pay for the cost of the computer within two years, just from improved penetration and follow-up to the members and recipients of an agency's services. Small business applications can expect results at least as favorable.

One of the newest additions to the PFS family of programs, *PFS:Proof,* can act as an electronic proofreader. It compares all the words in your correspondence with its 100,000 word dictionary. Any words that do not match the dictionary are highlighted for possible change. Unlike many spelling checkers, *PFS:Proof* provides the correct spelling in a single step rather than requiring the user to look up the word manually or use a separate command to provide alternative spellings. Words that are not in the dictionary but are in your specific vocabulary may be added to the dictionary at any time. As great as that is, that is not all. *PFS:Proof* also checks for irregular capitalizations and repeated words. All corrections can be made with a single keystroke. Chapter 5, *PFS:Write*—Writing Without Drudgery, and Chapter 6, *PFS:Proof*—Avoiding Mistakes, detail the uses and capabilities of word processing and text editing.

REPORT PRODUCTION

PFS:Report allows you to sort, add, subtract, multiply, and divide the numbers and other information that you have stored in *PFS:File.* If you are recording contributions received from members, for example, a quick run of *PFS:Report* can total the dollars you have received, subtract that figure from the amount pledged, and tell you the percentage of pledges received. It can tell you how often each film has been borrowed and count the number of people who have seen it at your showings.

Inventory control is another excellent application for *PFS:File* and *PFS:Report.* These programs can track your inventory of pamphlets, for example, and tell you which items should be reprinted or reordered. You can tell the quantity of each item that was distributed and find the grand total of all materials distributed during the month, quarter, or year.

Have you ever wondered about your penetration into different zip code areas? *PFS:Report* can tell you all of this and more. As long as you can gather the information, and include the proper spaces in the *PFS:File* forms for the information, *PFS:Report* can manipulate and summarize the data. The program is capable of deriving new data from existing data. For example, a new bit of information, let us say "response time," can be a calculation derived from subtracting the starting date of a project from the completion date.

An automatic function of *PFS:Report* is that of alphabetizing data and arranging it in numeric order. *PFS:Report* is very flexible in that it can provide reports from *PFS:File* sorted in as many different ways as you choose. One list of members alphabetized within zip code areas can be generated as quickly as a complete alphabetized membership list or a list of unpaid members. All of these reports, and more, can be generated from a single data file. See Chapter 3, *PFS:Report*—Selecting, Sorting, and Presenting Information for all of the ways that data for *PFS:File* can be listed and reported.

GRAPHIC SUMMARIES

PFS:Graph delivers the power of a sophisticated business package at a very reasonable price

```
May 1, 1985

*Fname* *Lname**Ext(, Jr.)*
*L2 (T)*
*L3*
*L4 (T)* *Zip*

Dear *Title (Dr.,Ms.)* *Lname (T)*:

     As one who has utilized the services provided by our
agency, you may want to consider supporting our agency by
becoming a member.  This support will allow us to be involved
in more projects, thereby helping even more people.

     Our organization is a certified 501 (c) 3, not-for-
profit organization and all contributions are tax deductible.
Please take a moment to consider this important opportunity.
A membership form is attached to the back of our
informational brochure.  A check may be enclosed, or
convenient credit information may be supplied in payment.

     We hope that you will decide to join.  Membership, of
course, is not necessary in order to receive the services of
our organization.  We hope that you will continue to utilize
our services.

Sincerely,


Kathryn R. Burton
Membership Chair
```

Fig. 1-3. Follow-up individualized form letter used to increase membership.

and in a very friendly format. Marshall McLuhan correctly observed that the manner in which information is presented is often more important than the actual information being transmitted. The art of persuasion, which comprises a good portion of our communications, can be dramatically enhanced by the proper visual cues. "Dog and pony shows" that sell ideas or make reports look better are not complete without a few charts or graphs.

PFS:Graph allows the user to print graphs on 8½ × 11-inch format or in 3 × 4-inch format or store graphs on the disk as "pictures" for the purpose of incorporating them directly into the body of a document. *PFS:Graph* is most frequently used to display data stored in *PFS:File*, but it can graph information you provide directly through the keyboard or even graph information from spreadsheet programs such as *VisiCalc* or *SuperCalc* created by other companies. The PFS spreadsheet will, of course, be made to interact with *PFS: Plan*.

PFS:Graph is a lot of fun to use, in addition to being useful. It supports bar charts, line graphs, and pie charts. Bar charts may be stacked on top of each other. Figures may be considered separately or in a cumulative fashion. Bar charts and line graphs may be used in the same chart. Information can be provided on monochrome or color displays. Chapter 4, *PFS'Graph*—Worth a Thousand Data Points, details the uses and limitations of this graphics package.

COMMUNICATION BY COMPUTER

Date communications is a field that is potentially useful to many organizations and businesses. Organizations that have satellite offices or different levels such as local, state, and national can benefit most significantly. An organization that has an advocacy function can often become involved in lobbying efforts in Washington, D.C. and in 50 state capitals. The accurate and timely exchange of information and the ability to communicate with the proper parties can often be the difference between success and failure. *PFS:Access* is a communications package that allows you, through the use of a modem, to connect your computer with the rest of the world. Complete documents created with *PFS:Write* on *PFS:Report* can be transmitted over telephone lines in a matter of seconds. Mass mail campaigns can be carried out automatically using MCI Mail or Western Union EasyLink, or even the U.S. Mail service.

Data communications is becoming the fastest growing area in microcomputers. Services such as The Source and CompuServe are becoming clearinghouses of tremendous amounts of information. Dow Jones provides stock information previously available only through large brokerage firms. Home banking and catalog shopping are becoming much more commonplace each month. Bulletin boards keep people with similar interests in touch without the annoyances of trying to catch people at home. *PFS:Access* makes dial-up and sign-on procedures quick and easy. Finally, and importantly, *PFS:-Access* provides data encryption to assure the privacy and security of your information. On-line connection charges and telephone bills are kept to a minimum because documents are created ahead of time and sent/received in a matter of a few seconds, and then read off line. Chapter 7, *PFS:Access*—Talking with the World, recounts the capabilities of this new telecommunications software.

COMPUTER CHOICES

As we begin to explore the capabilities of the PFS programs and consider applications for your own uses, it will be useful to consider the computer systems that will handle the information.

First of all, consider the importance of a system with built-in upper- and lowercase letter capabilities. All major systems currently being manufactured have upper- and lowercase capabilities. However, what if you get a terrific deal on an Apple *II* +, a system that did not come equipped with lowercase capabilities? Should you take it? I would say "No!" *PFS:File* will run on it as will *PFS:Report* and *Graph*. However, *PFS:Write* will not because that program even uses keys that are not on the Apple *II+* keyboard. With that system, everything is stored in uppercase letters on *PFS:File* and *PFS:Report*. All uppercase letters minimizes its effectiveness in merging information. Also, if it were to be used for mailing lists, it would cause envelopes and printed labels to have a definite "computer-generated" look.

Second, consider the cost-per-power-ratio of a system with two disk drives. Some misinformed advisors will tell you that the only function of a second disk drive is for the ease and convenience of making backups of your data. That statement may be true for some packages, such as some word processors or a BASIC programming language, but using *PFS:File* with a single disk drive system will definitely cause a loss of some of its power and capability—with every system mentioned. Single disk drive users will be able to use the *Disk Operating System (DOS)* supplied with their computer to make backup copies of their data by copying entire disks. They will not, however, be able to use the COPY command on *PFS:File* to copy a form design onto another data base. Nor will they be able to modify a form once it has been designed. Beyond that, we will learn that the capabilities of using other PFS modules in combination with *PFS:File* are severely limited or completely eliminated when trying to use a single disk drive. The Apple Macintosh is the only system that should be functional with the use of a single disk drive. However, the space available on a single disk drive is severely limited because a large amount of space is required for the system files. Functionally, the size of the data files that can be manipulated will be limited.

How Much to Invest?

I realize that cost is an important consideration to almost all organizations. A comparison is provided (Fig. 1-4) to compare costs of purchasing a system that is capable or will soon be able to run the entire series of PFS programs, including the capability of integrating information from one program onto another. Prices in the computer industry are

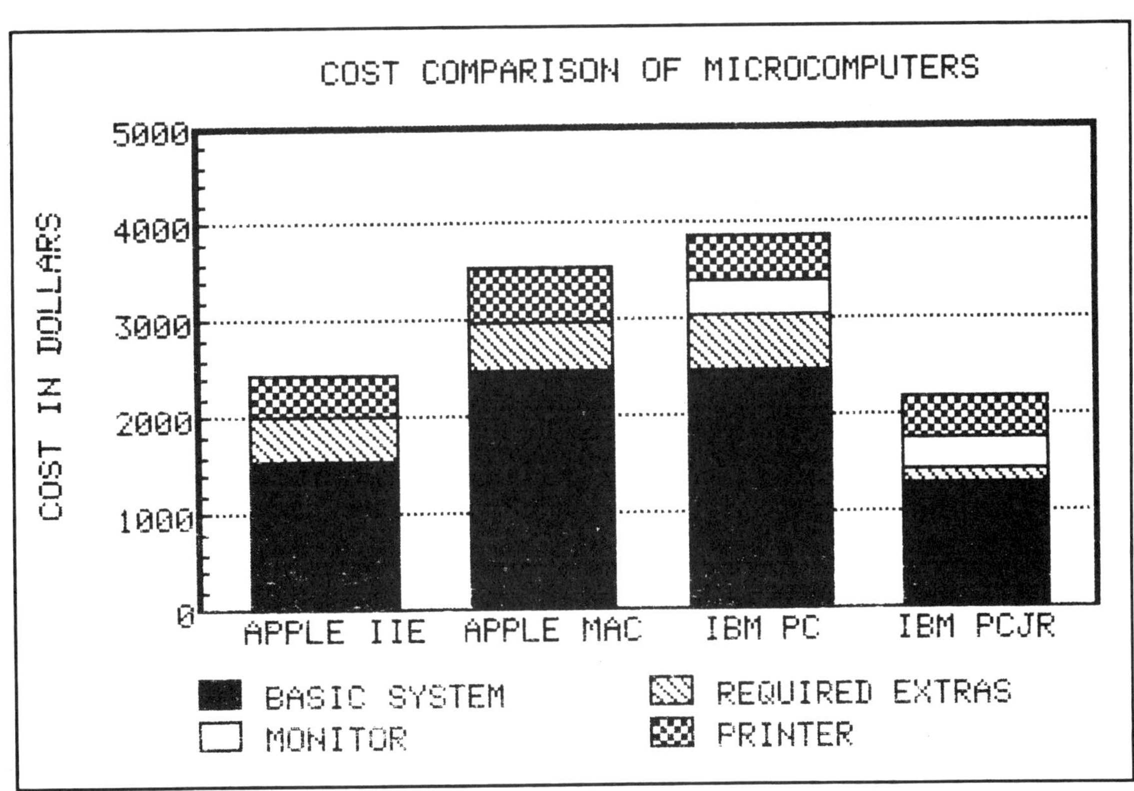

Fig. 1-4. Chart illustrating cost comparison of popular microcomputers. Prices subject to change.

far from stable. Use Fig. 1-4 only for rough comparison. Check with dealers to find actual prices available. Remember that the price of a system can be expected to be depreciated over a period of time. Curtailing future expandability in order to save a few hundred dollars is not a recommended procedure. In this, and future comparisons, IBM PC will also represent TI Professional, Tandy Model 2000, COMPAQ and other "IBM compatible" computers. Generally speaking, they are in the approximate price range and have features comparable to the PC. IBM was there first and was creator of the standard by which all of the "compatible" systems are compared.

This graph (developed using *PFS:Graph*) includes all of the hardware components required to have the potential of a fully operational PFS series. The base price of a computer system can be very misleading. The current list price of $1295 for the IBM PCjr, for example, is not so attractive when you learn that if you want to use it, you must pay extra. Why? No DOS (Disk Operating System) is included and the DOS is essential to use the disk system at all! (Oh, you want to use the disk drive?) No cables are included to attach the computer to a monitor. (Do you need to see what you're doing?) Some systems include the monitor in the base price. That is both the case with the Apple Macintosh and, effectively, with the Apple *II*e if you purchase their "Starter Package," which includes a monochrome display. When they are not included in the base price, cables and DOSes fall into the "Required Extras" category, as do second disk drives.

Printers in Fig. 1-4 were estimated as a moderately priced dot matrix unit at about $500. Letter quality printers can easily cost three times as much

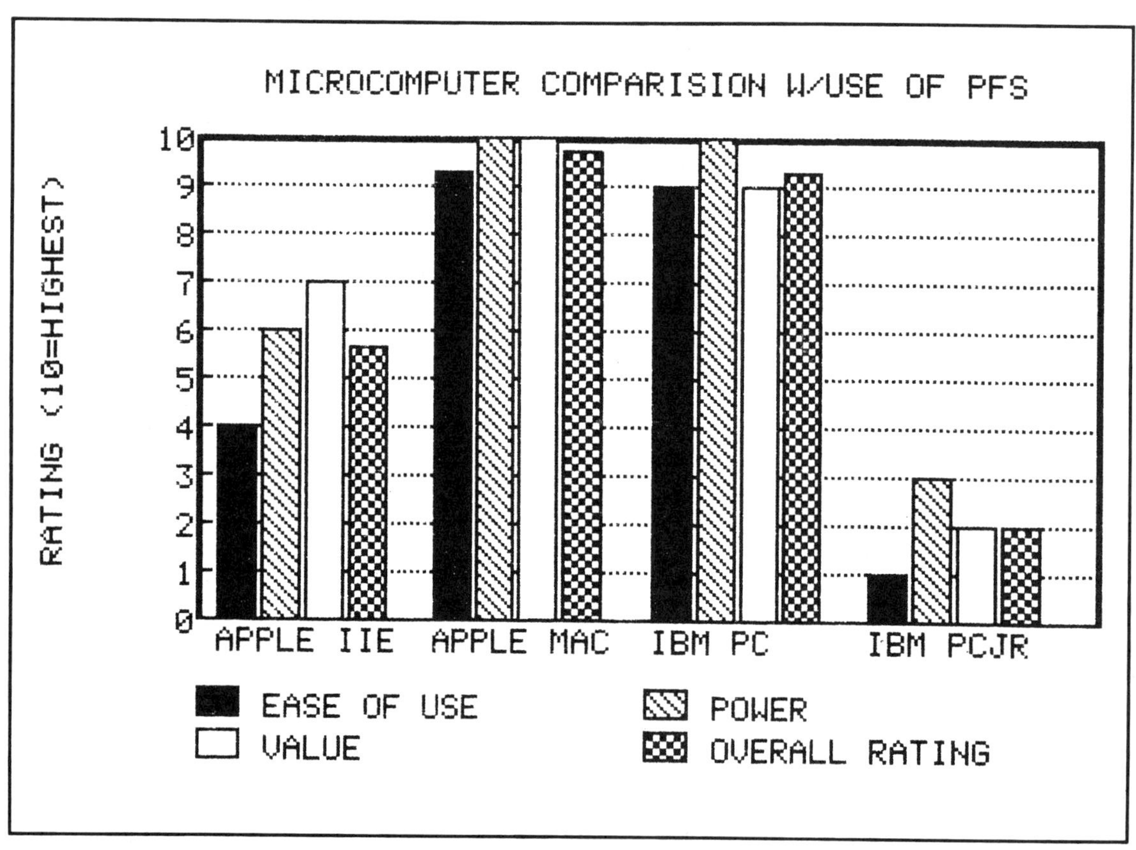

Fig. 1-5. Subjective microcomputer performance comparison.

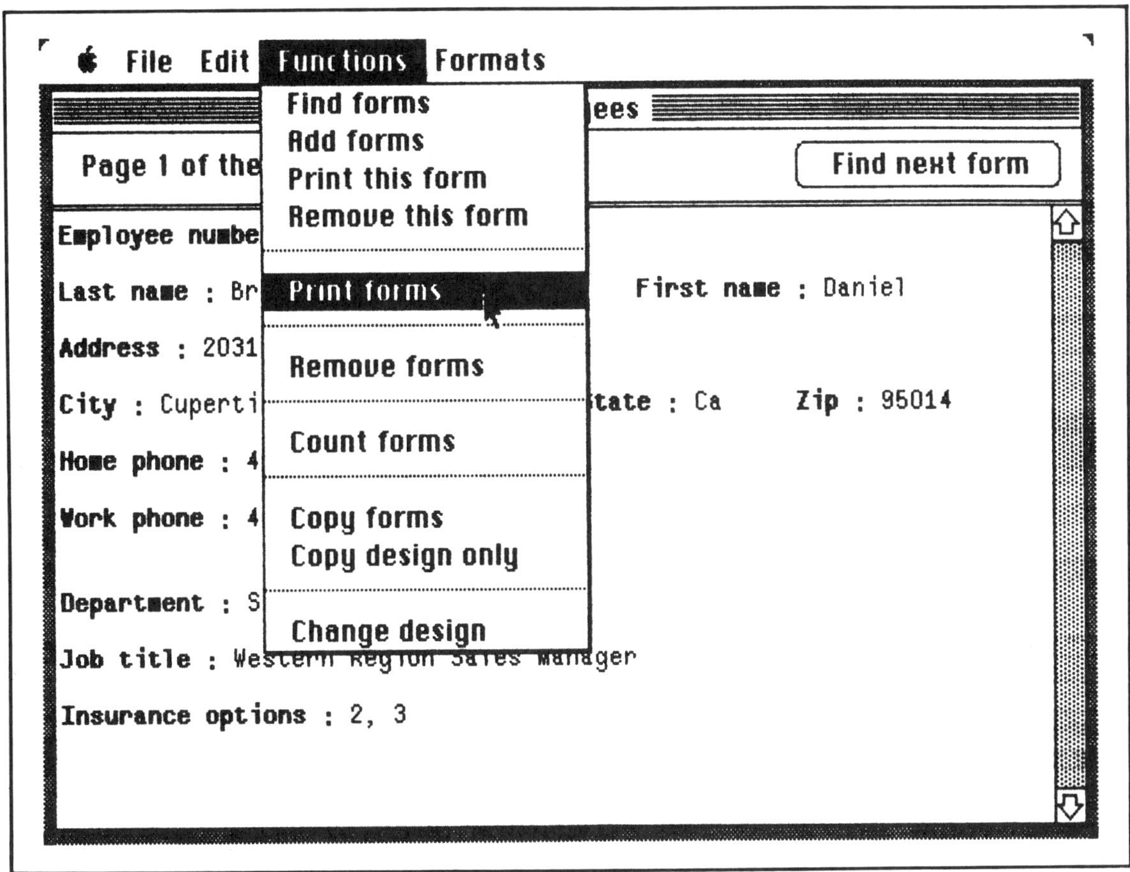

Fig. 1-6. Macintosh pull-down menu for *PFS:File*.

and more. Please refer to the Printers in Perspective section later in this chapter for more details on printers.

Which Is Best with PFS?

Figure 1-5, "Microcomputer Comparison with Use of PFS," illustrates a subjective rating on three scales, with a fourth representing an overall average rating of the ability to utilize the PFS series of productivity software. (This graph was also produced using *PFS:Graph.*) It is clear to see that for full implementation and ease of use, the Apple Macintosh and IBM PC set themselves apart from the pack. It is also clear that the Apple *II*e/c provide good value for the price.

In the "Ease of Use" category, Apple Macintosh has a slight edge over the IBM PC and is miles ahead of the other systems. Pull-down menus, such as the one shown in Fig. 1-6, and use of the mouse as a cursor controller are Macintosh features that create a kind of intuitive ease of use not matched by conventional systems. Function keys on IBM PC and compatible systems have many advantages over systems without function keys. Pull-down menus and the mouse controller for the Macintosh are different, but roughly comparable to function keys in ease of use. The lack of a separate numeric keypad is a minus for the Macintosh, but is available as an option. Those who deal with lots of numbers will find one invaluable. Additionally, Macintosh topped IBM and the others in this category in such performance features as modifying forms. The process of adding a field to a simple *PFS:File*, for example, could take 10 minutes on the Apple *II*e, 6 minutes on an IBM PC, and be completed in about four minutes on the Macintosh, without the use of two disk drives, and without extensive reading and writing back and forth between the drives. The Apple *II*e/c is functional, but awkward. Without function keys or a mouse, a lot of CTRL key sequences must be memorized. Program disks must be left in the first drive in order to operate *PFS:Write*, whereas the IBM PC does not need the program disk resident in the disk drive after it has been loaded unless you want to access a help screen. The IBM PCjr's standard keyboard renders it almost useless as a word processor. Function keys are used through combinations of keystrokes. Displays on the screen are difficult to read, sometimes losing the first letter of a field where the screen begins to wrap around.

The second category, "Power," reveals that the PC and Macintosh are both able to utilize the full range of features available, and are essentially equal in their capabilities. The Apple *II*e was marked down for limited disk space, slow input and output operations, and its inability to use two data disks without the program disk in the drive, the latter slowing the speed and ease of making backups. The PCjr gets marked down for its lack of expandability and ineffective screen displays. Its memory constraints limit the size of spreadsheets that can be used, and therefore the uses of *PFS:Graph*.

The third category, "Value," attempts to deal with the very real issue for some—the alternative of an inexpensive system or no system. Given that the system may be less than super easy to use, and may have some limited capabilities, the value per dollar nod in this subjective evaluation goes clearly for the Apple *II*e/c over the IBM PCjr. These categories, however, should probably be taken with a grain of salt. In today's competitive marketplace, the features and prices of these systems will be in continual flux, and ultimately many decisions will be made on the basis of personal preference. It is well known, for example, that there is a new keyboard in the wings for the IBM PCjr. With a better keyboard and more memory, the scales may have to be significantly revised.

The fourth category, "Overall Rating," is simply a numerical average of the previous three categories. It is the single rating that attempts to reflect all aspects of the systems available.

PRINTERS IN PERSPECTIVE

The people responsible for the operation of an effective office must carefully consider the type of printer that is to be used. The decision is second in importance only to the selection of the computer. *Letter quality* printers are so named because their output is of a high quality, similar to typewriter print. Many letter quality printers produce output that is camera-ready for even the most demanding of requirements. Typically, they use a thimble, wheel, or ball that strikes a ribbon and places text on paper. A sample of the quality of output of a letter quality printer is shown in Fig. 1-7. Letter quality printers are recommended for applications that require substantial amounts of personal contact or require a preparation of materials that are to be photographed and printed by an offset press or mimeograph machine. Their chief drawbacks are that they are slow by computer printer standards, quite expensive, and noisy. The less expensive they are, the slower they are. Also, letter quality printers usually sacrifice graphics capabilities and can print only letters and numbers, not charts and graphs.

Most letter quality printers have friction paper feed mechanisms that allow single sheets of stationery to be fed through the printing surface. Some have options that allow for *pin* or *tractor feed* paper feeding mechanisms. Tractor fed paper has an additional margin containing two perforated and detachable strips of paper with sprocket holes that feed the paper through the printer. The advantage of a tractor feed mechanism is that no one has to manually feed sheet after sheet of paper into the printer when large quantities of letters are to be automatically processed. For correspondence, your letterhead can be printed on continuous form paper.

Another option for a printer selection is a *dot matrix* printer. Rather than having letters forged and striking a ribbon, this kind of printer forms

```
ABCDEFGHIJKLMNOPQRSTUVWXYZ[®]©_°abcdefghijklmnopqrstuvwxyz§¶†™
ABCDEFGHIJKLMNOPQRSTUVWXYZ[®]©_°abcdefghijklmnopqrstuvwxyz§¶†™
ABCDEFGHIJKLMNOPQRSTUVWXYZ[®]©_°abcdefghijklmnopqrstuvwxyz§¶†™
ABCDEFGHIJKLMNOPQRSTUVWXYZ[®]©_°abcdefghijklmnopqrstuvwxyz§¶†™
ABCDEFGHIJKLMNOPQRSTUVWXYZ[®]©_°abcdefghijklmnopqrstuvwxyz§¶†™
ABCDEFGHIJKLMNOPQRSTUVWXYZ[®]©_°abcdefghijklmnopqrstuvwxyz§¶†™
ABCDEFGHIJKLMNOPQRSTUVWXYZ[®]©_°abcdefghijklmnopqrstuvwxyz§¶†™
ABCDEFGHIJKLMNOPQRSTUVWXYZ[®]©_°abcdefghijklmnopqrstuvwxyz§¶†™
ABCDEFGHIJKLMNOPQRSTUVWXYZ[®]©_°abcdefghijklmnopqrstuvwxyz§¶†™
ABCDEFGHIJKLMNOPQRSTUVWXYZ[®]©_°abcdefghijklmnopqrstuvwxyz§¶†™
ABCDEFGHIJKLMNOPQRSTUVWXYZ[®]©_°abcdefghijklmnopqrstuvwxyz§¶†™
```

Fig. 1-7. Sample of letter quality print.

different matrices of individual dots that collectively form letters and numbers. The range of quality of type produced ranges from poor *draft* to quite good *correspondence* quality. Some dot matrix printers have a switch that can be set to draft quality for rapid printing and correspondence quality for denser, more readable characters. Some can print in different colors. Almost all can print in different fonts, such as pica, compressed (narrower), expanded (wider), and double strike (darker). Most dot matrix printers are capable of fairly impressive graphs and charts. The dot matrix printers that the PFS series currently support for *PFS:Graph* are printers that have the same printer control codes as IBM Graphics, Epson, IDS, Okidata, NEC, C.Itoh, and Apple Printers. Dot matrix printers are less expensive as a class (although the most expensive dot matrix printers are more expensive than the least expensive letter quality models) and print much more rapidly. Figure 1-8 illustrates dot matrix printer output.

The Imagewriter printer, supplied with the Apple Macintosh, is capable of some of the most astonishing graphics outputs to be seen yet. (See Fig. 1-9.) A printer like that could add a boost for design of pamphlets and posters.

Thermal printers require special paper for printing and are typically of poor quality. However, the Panasonic Sr. Partner includes a thermal printer right in the case of the IBM PC compatible system so that printing capabilities become as portable as the system.

```
:;<=>?@ABCDEFGHIJKLMNOPQRSTUVWXYZ[\]^_`abcdefghijklm
^_`abcdefghijklmnopqrstuvwxyz{|}~▦ !"#$%&'()*+,-./01
"#$%&'()*+,-./0123456789:;<=>?@ABCDEFGHIJKLMNOPQRSTU
FGHIJKLMNOPQRSTUVWXYZ[\]^_`abcdefghijklmnopqrstuvwxy
jklmnopqrstuvwxyz{|}~▦ !"#$%&'()*+,-./0123456789:;<=
./0123456789:;<=>?@ABCDEFGHIJKLMNOPQRSTUVWXYZ[\]^_`a
RSTUVWXYZ[\]^_`abcdefghijklmnopqrstuvwxyz{|}~▦ !"#$%
vwxyz{|}~▦ !"#$%&'()*+,-./0123456789:;<=>?@ABCDEFGHI
:;<=>?@ABCDEFGHIJKLMNOPQRSTUVWXYZ[\]^_`abcdefghijklm
^_`abcdefghijklmnopqrstuvwxyz{|}~▦ !"#$%&'()*+,-./01
"#$%&'()*+,-./0123456789:;<=>?@ABCDEFGHIJKLMNOPQRSTU
FGHIJKLMNOPQRSTUVWXYZ[\]^_`abcdefghijklmnopqrstuvwxy
jklmnopqrstuvwxyz{|}~▦ !"#$%&'()*+,-./0123456789:;<=
./0123456789:;<=>?@ABCDEFGHIJKLMNOPQRSTUVWXYZ[\]^_`a
```

Fig. 1-8. Sample of dot matrix sample print.

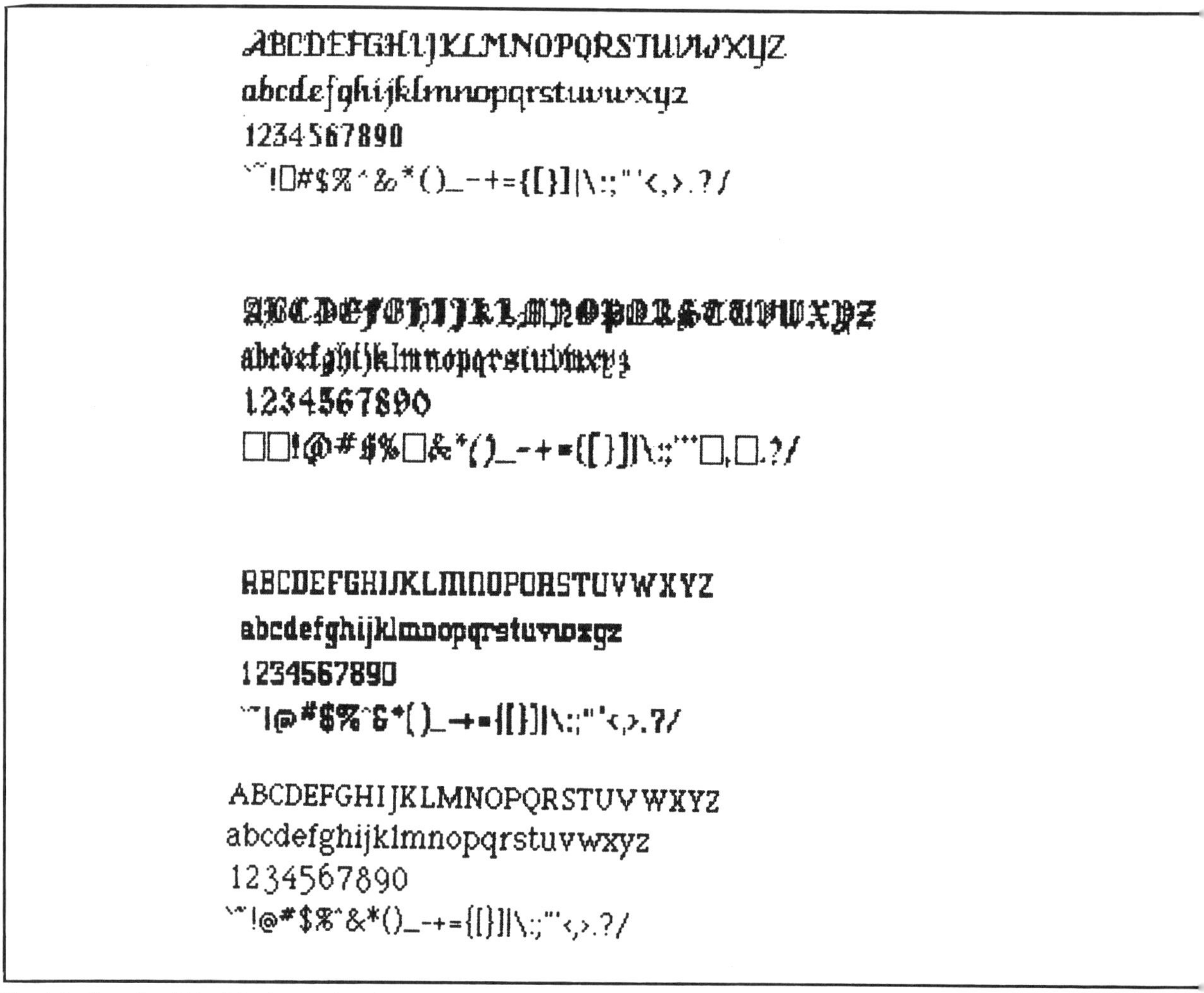

ABCDEFGHIJKLMNOPQRSTUVWXYZ
abcdefghijklmnopqrstuvwxyz
1234567890
`~!□#$%^&*()_-+={[}]|\:;"'<,>.?/

ABCDEFGHIJKLMNOPQRSTUVWXYZ
abcdefghijklmnopqrstuvwxyz
1234567890
□□!@#$%□&*()_-+={[}]|\:;"'□,□.?/

ABCDEFGHIJKLMNOPQRSTUVWXYZ
abcdefghijklmnopqrstuvwxyz
1234567890
`~!@#$%^&*()_-+={[}]|\:;"'<,>.?/

ABCDEFGHIJKLMNOPQRSTUVWXYZ
abcdefghijklmnopqrstuvwxyz
1234567890
`~!@#$%^&*()_-+={[}]|\:;"'<,>.?/

Fig. 1-9. Sample of Macintosh sample print.

Ink jet printers are a new innovation that pretty successfully combines speed and quality by using a spray of ink that eliminates the look of tightly packed dots found in dot matrix printers. The $500 Hewlett-Packard "Thinkjet" print quality is shown in Fig. 1-10. The printer addresses particular locations just as the dot matrix models do, but ink fills in the gaps between the dots. An additional advantage to ink jet printers is that they are very quiet, a factor that can be critical in some offices. New developments in this technology have brought ink jet printers into the cost range of dot matrix printers.

Laser printers are also available. They are very nice, but also very expensive. Prices for laser printers begin at about $3500. They can be loaded with different cartridge fonts for versatility. They are the type of printer that may be found in a print shop and do not fall within the price range of most of us contemplating the purchase of a computer printer. They are used by some of the large electronic mail services, and can even accurately duplicate and print letterhead long distance.

Finally plotters are devices that are used almost exclusively for graphic output such as the drawing of figures, charts, and graphs. These devices utilize computer controlled pens that can even

ABCDEFGHIJKLMNOPQRSTUVWXYZ
abcdefghijklmnopqrstuvwxyz
1234567890
`~!@#$%^&*()_-+={[}]|\:;"'<,>.?/

ABCDEFGHIJKLMNOPQRSTUVWXYZ
abcdefghijklmnopqrstuvwxyz
1234567890
`~!@#$%^&*()_-+={[}]|\:;"'<,>.?/

ABCDEFGHIJKLMNOPQRSTUVWXYZ
abcdefghijklmnopqrstuvwxyz
1234567890
`~!@#$%^&*()_-+={[}]|\:;"'<,>.?/

ABCDEFGHIJKLMNOPQRSTUVWXYZ
abcdefghijklmnopqrstuvwxyz
1234567890
`~!@#$%^&*()_-+={[}]|\:;"'<,>.?/

This is a sample of the new Hewlett Packard 2225B "Thinkjet" printer. As you can plainly see, it has a higher quality output than standard dot matrix printers. However, it is not quite letter quality in appearance.

Ah, the quiet. Listen to the quiet.

Fig. 1-10. Sample of ink jet print.

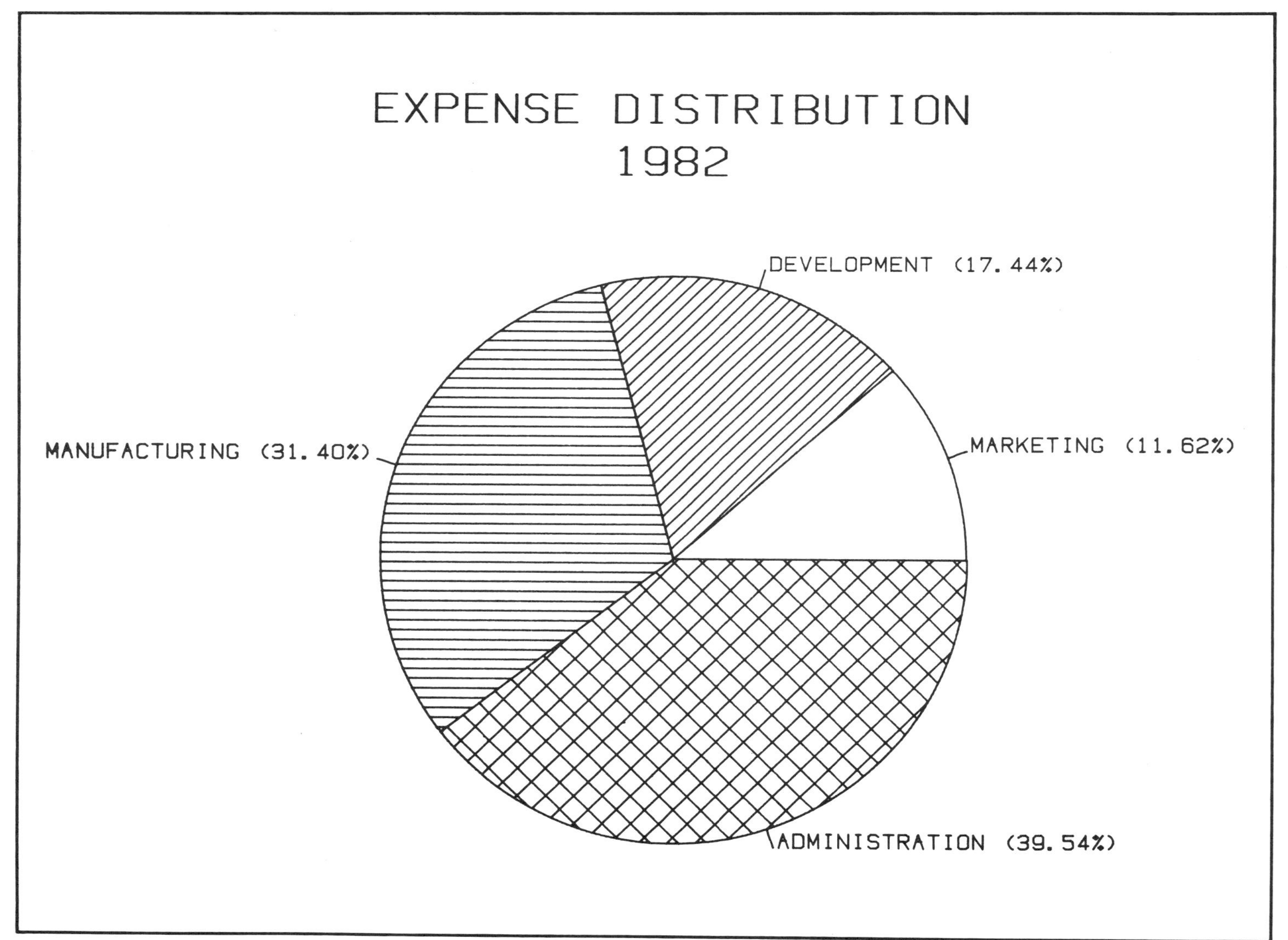

Fig. 1-11. Sample of plotter output.

display very nice three-dimensional perspective and highly stylized graphs and charts. See Fig. 1-11 for a sample of a pie chart drawn with a plotter.

In planning for the purchase of a printer first assess your primary and secondary needs, and your budget. Then find a place that will provide quick, reliable service, even including the supply of a loaner machine should yours fail. It is sometimes amusing how dependent on high technology equipment an office can become. Yet it is less than amusing when the high tech equipment fails. It can be almost totally devastating. If presented with the choice of purchasing a printer locally for a few dollars more than through a mail-order outlet, I recommend, (speaking from experience) you spend the extra money to make a valuable friend and have a backup.

WHAT YOU GET FOR YOUR MONEY

When you purchase PFS software, you get more than just a disk. With each package come the essentials, further discussed in the ensuing paragraphs.

Two Program Disks or One Program Disk with Instructions for Making a Backup Copy

The program disk contains the computer instructions (software) that turn your computer into a word processor, database manager, report producer, graphing program, or communications system.

Each program disk loads the program into the computer's memory and prepares the system so the user can input information from the keyboard. On most computers the program loads into memory on the initial spin of the disk drive and the program disk can then be removed from the disk drive. Usually you proceed by removing the program disk and inserting data disks that will be used to store and retrieve the documents you create. The program disk need be in the drive only when the user wants to utilize the help features found on the disk.

The second program disk in each package is an exact duplicate, or backup, of the first program disk. This arrangement is a happy compromise intended to protect the publisher and the user. Most industry investigations report that there are as many as ten programs in use through illegal copying for every program that is actually sold. This unfortunate phenomenon is the Achilles' heel of the software industry and makes the entire business risky. In order to slow that process down to manageable proportions, Software Publishing Corporation has *protected* their program disks so that normal efforts to duplicate them will fail.

On the other side of the coin, the user becomes very dependent on the program, and must be able to access the information that he or she has so painstakingly entered. Disks do wear out. Dogs really do chew up disks. Soft drinks and coffee do get spilled on them. The second program disk, or backup, can be thought of as disaster insurance. If something happens to your program diskette, you are covered by the publisher's replacement policy, which is to replace any defective merchandise within 90 days after purchase, or after 90 days to replace a damaged disk for a fee of about $15 to cover the cost of the disk plus the cost of postage and handling.

Please note that only the program disks are protected. The documents you enter and save on your own data disks may be duplicated, or backed up, as many times as necessary.

One Sampler Disk

The sampler disk included with some packages contains samples of different types of documents and files, and allows the user to work along with the instruction manual (called *documentation*) to learn tutorial style. The sampler disk includes samples of documents and files ranging from simple memos to complex graphs. With the word processing program, *PFS:Write*, there are examples of how to merge graphs created by *PFS:Graph* into the body of a letter as well as examples illustrating how to use the Search and Replace function of the word processor to merge text with information stored in *PFS:File*. Finally, there are programs on the disk that allow the user to set up PFS for use with a hard disk. A *hard disk* is a mass storage device similar to standard *floppy* disks in that it stores the information that the user creates, but different in that the storage area is permanent and does not use individual disks that are inserted and removed.

A User's Manual

The user's manual, or documentation, has often been the weak link in making useful programs comprehensible to a wide audience of users. Most often, novice users throw up their hands in frustration while seasoned veterans compare their favorite documentation horror stories. Fortunately, the materials that accompany PFS are an exception to this rule.

The documentation is supplied in a spiral binder that encourages opening and using of the manual along with the computer. The materials do not assume that the user has any prior knowledge of computers and do a good job of walking the user through each of the features of the program. The materials are organized in a logical manner and cross referenced in an index. A glossary is also included that explains any terms the user may be unsure of. Screen pictures show individual steps of complex operations; summaries of program commands are at the end of each chapter. Both of these features are considered state-of-the-art for user manuals.

A combination of easy-to-follow instructions with easy-to-use programs are the key elements of the PFS marketing success story. There are, however, some compromises that were made in creating such a user-friendly program. The manual naturally does not mention the things that the system cannot do and features that it does not have. Looking for features such as justification in *PFS:Write's* initial release, for example, will be futile.

User's Group Enrollment Card

Not to be ignored in these packages is the User's Group Enrollment Card. It looks like a standard user survey card bound into the front page of the manual. Although it does include all of the standard questions about your system configuration and occupation, it is a lot more. A user who doesn't bother to fill it out will be cheating him/herself. Filling it out ensures the user of a free replacement if any of the disks should fail within 90 days of purchase. More importantly, filling out the card puts you in touch with the company's customer support system, which is becoming one of the best in the business.

Filling out the enrollment card will get you on the mailing list of *PFS:News*. *PFS:News* is a slick little newsletter, published quarterly, that will keep you up to date with new product releases, such as the new *solutions* series of templates for *PFS: File*. It will provide some interesting tips and examples of successful applications for the entire series of programs. It will make you aware of program updates that will be made available at a moderate price to owners of the program. Some of the features that will be listed in this book as unavailable or missing will surely be added with subsequent updates and releases. Software Publishing Corporation is not in business to make a quick sale, take your money, and run. They know that by keeping in touch and servicing their customers they will generate an after-market of sales. The point is that their approach benefits the user as well as the publisher.

PUTTING YOUR COMPUTER TO WORK

First of all, blank disks will have to be purchased as the storage media for your documents. Get ready for some future shock. The salesperson may ask "Single sided, double sided, or flippies? Single, double, or quad density? Hard or soft sectored?" Do not be intimidated. By telling the salesperson the type of system you have and opening your wallet, you can come home with a suitable box of disks (usually sold in boxes of 10). In case you want to be adroit and respond "Double sided, double density for my IBM" or "Single sided, single density for my Apple," read on.

Disks can be thought of as a type of small record. In order to prepare them to receive information, they have to be *formatted* or *initialized*. That can be thought of as setting up the groves on the record. Rather than having one continuous groove, disks are subdivided into tracks and sectors.

Historically the first distinction was made between hard and soft sectored disks. *Hard sectored disks* were divided into sectors using permanent methods, such as a ring of holes in the disk itself.

Soft sectored disks, in contrast, marked the beginning of each sector by placing a magnetic mark on the disk that will be detected by the system. Although some of the old systems still require hard sectored disks, soft sectored disks, and disk drives have become a defacto standard that all of the popular microcomputers have endorsed.

Hard sectored disks should not be confused with *hard disks*. Hard disks contrast in that they are permanent storage devises, and can store up to millions of characters of information. Systems that have hard disks almost always include a regular *floppy disk* drive, so that commercially purchased software can be loaded into the computer and then saved as a permanent file within the hard disk. The chief advantages of hard disks are that they eliminate much disk swapping, and there is tremendous space for data storage. The major disadvantages are that they are expensive and can lead to difficulty in providing adequate backups of data should equipment fail.

After soft sectored disks became a standard on most microcomputers, the next distinction became the *density* of a disk. Information can be recorded and stored on a disk in different formats. Disk systems such as the Apple II series originally recorded on, or *wrote to*, a disk with 35 tracks in *single density*. As time went on, other systems typically chose 40 track formats and packed more information (more densely) into each track. In order to reliably hold the more thickly packed data, disks became rated for use with single density or *double density* formats. A few systems have even developed *quad density* for their data formats. A disk rated for a higher density can be reliably used on a machine with less density requirements. In other words, if disks have been rated for double density, no harm will come of using them on single density disk drives. Single density disks cannot be used reliably on double density systems, such as an IBM PC. Single density disks are, however, somewhat less expensive than disks rated for double density.

Typical single density disks can hold anywhere from 85,000 to about 140,000 characters, or *bytes*. Because of their rather limited storage capacity and because they were expensive at first, some people began to cut a slot on the other side of the disk and flip it over to be able to record on both sides of the disk. Some manufacturers jumped on the idea and supplied such disks commercially as *flippies*. Flippies have a fundamental problem in reliability. While the disk drive read/write head moves back and forth over the first side of the disk it moves against the grain of the under, or flip side; the net effect is like rotating your turntable backwards while playing a record. So flippy disks are bound to wear out with extended use and should be avoided. If the information is worth saving, it is worth saving on reliable media.

Even though double density formats boosted the amount of storage per disk to about 160,000 characters, smart manufacturers determined that they could double storage to 320,000 characters by utilizing the second side of a disk. True double sided disks evolved. Rather than having to flip the disk and allow the write head to rub the other side the wrong way, computer equipment was designed so that the write heads could record simultaneously on both sides of the disk. Most IBM systems are now supplied with double sided, double density disk drives as are TI Professional and Tandy Model 2000 computers. Each double sided disks costs a dollar or so more than a single sided disk, but storage capacity has improved up to four times as a result.

Getting the Disk Set

Once data disks have been formatted, they will receive the information you input with your PFS programs. But how do you get the disks ready?

The manuals and materials that accompany a new computer include a DOS (Disk Operating System) disk, sometimes called a system master, and a manual. Some kind of DOS is required with all computers that have disk drives. DOS is responsible for input and output (I/O) to and from the disk drives as well as a number of other functions. Check the index and turn to the correct page and it will tell you all you need to know about formatting (or initializing) disks. With IBM and other MS DOS Systems (MicroSoft Inc. of Bellevue, Washington, developed the DOS that the family of IBM personal computers utilize as well as DOSes for several other powerful microcomputers). It is as simple as typing.

FORMAT B:

and pressing ENTER.

A note of caution on IBM DOS is vital. IBM has released DOS 1.0, 1.1, 2.0 and 2.1 at this writing. Other DOS updates are likely. It is prudent for you to take care to use the same DOS and DOS format programs for all modules of PFS. If, for example, you purchased *PFS:Write* first and transferred DOS 1.1 to the disk, and later purchased *PFS:File* and subsequently DOS 2.0 and transferred it to the *File* disk, files on *Write* will be incompatible with files on *File*. If, after typing the names of several hundred people on *PFS:File* to send them an "individualized form letter" created on *PFS:Write*, you get a FILE NOT FOUND message, you will be disheartened, to say the least.

Apple II systems automatically format, or initialize data disks from within the PFS programs. If you give the command to save a document or form onto a disk that has not been prepared, you will be informed of that fact with a message similar to the following one:

The diskette in Drive 2 is not a PFS:WRITE diskette. Your options are:

1) Insert a *PFS:Write* diskette in the drive.
2) Leave the current diskette in the drive, and create a *PFS:Write* diskette.

Press CTRL C to continue

After formatting the blank disks that you are going to use to receive data and documents, you will be ready to load and start, or *boot,* the program disk.

Booting the Disk

Getting the program disk to run is commonly referred to as *booting* the disk or getting the disk to *boot*. The term boot is a shortened version of the old computer term "bootstrap," which alluded to a system's using its own action to initiate or sustain itself. The procedure for getting the program running varies with the type of computer you are using.

The PFS program disks that you receive for Apple computers are ready to run. You just put them into the computer and turn the computer on. The Apple company developed the architecture of the Apple and tailored its corporate policy to encourage software development. So for a nominal fee to the publisher, Apple allows software houses to put Apple DOS on their disks. For this reason, you do not have to do anything but turn the computer on to boot the Apple PFS disks.

The story is a bit different with IBM software. A PFS program disk is not quite ready to run when it is packaged for IBM and other MS-DOS systems. Because the makers of those systems have taken every effort to protect their company's inventions, their DOS is considered proprietary and no third party publishers are given the license to distribute it. As a user, this leaves you two options.

You can turn your computer on with your DOS disk in the disk drive. After the computer checks itself and its memory you will see a prompt asking for the date. It is not necessary to answer the prompt. You may just press ENTER. However, it is wise to take the couple of seconds to input the information requested. The information that is stored on disk is automatically date- and time-stamped when it is recorded so that additional information can sometimes provide a needed clue for finding the file you need.

Next a prompt asking for the time will appear. Again, answering this prompt is optional. Some people will use the same logic I used for the date prompt and point to the benefits of knowing whether a file was saved in the morning or afternoon. I do not answer the time prompt; I only press ENTER. That way the real time clock starts at 0:00. When you complete a task and quit the PFS program, you are returned to DOS. Then I type TIME and press ENTER. The amount of time I have spent on the project is displayed—a kind of temporal odometer for the inevitable time and motion surveys.

After responding to the time prompt, you will see a prompt that looks like this:

A>

Remove the DOS disk, insert the program disk and type the program name, such as WRITE, FILE, REPORT, or GRAPH, and press ENTER. Booting a disk in this manner bypasses a display of the PFS logo, that will otherwise appear every time you boot one of their programs.

The alternative method is to transfer the DOS permanently to your program disk. You can only transfer DOS 1.0 or 1.1 as DOS 2.0 is too large to fit on the space remaining of the program disk. To perform this transfer, boot DOS in drive A, place the program disk in drive B, and type INSTALL. Appropriate instructions are included in the manual for single drive systems. Using this method, you can just insert the program disk in the drive when you turn on the computer, saving a swap of disks. However, please note that the FORMAT command is not transferred in this process and you should be sure the DOS that formats your data disks is the same one that boots the program.

SAFEGUARDING YOUR LABOR

Every manual and text that you ever read about microcomputers and programs will caution you to make backups, or copies, of your data. Typically, it is only after an error that the user seriously heeds this advice. The time required to execute a backup procedure is usually negligible, although I have seen files of approximately 2500 pages (records) require 10 minutes to completely back up. Usually, it is a matter of a couple of minutes or less. The cost of disks are quickly coming down to the two- to three-dollar range, or approximately the value of a few minutes of paid work time. The time needed to reenter all the information stored on a disk could run into the hundreds of hours (and dollars). Finding the lost information may be impossible. The cost of losing information in the bit bucket may not be calculable.

For best results, I recommend that you use a minimum of two backups in addition to the original data disk, and alternate between them. This procedure protects you from the occasional system failure and the more frequent occurrence of operator error. If you update your data on a daily basis, one backup disk could be a "Monday, Wednesday, Friday" while the other might be a "Tuesday, Thursday, Saturday" backup disk.

The quality of disk drives, and the way that they protect against accidental erasure has steadily improved over the last several years. It is highly unlikely that a power failure will damage two disks at once, although it certainly has happened when lightning has struck. It is much more likely that you will inadvertently erase the data on a disk by using an improper command. For example, the FORMAT command on MS-DOS does not caution the user that there is already data on a disk that is to be formatted. Any data on the disk will be lost during a format procedure. (This possibility also lends credence to the warning—"Label your disks!" All too often users format the wrong disk simply because they fail to properly label it.)

The real advantage of a third disk is to provide a degree of protection against the careless operator. As an example, consider a situation where you have a change in the status of the Ken Smith file. You search for his file, make the updates, and proceed with your work, and then faithfully back up the disk. It is only now that you realize that you updated the file for the wrong Ken Smith. If you had only the original and a backup, the information that you obliterated would be forever lost in the old bit bucket again. However, if you have a third (or even a fourth disk that is updated infrequently) you will have a reference for finding the prior, correct information. Of course, that amount of insurance can also be obtained by occasionally printing out all the information on disk.

Finally, it is important to realize that the information stored on disks is stored in a magnetic format. It is very possible to lose all of the data (or destroy your program disks) by allowing disks to come in too close contact with a strong magnetic field. Electric appliances create strong electric fields. Running a vacuum cleaner too close or leaving disks next to a ringing telephone can erase a disk. X-rays will also destroy magnetic information. For safest storage of disks, a metal cabinet is the best place to keep useful disks.

PFS:File—Organizing Creativity

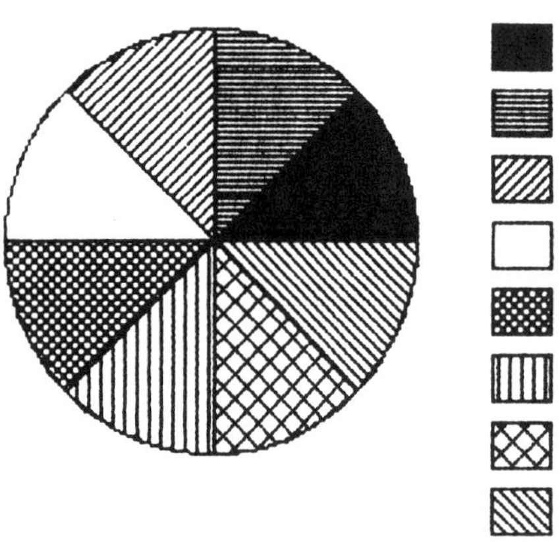

Chapter 2

Word processing is . . . I was ready to say that word processing is my favorite microcomputer productivity tool. Well, word processing is nice. It saves enormous amounts of time that would be spent on repetitive tasks and gives my correspondence a more finished quality. But I must say that as much as I enjoy word processing, it is, after all, merely an improvement on an old way of doing things. *PFS:File* is really my favorite application because it is revolutionary—it allows for the instant retrieval and cross referencing of information. *PFS:File* saves me from the endless aggravation that results from losing something. As long as I can remember anything at all about a misplaced bit of information that I know is on *File*, I can retrieve it. Creativity without a measure of organization usually will not get the job done. Thank you, *PFS:File*, for keeping track of the who, what, where, and when of daily business.

PFS:File allows you to keep track of almost anything. Your appointments, mailing lists, inventory, accomplishments, and projects can be swiftly and easily categorized, cross referenced, and filed electronically. You are only limited by your imagination. *PFS:File* can be used to create any number of different data bases. After the program is loaded into the computer's memory, it then can be used to create and retrieve from as many different forms as you want to create. Different forms are usually kept on different data disks. It is possible, but *not* recommended, to have more than one data base on each data disk, as long as it is given a distinct filename.

Before you decide to set up a *PFS:File* form, there are a few common sense questions you should ask to determine whether or not you will really benefit from creating a data base. Remember, the procedure will take a fair amount of thought and planning. It will be an investment of time. Benefits will only be evidenced "down the road." The more frequently you use the system, the higher your return on the initial investment.

Will you have to cross reference materials? Cross referencing is the most significant advantage over paper and pencil filing systems. Files that are only referenced in one manner might as well be kept on 3 × 5 index cards, so when you need something from it, at least you do not have to find your disks and boot up the program. If, however, you have ever found yourself wondering what was the last name of that man named Ken who you met at the sales meeting who had such a terrific deal on that product you suddenly need, electronic filing is for you. Indeed, if you would like to see all of the suppliers of that product, a database manager is for you. What if you only remembered that the man was from Alabama? You can see that it would take four sets of index cards to do what *PFS:File* can do with one. Once the form has been designed, it takes no longer to enter all of the pertinent information on the computer than it would take to enter it on an index card. The first card will be the "expensive" one. The accrued benefits will be an improved information retrieval system.

Will you have the occasion to frequently reuse the items that you will be filing? If you are only going to contact a person once and then throw his card away, there will be no benefit to entering his or her name into a permanent data base. It will be quicker to type the name and address onto an envelope once. If however, there are people that you frequently contact, a single entry in the data base can be used as many times as you need it. If you had a Board of Directors consisting of 40 members who receive a monthly financial statement, you would have to type 480 addresses on envelopes with a typewriter. The same task can be accomplished by typing only 40 addresses into *PFS:File*. Just type them in once and use them over and over again. With one thousand members who receive a quarterly newsletter you could save typing 3000 envelopes the first year and 7000 by the end of the second year. That savings can manifest itself in a reduction in labor cost, or more likely, in more creative and productive use of time by the staff.

Will you ever need to use multiple factor searches? For example, will you need to have a listing of people who contributed to your organization two years ago, but not during the past year? If so, *PFS:File* is for you. How about finding the people who utilized your services during the first quarter of last year, or people who receive monthly newletters but who have not joined your organization? Searches like these, until recently, caused researchers to tear at their hair. They are child's play for *PFS:File*.

Will you benefit from an automatic tickler file? Would it be convenient to set deadlines for yourself that can automatically be sorted into the "behind schedule" status? If so (you guessed it), *PFS:File* is for you.

The operation of *PFS:File* will be dealt with in this chapter primarily as a stand-alone piece of software. It is very competitive with other database managers on the market. You get good power and performance for the dollar, plus the industry's standard in user-friendliness. You do not have to make too many significant sacrifices in either area. The real power of *PFS:File* is that it interacts with the other modules of the Personal Filing System arsenal of programs. As a single-wheel program, it is good. Combine it with the other three "wheels," and you can really get somewhere.

EFFECTIVE INFORMATION RETRIEVAL

The effectiveness and quality of information you will be able to retrieve is directly related to the completeness of the form you design. *PFS:File* uses a free-form design that allows you to design and implement your own system. Generally, it is wise to plan the form ahead of time, set it up, and test it with some data. Try to design it so it provides an easy way to search through fields that you know you will use, yet provides for the unexpected through "open" fields.

To use *PFS:File* you do *not* have to know the difference between fields and records, or know Boolean logic. In order to establish a common vocabulary, we will introduce the terminology. They are the basis for what happens in a database manager and are not really abstruse topics.

Record. A record can be conceptualized as a single sheet, or index card, of information within the total file.

Field. A field is an item that is designated as a characteristic that you will need to search for.

Examples are "First Name," "Last Name," "Date," and "Notes." *PFS:File* allows a maximum of 100 fields on every page of the form. Since there are 32 possible "pages" per form, the form can be designed to have a maximum capacity of 3200 fields. In creating the *PFS:File* form, a field is defined by using a colon (:) after the words describing the field. The first field of a form has particular importance. An exact match of the first field can be located by the program within a second or two, even in very large files. This is because each *record* (see below) is stored under the name of its first field, and the program can access that record directly (through random-file access) rather than by searching in a page by page fashion (sequential file access) required for all of the other fields.

Boolean logic.Searches are carried out according to *logical operands* that the user supplies. *PFS:File* typically uses an AND search when more than one item is specified for a search criteria. It is actually the intersection of two sets. Searching for people who contributed time *and* money to the organization is one kind of an AND search. Both specified criteria must be met in order to be a match as illustrated in the diagram of Fig. 2-1.

An OR search is another kind of search that is the union of two sets. An example of an OR search would be to find the names of people who have contributed dollars *or* volunteered time. Figure 2-2 illustrates an OR search or a union of sets. *PFS:File* has to use two passes, or searches, to complete such an OR search. Through the use of the option allowing the selection of specified forms, *PFS:File* is capable of advanced logical operations such as finding people who are women AND who live in California, OR who are men AND who live in New York. (See Fig. 2-3.) You can also find people who do NOT live in the United States AND do live in English-speaking countries.

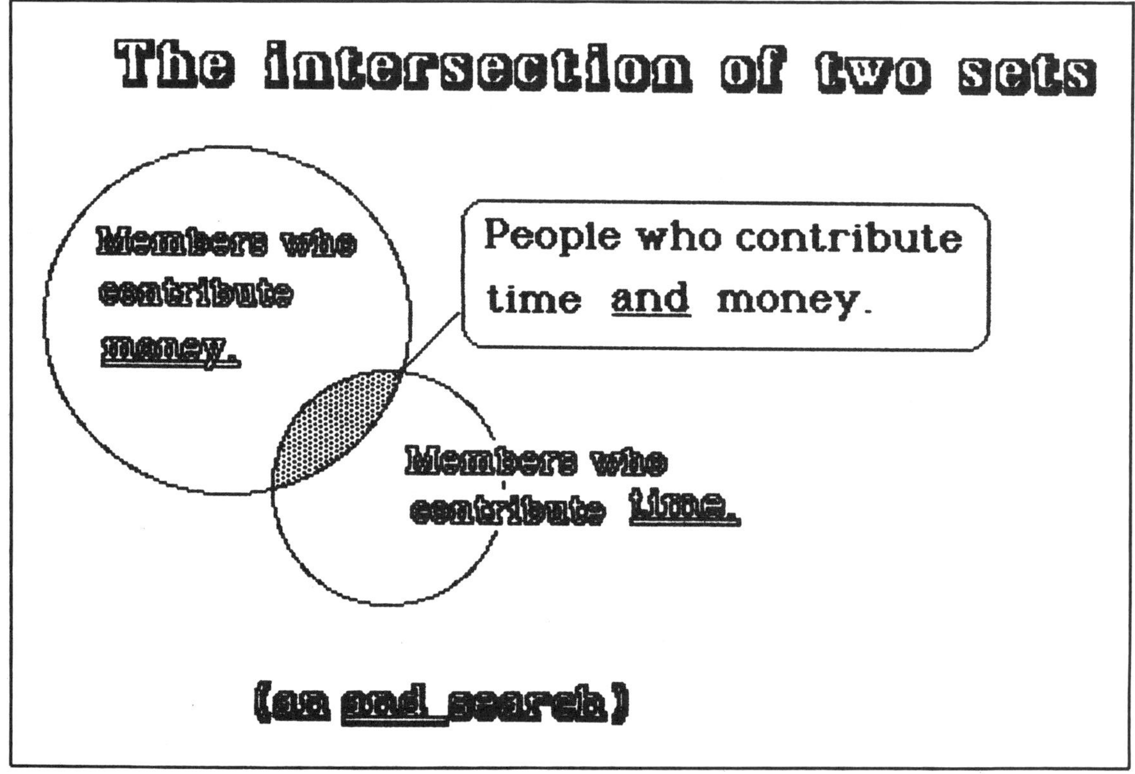

Fig. 2-1. Diagram showing the intersection of two sets.

Also, searches can be done for numbers "greater than," "less than," or "equal to" other values. Ranges of values can also be identified as search criteria. For example, we could find members who have joined the organization within the last year, or list all of the members who have volunteered more than 10 hours, but less than 50 hours.

GETTING STARTED WITH *PFS:FILE*

As with all of the modules of Software Publishing Corporation's Personal Filing System, *PFS:File* expects you to be able to supply formatted data disks. Following your DOS instructions, format at least three blank data disks. Next, boot the system disk following the procedures described in Chapter 1. (Turn on an Apple with the program disk inserted in drive 1 or type FILE and press ENTER at the > prompt on MS-DOS systems.

If you are using an MS-DOS system remember to use the same version of the DOS that you use for other modules of the PFS series. Following the same procedures will ensure that the different modules will be able to pass information back and forth. After the program has booted, the program disk may be removed. It will not be needed any more until the next time the program is to be started. In fact, there are not even any help functions on *PFS:File*, as there are on *PFS:Write*, so it is wisest to remove the disk and return it to a safe place.

The first screen that appears is the PFS:File Function Menu. (See Fig. 2-4.) Selections are made by typing the number corresponding to the function you want to use following the SELECTION NUMBER: prompt, and typing the name you are to assign or have assigned to your file following the FILE NAME: prompt. The TAB key causes the

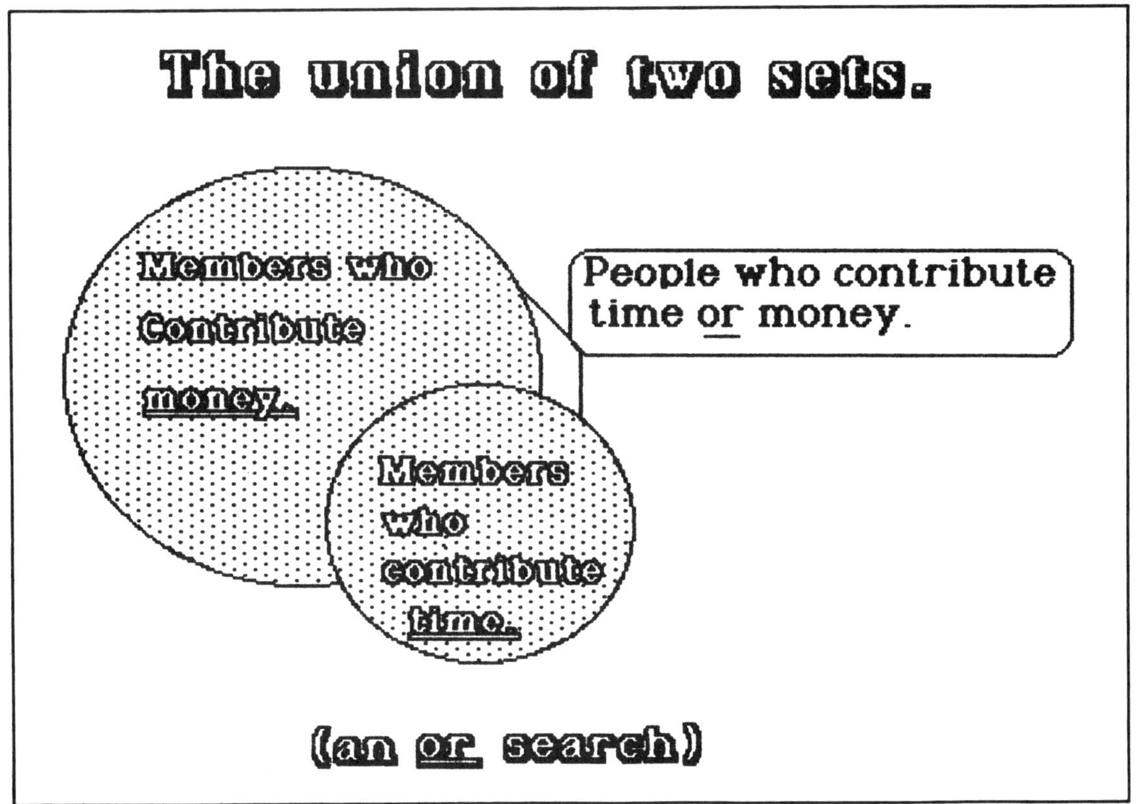

Fig. 2-2. Diagram showing the union of two sets.

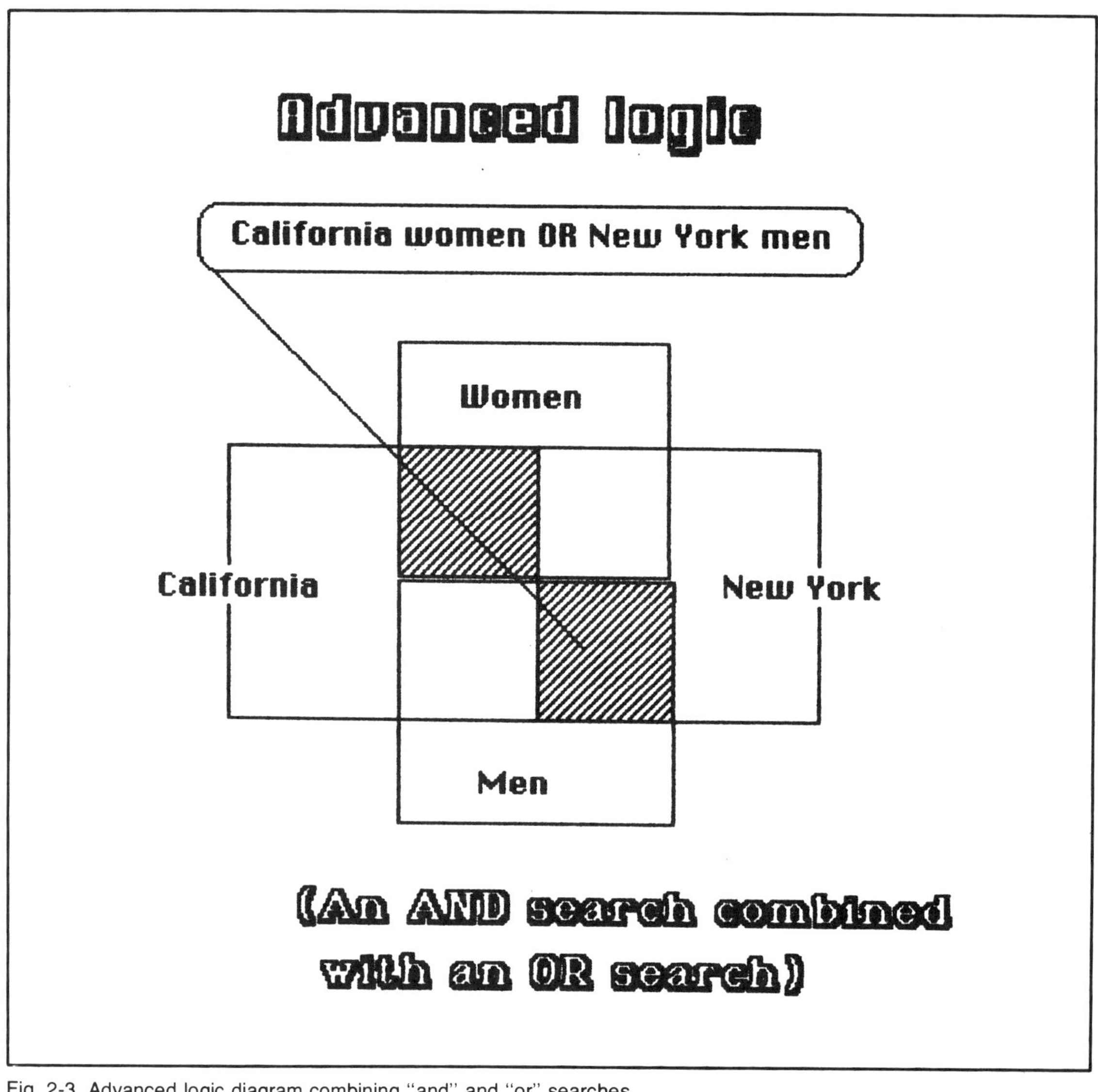

Fig. 2-3. Advanced logic diagram combining "and" and "or" searches.

cursor to jump from one prompt to the next. The RIGHT ARROW key is used on Apple II+ systems. The Apple II+ does not have a TAB key. Press the F10 key on keyboards with function keys or press CTRL and C on keyboards without function keys to signal the program that you want to *continue*.

The following brief descriptions will summarize the functions available. Each function will be described in detail later in the chapter.

1 DESIGN FILE. DESIGN is used to create the *form* that will be used to store information. You will enter the names of the item fields that you want included and determine the amount of space that is to be allowed for each field item. This option also includes provisions for changing a file that has already been created.

2 ADD. ADD is the selection to use when you are going to add information onto one of the forms that has been previously created. After selecting ADD, you will see the working form and be expected to begin entering new information. Pressing ESCape terminates this operation.

3 COPY. COPY can actually be used to perform three different operations. The entire file of all records can be copied to provide the user with a backup data disk. The design of the form can be copied for use with another application or for preparing subsets of the whole file without copying any of the individual records. Finally, selected forms may be copied onto another data disk. Information from records that match a criteria you have selected will be read from the original file, and transferred onto another disk. The information transferred will only be for items that have identical field item identifiers. That is, information such as "LName" that has an identical field on the old and new forms will be transferred. There will be no damage to the original data disk, and the information that has been transferred will also remain on the original data disk.

4 SEARCH/UPDATE. This option allows for the continual updating of information on your data base. When this function is selected, you are asked to supply the retrieval specifications. Full and partial matches are allowed as well as various numeric, range, and NOT searches. After the retrieval specifications have been supplied, the forms that meet the specified criteria are displayed on the screen, one after another. Displayed forms may be reviewed, altered, removed, or printed while they are on screen. When the search is completed the number of forms found that matched the given criteria will be displayed.

5. PRINT. The PRINT function is similar in many respects to the search/update function. Retrieve specifications must also be supplied for this selection. However the output will be automatically sent to the printer rather than the monitor. The user will also select the portions of the form that should be printed, as well as whether the field item names should also be printed. The user may specify the length of the forms to be printed and the number of

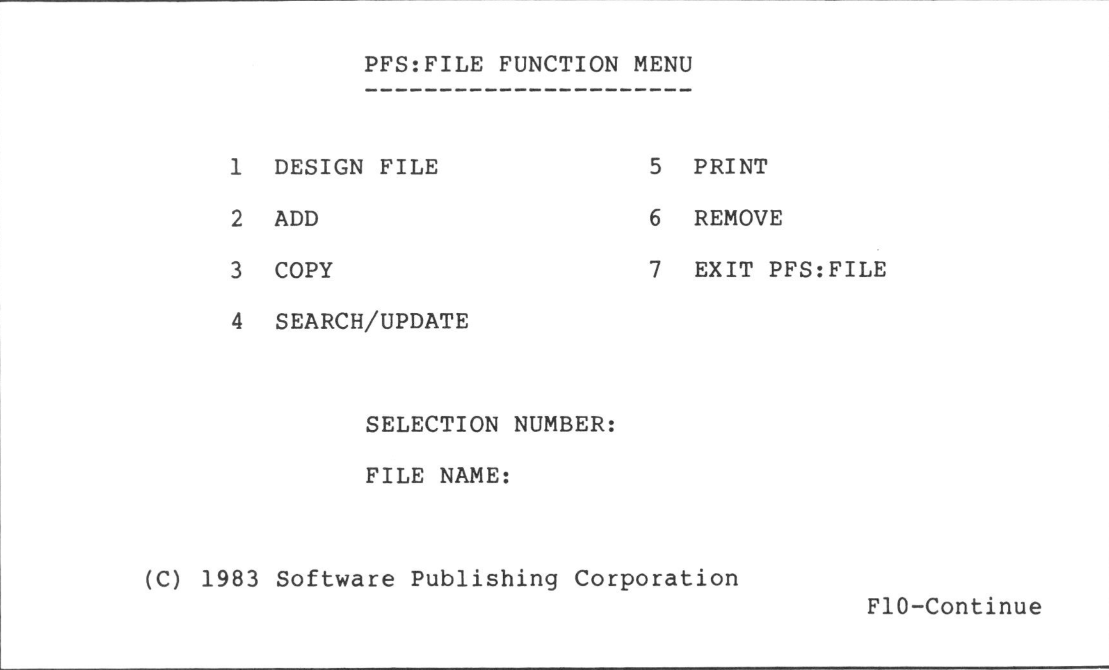

Fig. 2-4. PFS:File Function Menu—the first menu screen that appears in the *PFS:File* program.

copies of each to be printed. The total number of forms printed will also be summarized following the print run.

6 REMOVE. The REMOVE option allows the user to remove all forms that match a set of specified criteria. This function could be used, for example, following a COPY operation that has copied selected forms to another data disk. Individual forms can also be removed with the SEARCH/UPDATE option, which offers the advantage of allowing the user to review each form before its removal.

7 EXIT PFS:FILE. This function exits the program and returns to the DOS. It is not essential to use this option to exit the program, but it is good operating procedure. The data disk should only be removed when the main PFS:File Function Menu is displayed or after using the EXIT command. To do otherwise will risk permanent damage to the data disk in use. Making a habit of using the EXIT command will guarantee that no damage is done to the data due to careless operation. EXIT returns the user to the DOS > prompt. At that prompt, it is possible to immediately begin another program, such as *PFS:Write* by typing WRITE and pressing ENTER.

The EXIT command is not an option on the Apple *II* +/e version of the program. People who use that system will have to remember to remove the disk and turn the machine off only when the main menu is displayed.

PFS:FILE WITH APPLICATIONS

Many management courses suggest the institution of a simple "Do-Doing-Done" chart in order to effectively record tasks. It also provides a system of reinforcement for remembering one's accomplishments. We will begin to demonstrate *PFS:File* by setting up such a chart and show why the computer implementation of such a system will be superior to a board with three pegs and a set of index cards.

After booting the disk (see Chapter 1), remove the *PFS:File* disk from the disk drive. The program disk does not have to stay in the disk drive. From the (main) PFS:Function Menu, type 1 to select DESIGN FILE. Press the TAB key to move the cursor to the FILE NAME: prompt. Let us assign

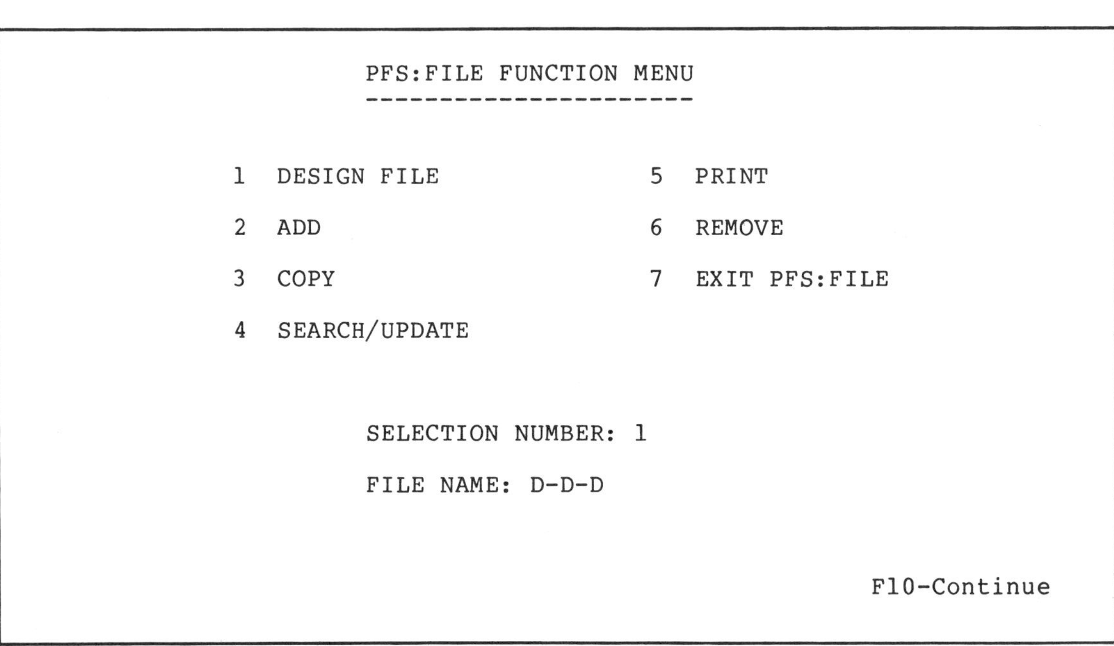

Fig. 2-5. A Function Menu completed for designing a form.

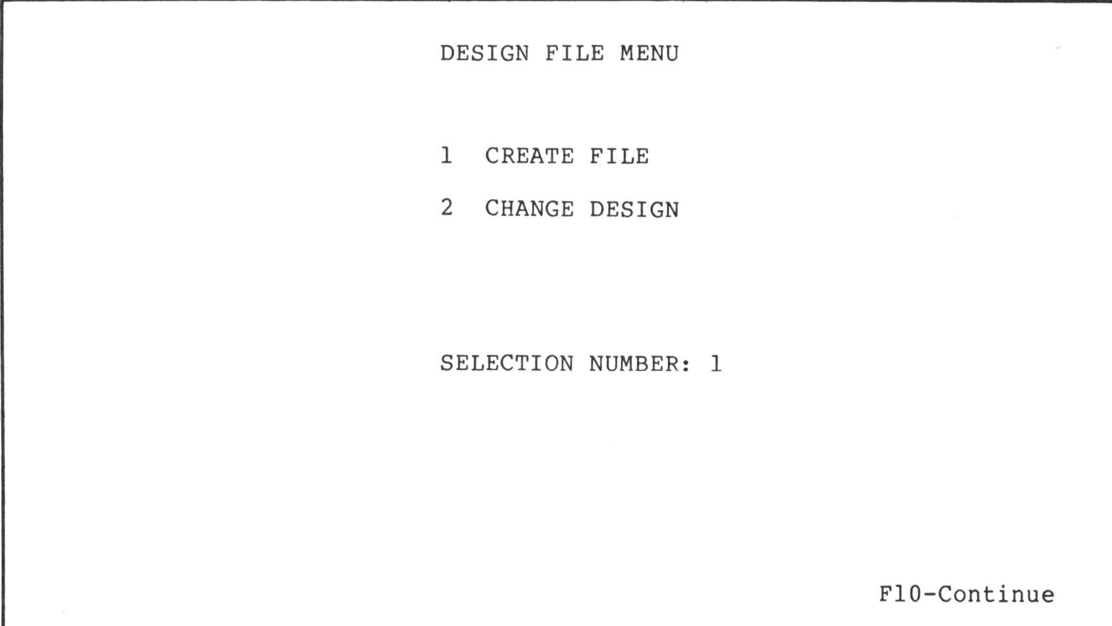

Fig. 2-6. The inner Design File Menu completed for creating an original form.

the filename as "D-D-D" as shown in the completed Function Menu of Fig. 2-5. Filenames can have a length of one to eight characters. One should try to use easily remembered filenames, and mark the labels on each disk clearly so that you can easily use the data disk at any time. You cannot enter the data base without first entering the filename.

If you have a data base that you feel is confidential, let's say "Payroll," you may choose not to label the filename on the disk. Since you cannot enter the file without the filename, and since the program will not list a directory of the disk files, there you have a first (albeit slim) margin of protection from people who know how to operate the program, but know little else about computers. Ideally, though, magnetic media should be protected the same way confidential papers are secured—in a locked cabinet.

If you create a data base for which you forget the filename, you will have to use your computer's DOS to get a directory of the files on the disk. To do this on an IBM or MS-DOS system, boot your DOS, put the data disk into the first drive, type DIR, and press ENTER. The filenames of the *PFS:File* data bases are stored in the same manner as other programs. Apple systems will have to use a Pascal system disk to view the CATALOG and listing of filenames. Make note of the filenames, and enter the information after the FILE NAME: prompt once the *PFS:File* program is booted.

After indicating that you want to DESIGN FILE, you will be presented with the DESIGN FILE MENU illustrated in Fig. 2-6. Since we are creating a new file, we will choose 1, CREATE FILE. Later the use of CHANGE DESIGN will be illustrated. After indicating that we are going to create a file, we are presented with a screen that is almost blank, except for some notations on the bottom of the screen. (See Fig. 2-7.)

The filename is displayed in the lower left corner (in this case, D-D-D). The word "DESIGN" appears centered under the bottom line, indicating the phase of operation in progress. "Page 1" appears in the lower right corner, and will be updated appropriately as successive pages of the form are created. "F5-Date" and "F6-Time" indicate that pressing either of those function keys will result in the automatic input of either the time or the date.

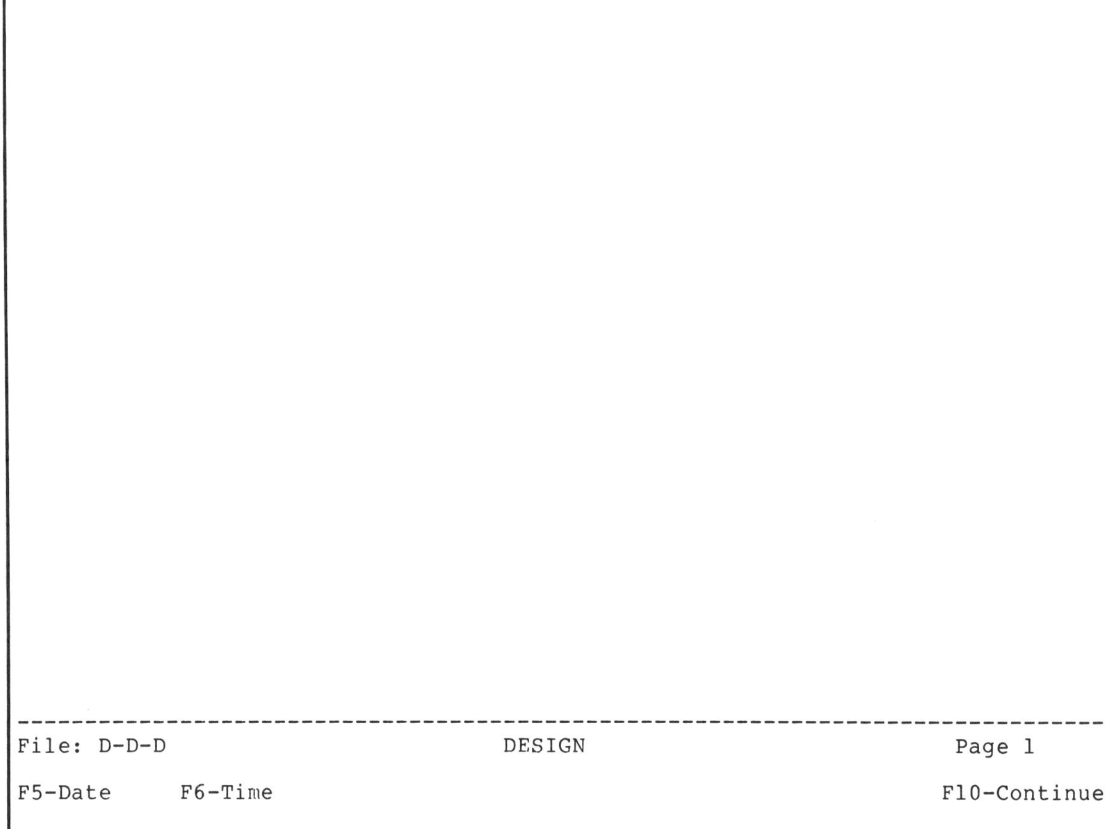

Fig. 2-7. A blank design form screen ready for the creation of a form.

Apple *II* +/e users do not have this option because those systems do not have real time clocks.

The screen is blank, and the program is awaiting the creation of the form. A white block will also appear in the top left corner. That block is the *cursor*, which marks the spot where typed letters will appear on the screen. Each field is identified by terminating the field identifier with a colon (:). You may add, delete, and change any of the information you choose, using the normal conventions for cursor control, such as INSERT and DELETE keys, until you press F10 or CTRL and C to lock in the form.

PLANNING THE FORM

Planning the form is the most important part of effective information retrieval, so let us first consider the key field items that we want to include. First, of course, we want space for a name of the project. Since the project title does not always adequately describe the job, we shall create another field item, "Job Description," and leave ample space for a complete description. Next, we will want a way to sort the status of whether a job falls into the (to) "Do," "Doing" (in progress), or "Done" (accomplished) classification. There are two basic ways we could reach our goal. We could create a single field identifier called status, and type STATUS and then enter "Do," "Doing," or "Done" for each form we create for each task. or, we could list three different field items as "Do," "Doing,"and "Done," and then simply place an "X" beside the appropriate status. Figure 2-8 illustrates a form design that uses one field for noting the status of a job. Figure 2-9 uses three different fields.

In this instance, we will choose the single designation, STATUS. The single item field designation leaves less chance for confusion. If we were to use the three field item identifiers, the "X" used to designate a "Do" status would have to be erased when the project is upgraded to "Doing" status, and then changed again when the project is completed. Or else, in data retrieval, there would have to be a combined search criteria. For example, in order to retrieve a listing of only the "Doing" category (and not jobs that are done, but were once in the "Doing" stage) one would have to mark an "X" beside the "Doing" category and a "/X" (not X) beside the "Done" field.

In data entry and retrieval there is too much of an opportunity for those changes to fall through the cracks, and have an "X" that is not erased or a "/X" that is not specified. Failure to do so would cause the same project to be categorized in at least two categories at the same time. The purpose of using this data base is to avoid confusion, so one item field is it. In the SEARCH/UPDATE phase, the person entering the status of any project can just add "ing" to "do," or type "done" for each status update.

Another function that we want the data base to be able to perform is to provide a tickler, or follow up, file to remind us when a job should begin. So, we shall put an ACT BY DATE field. We want to be able to search for dates that are approaching the designated date or that have fallen past the "Act by" date. To do so, we must put the date in a form that can be treated numerically. This is easily accomplished by printing the date in the format of YY/MM/DD. Using this format and being careful to use exactly two digits for year, month, and day

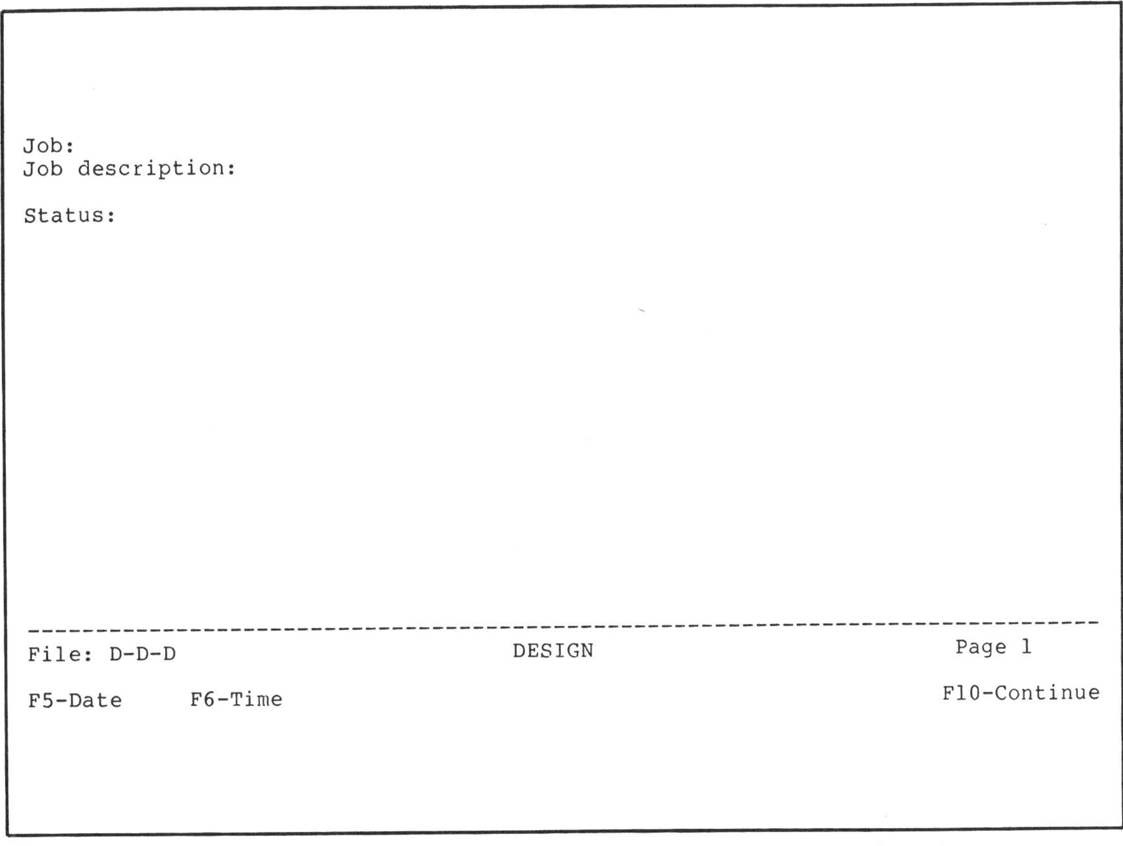

```
Job:
Job description:

Status:

--------------------------------------------------------------------------------
File: D-D-D                     DESIGN                          Page 1

F5-Date     F6-Time                                             F10-Continue
```

Fig. 2-8. Design form function in progress, using one field, "Status," to specify the progress of a project.

```
Job:
Job description:

Do (x):
Doing (x):
Done (x):









--------------------------------------------------------------------------------
File: D-D-D                         DESIGN                          Page 1

F5-Date       F6-Time                                          F10-Continue
```

Fig. 2-9. An alternate form design using three fields to keep track of project's progress.

(such as 03 for March), each successive day is numerically increased by a value of one more than the value of the previous day. A search for all dates before September 18, 1984, can be handled in the retrieve specifications of SEARCH/UPDATE by entering 84/09/18. This system will work very well through December 31, 1999. If you plan to be using the same system beyond that date, do not worry. Beyond that date, you may change the "YY" format to a four digit code that will have the effect of increasing the date's numeric value.

The slashes are ignored by the computer in numerical treatments of dates. Since that is the way it is done, it would be good practice to remind ourselves of the proper format anytime we are to enter a date. Therefore, we will make the field item identifier "Act By (yy/mm/dd)" as illustrated in Fig. 2-10.

Recording dates and times on *PFS:File* forms is made simple by having the program automatically insert today's date in the proper format by pressing the IBM's F5 key for the date or by moving the Macintosh's mouse to the appropriate block. Pressing IBM's F6 key will automatically insert the correct time. This feature is available only on systems with internal real time clocks, such as the IBM PC, TI Pro, or Apple Macintosh. In order to use these functions properly, you have to answer the initial date and time DOS prompts when the computer is initially turned on.

The "Act by" field is fine for a tickler, but how about accurately recording the date on which a project was completed. We need a "Date completed (yy/mm/dd)" field. We will learn in Chapter 3 that with *PFS:Report* it is possible to automatically calculate differences between different fields, so we could use *PFS:Report* to track the length of time required to complete a project if we only add a "Date Began" field. Also, when the infamous "Time and Motion" studies roll around, we can automatically punch in and punch out on jobs by using IBM's automatic time insertion key. FG, *PFS:Report* can be used to calculate the difference in beginning and ending times and dates. In order to provide for a meaningful analysis of our effort, we will, of course, have to reserve a field for indicating the classification of work. We will call that field, "Service Area" (See Fig. 2-11.)

Ample spaces are allowed after each of the date fields. It will be possible to use *PFS:File* to search for events that occurred between dates specified. If, for example, you choose to search for all events completed between January first and March 31, there will have to be enough room after the item to input the search criteria, which is =84/01/01 . . 84/03/31.

So far we have a very sophisticated 3×5 index card. In addition to the electronic capability of searching for dates before, after, or within a range of dates, we are providing for the capabilities of automatically calculating project times. Now let's really go to work and include everything we would ever want to know about the project.

How about volunteer hours and number of people benefiting from the project? You know what a hassle it can be to retrieve that kind of information. I have a hunch that *PFS:Report* will know how to add those figures together. Let's provide space to list volunteers. (There's no motivator like a little recognition.)

A good practice is to provide a free form area for notes or miscellaneous entries. We shall include

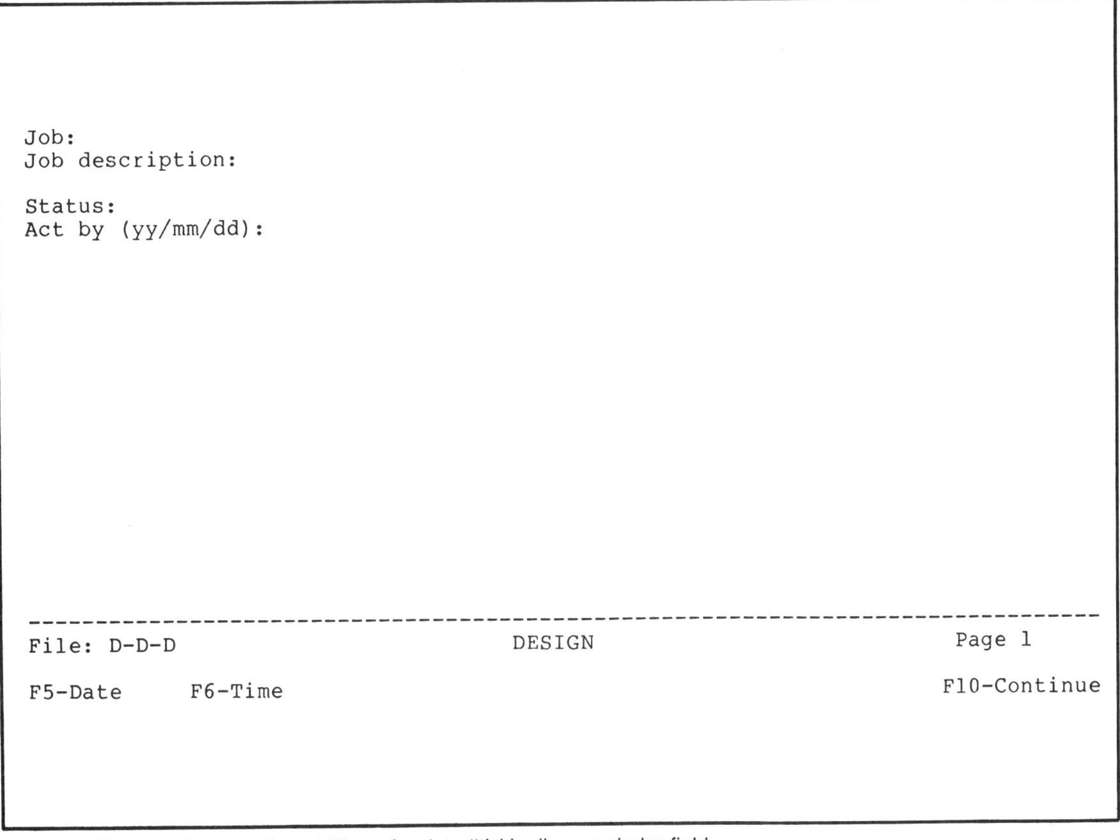

Fig. 2-10. Form design with the addition of a date "tickler," or reminder field.

```
Job:
Job description:

Status:
Act by (yy/mm/dd):

Date Began:                            Date Completed:
Time Began:                            Time Completed:

Service area:









------------------------------------------------------------------------
File: D-D-D                            DESIGN                      Page 1

F5-Date      F6-Time                                         F10-Continue
```

Fig. 2-11. Form designed to allow for the calculation of beginning and ending dates and times.

the field item "Notes" and plenty of space to write descriptions, explanations, and reminders. Each form can automatically have an *attachment* appended onto the standard form. The attachment is accessed by pressing the PgDn key on the numeric keypad or CTRL and N on small keyboards after the last regular page of the form. On the attachment page you may use a text editor to insert any additional information that could not be included on the original form. Conceptually, it is similar to using the back of a 3×5 index card. The information is there, but there is no way to search for materials included on it. The advantage of including the field "Notes" on the main form is that the search function will look through a free form space like "Notes" if it is on the main form. For example, if we had an event in which we used balloons, we could search the "Notes" field with the criteria " . . balloon . . " to find a mention of balloons in the notes on an event. The two periods used in a search procedure are "wild cards" and the statements means "ignore everything before or after, but select all forms containing the letters "balloon" in sequence.

Remember that a colon is used at the end of each field item to indicate the place where the field item name ends, and inserted information will begin.

Now we have a more fully developed form. (See Fig. 2-12.) It is still kind of a small form when you see it on a large 80-column display. Obviously, you could leave room for subdividing your projects into phases, include milestones to check off on completion, and do other more elaborate fields. We will forget doing this for now so that we can illustrate the CHANGE DESIGN option later. For purposes of demonstration, this form is almost good enough. Almost?

Our current form's primary difficiency is the way the first field has been designed. The retrieval of an exact match of the first item in the form happens almost instantaneously while other searches are done in a page by page fashion. If we average one job per day in our file, a form can rapidly become so large that it can take a minute or more to search through each page of a 300-page file, and few of us have minutes to waste. If we have the capability of accessing any form directly, we should take advantage of it. The first field "Job" is too flexible for the user to be able to accurately remember the exact wording of a job's name. In this example, we shall assign numbers to our jobs.

There will be little or no difficulty in remembering the last number during data input. If it was forgotten, it will be possible to use the "Search" function to quickly locate the last job input, and therefore see the last number. Also, *PFS:Report* can be used to provide printouts cross referencing numbers and jobs. *PFS:Report* has a nasty quirk in requiring that the same number of digits be used if they are to be provided in ascending order at report time. The sort "looks" at the first digit first, regardless of whether it resides in the ones, tens, or hundreds place. I can live with that minor annoyance and enter my first job as "001."

If I wanted quick sorting and retrieval of jobs by service areas, I could devise a numbering system to accommodate that need. For example, by designating community education with an identifying digit of "1," direct services as "2," and social action as "3," jobs could easily be listed as 1/001, 1/002, 3/001, and so on. PFS programs ignore the slash when treating the column numerically. With this numbering system, jobs could automatically be sorted by service area in a standard report of ascending job numbers.

In our demonstration, we will plan to start with the number 001, and increase each job by a value of 1. To modify the form, it is possible to use the arrow keys to position the cursor, and then simply type over the existing letters until the form meets your satisfaction. The form we've designed is complete in Fig. 2-13 but nothing will be saved until it is locked in by the signal to continue.

To indicate we are satisfied with the design of our form, we press the continue key. The form will then be recorded onto the formatted (or initialized) data disk that we have inserted into the disk drive, and the PFS:File Function Menu will appear again, but this time with our current filename proudly displayed. (See Fig. 2-14.)

If we press 2 for ADD, 4 for SEARCH/UPDATE or 5 for PRINT, we will see that the

```
Job:
Job description:

Status:
Act by (yy/mm/dd):

Date Began:                              Date Completed:
Time Began:                              Time Completed:

Service area:
People benefiting:
Volunteer hours:
Volunteers:



Notes:




-----------------------------------------------------------------------------
File: D-D-D                              DESIGN                        Page 1

F5-Date     F6-Time                                              F10-Continue
```

Fig. 2-12. A "Do-Doing-Done" form that has only one shortcoming—a "job #" field for quick retrieval.

```
Job #:                  Job:
Job description:

Status:
Act by (yy/mm/dd):

Date Began:                        Date Completed:
Time Began:                        Time Completed:

Service area:
People benefiting:
Volunteer hours:
Volunteers:



Notes:




--------------------------------------------------------------------------------
File: D-D-D                        DESIGN                          Page 1

F5-Date     F6-Time                                          F10-Continue
```

Fig. 2-13. A completed "Do-Doing-Done" form ready to be saved on the disk.

appearance of the form has changed. The field names on the form we just designed are highlighted with a white background behind their names. (See Fig. 2-15.) Also, there is an additional message, "F2-Print Form," in the lower left corner. A convenient option, F2 allows the user to print the current form that is displayed rather than having to return to the main menu, select 5 PRINT, and then type the retrieve specifications, print options, and print specifications. Using the F2 option has the disadvantage that it prints out the entire form, without allowing you to select item names, but has

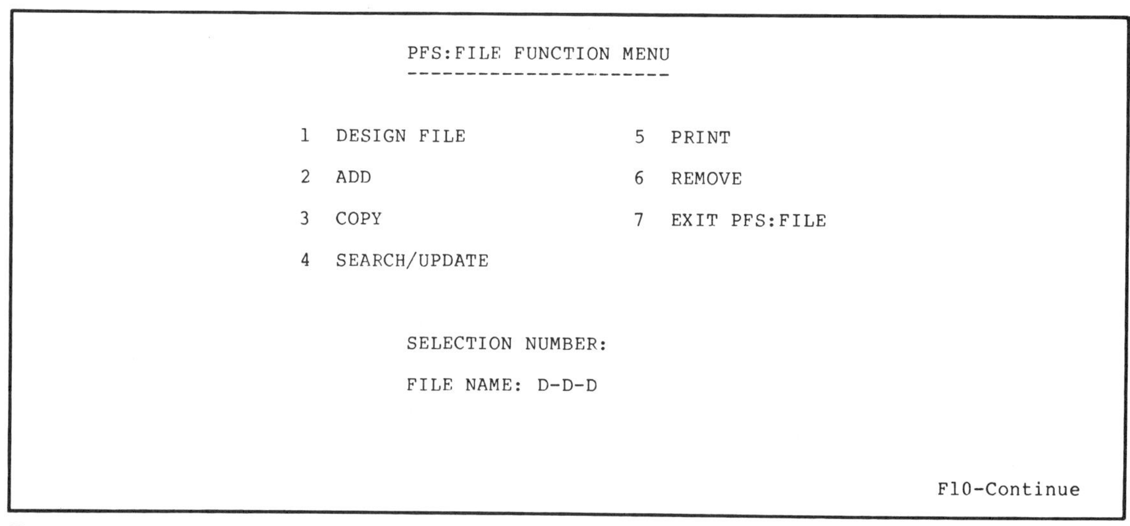

```
              PFS:FILE FUNCTION MENU
              ----------------------

      1  DESIGN FILE              5  PRINT

      2  ADD                      6  REMOVE

      3  COPY                     7  EXIT PFS:FILE

      4  SEARCH/UPDATE


              SELECTION NUMBER:

              FILE NAME: D-D-D


                                                  F10-Continue
```

Fig. 2-14, PFS:File Function Menu with filename automatically supplied.

the advantage that it does it quickly with a minimum of effort.

USING THE DESIGNED FORM

We are now ready to begin using the Do-Doing-Done file. Even though we are proud of it, we are not tied to its use forever. We can modify the form at a future time, so there is no need to feel like this is a point of no return. With an earlier version of *PFS:File* that I began using in 1981, the saving of a form *was* irrevocable. There were no facilities to modify forms. Nor were there options to copy selected forms onto another data disk. Nor were there as many different logical searches as are currently available. The old product has a maximum of fifty fields; the current product has a maximum of one hundred fields per page and a maximum of 32 pages per form, for a total capacity of 3200 fields per form. You may never need 3200 fields, but it is reassuring to know that the company is continuing to refine their products to supply the best possible. Examples like this illustrate the importance of filling in the User Group Enrollment Card. If the card is completed and mailed, Software Publishing Corporation will be able to let their customers know of these updates and improvements.

Even though the screen appearance may lead you to assume that you must fit all of your form onto one screen, or page, that is not the case. If we had preferred, a multiple page form could have been used. To do so, keep right on adding fields as long as you have fields that are important to retrieve. Use the PgUp and PgDn or CTRL and N (next) and CTRL and P (previous) keys to flip from page to page. As mentioned above there can be as many as 32 pages to a form. When part of a multiple page form is displayed on the screen, an asterisk (*) appears to cue you that there are other pages containing information.

Now is the time to test the design of our form by entering some data. After the continue key has been pressed to lock in the form during the design phase, the user will be presented with the PFS:File Function Menu, hereafter referred to as the Main Menu. As noted, the FILE NAME prompt continues to display D-D-D. Once a filename has been

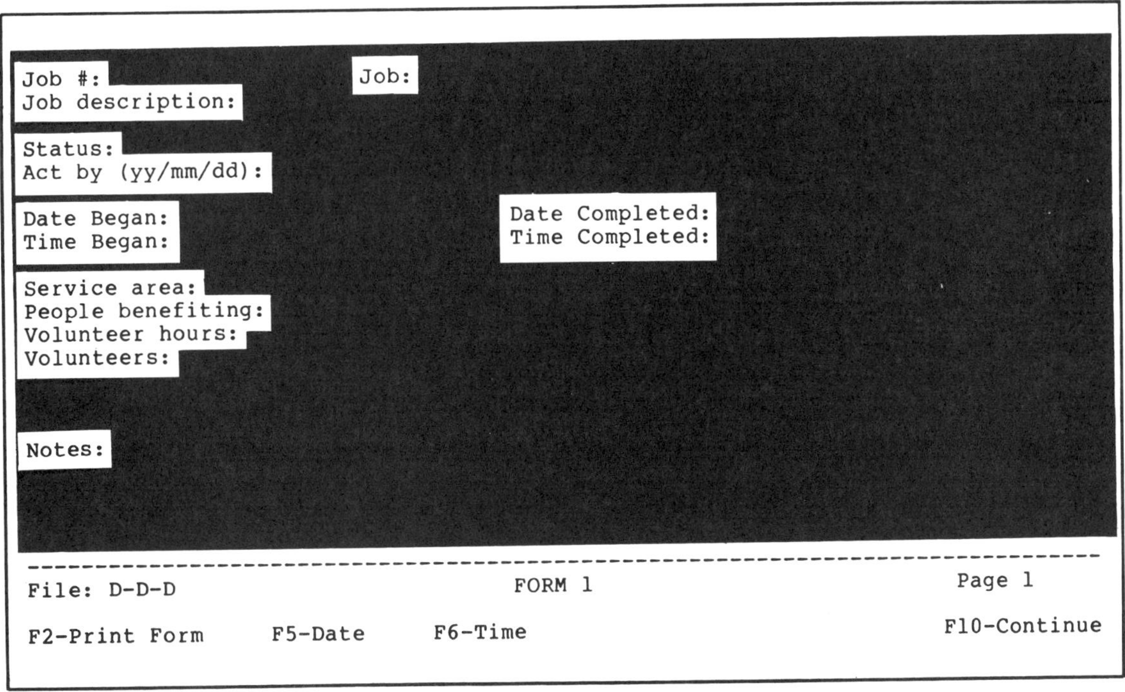

Fig. 2-15. Completed "Do-Doing-Done" form showing the way that fields are highlighted in the data entry procedure.

```
                COPY FUNCTION MENU



            1   COPY DESIGN ONLY

            2   COPY SELECTED FORMS

            3   COPY WHOLE FILE



                SELECTION NUMBER:

                NEW FILE NAME:

                                              F10-Continue
```

Fig. 2-16. Copy Function Menu of *PFS:File*.

entered, it will remain until the user changes it in order to work with a different file. It is a matter of convenience not to have to type the file name with each operation. We have only to choose our selection by typing the number corresponding to the operation that we want to perform. We are anxious to try out our form, I realize, but first let us protect our time investment by making a backup of our form.

Insert a formatted, or initialized disk, into the second drive. The second drive of an IBM PC is named drive B while the second Apple drive is named drive 2. Select COPY by pressing the 3 key and the continue key, F10, or CTRL and C. You will immediately be presented with another menu, the Copy Function Menu, shown in Fig. 2-16. Since our original file does not contain any entries thus far, the net results of choosing 1 COPY DESIGN ONLY or 3 COPY WHOLE FILE will be identical. Under normal circumstances 1 would be selected if a working file became completely filled or to prepare to use the option 2. If you wanted to copy selected forms, a form onto which the information could be copied would have to exist. In this backup procedure you are prompted for the new filename. As is normally the case, the TAB key on most systems (or <RIGHT ARROW> key on Apple *II*+ systems) moves the cursor to the next prompt. Per normal backup procedures, I will use option 3 COPY WHOLE FILE.

The new filename can be any name you choose, even the same name you gave the original file. It is, however, a good practice to supply all of the backup disk files with unique filenames. Providing a unique filename will decrease the possibility of accidentally updating the wrong disk. Apple *II*+/e/c systems will automatically provide the proper prompts to complete the backup procedure. I shall call the second disk D-D-D2.

IBM PC and other MS-DOS-based systems must have the drive of the backup disk specified. In our example, we will use "B:D-D-D2." Failure to designate the drive will cause the program to assume that the *destination disk* is in the first drive and cause problems. If you follow the practice of providing another name for the backup file, the worst that can happen is that there will be two data files on the same disk. If you forget to designate

```
COPY FUNCTION MENU

1  COPY DESIGN ONLY

2  COPY SELECTED FORMS

3  COPY WHOLE FILE

SELECTION NUMBER: 3

NEW FILE NAME: B:D-D-D2

                                        F10-Continue
```

Fig. 2-17. PFS:File Copy Function Menu completed to produce an exact backup, except with a unique filename.

either the use of a second drive OR a unique filename, the computer will inform you that NEW FILE MUST HAVE A UNIQUE NAME. Figure 2-17 illustrates how the Copy Function Menu should look to create a backup, or exact duplicate, of the original file.

In this case, since it is our first backup, the duplicate disk will be created automatically, without delay, after pressing the continue key. However, in the normal process of repeatedly making backup data disks on MS-DOS systems, you will see the message shown in Fig. 2-18 when updating a backup disk whose filename already exists.

This message is to remind you that when you use this process on magnetic media, only the most recent changes are saved. That is the primary reason that I recommend the use of an original disk and two backup disks. (See the section on Safeguarding Your Labor in Chapter 1.)

Apple *II*+/e/c systems provide this general warning:

PUT FILE IN DRIVE 1
PUT A DISKETTE IN DRIVE 2
WARNING
THE DISKETTE IN DRIVE 2 WILL
BE COMPLETELY OVER-WRITTEN
PRESS ESC TO ABANDON THIS OPERATION
PRESS CTRL-C TO CONTINUE

```
THE FILE ALREADY EXISTS

Press ESC to leave it and abandon this operation

Press F10 to delete it and continue
```

Fig. 2-18. Warning message that is displayed when a backup will replace an existing file.

In this case, the word "File" refers to your data file—*not* the *PFS:File* program disk. When the program disk is being referred to, the entire name, *PFS:File,* is used. The Apple backup procedure produces the entire backup, including the initializing of the disk.

ADDING TO YOUR FILES

Adding information to your files is a cinch and if the file has been well designed, retrieving information from it will be a cinch too. To get started adding forms to the file, simply select the second choice from the Main Menu, 2 ADD. The outline of the file appears with the field items highlighted on a white background. A blinking cursor will be beside the first field item. Also note that FORM 1, rather than DESIGN, appears in the bottom center of the screen. The number of the form will be incremented each time you add another form.

Start adding information to each field. Use the TAB key (or RIGHT ARROW key on Apple *II+* system) to move to each successive field. It is all right to leave fields blank. IBM and compatible systems as well as Apple *II*e/c systems automatically provide *word wraparound* to avoid splitting words in fields that have more than one line. Apple *II+* users must manually arrange the ending of lines so as not to split words in half. When each form is complete, as the one in Fig. 2-19 is, press the continue key to go on to the next form. In order to terminate the process of inputting new forms, press ESC. Do not press ESC *before* pressing the continue key upon completion of a form, or it will be lost.

Finding/Updating Information

Let us assume that we have logged in about a dozen jobs to complete, press ESC to terminate the input phase, and are ready to do some of our chores. Let us go back and retrieve the first job. We will press 4 SEARCH/UPDATE and then the continue key. The form is displayed again, only this time the centered status line says, RETRIEVE SPEC. (See Fig. 2-20.) We are to supply the information necessary to find the form or forms we want. In this case, let us start at the beginning, and retrieve Job # 001. We type 001 into the first item

```
Job #: 001                Job: Print depression pamphlets
Job description: Print 5000 "What is Depression" pamphlets.  Black on white.
trifold.
Status: do
Act by (yy/mm/dd): 84/03/24

Date Began:                          Date Completed:
Time Began:                          Time Completed:

Service area: Public education
People benefiting:
Volunteer hours:
Volunteers:



Notes:




-----------------------------------------------------------------------------
File: D-D-D                          FORM 1                          Page 1

F2-Print Form     F5-Date      F6-Time                          F10-Continue
```

Fig. 2-19. A completed first form ready for saving on disk.

```
Job #:                         Job:
Job description:

Status:
Act by (yy/mm/dd):

Date Began:                               Date Completed:
Time Began:                               Time Completed:

Service area:
People benefiting:
Volunteer hours:
Volunteers:


Notes:



--------------------------------------------------------------------------------
File: D-D-D                               RETRIEVE SPEC                     Page 1

F5-Date     F6-Time                                                 F10-Continue
```

Fig. 2-20. RETRIEVE SPECS screen on which the user provides the information to be matched in the Search/Update phase.

field, press the continue key, and immediately see the first form. Along the bottom status line, new options have appeared. F2-Print Form and F3-Remove Form are options on IBM-like systems. CTRL and O (output), and CTRL and R (remove) are equivalent Apple commands. It is possible to delete a page or record by pressing F3 or CTRL and R. If, however, the remove key is pressed by mistake, there is a chance to cancel that action because the message in Fig. 2-21 is shown.

In this case, we do not want to remove the form, so we will press the Space Bar on MS-DOS (or the RETURN key on Apple *II*+/e/c keyboards) to retain the form in our file. The form may be updated as we complete the project.

Notice that pressing F6 (MS-DOS) will automatically input a time stamp in a 24-hour, or "military" format as shown in Fig. 2-22. F5 will automatically insert the date in YY/MM//DD format. That is good as the start time can be subtracted from the completion time in *PFS:Report* to accurately track our time on each project. Each time we update a form and press continue, only the most recent version is stored. Following any search, a summary of the matching forms found will be summarized as it has been in Fig. 2-23.

There are five different ways that forms may be found using *PFS:File*:

- Full item match.
- Partial item match.
- Numeric item match.
- Numeric range match.
- Not match.

Searching for Job # 001 is a full item match. In order to find a desired file using a full item match, all

```
CURRENT FORM ABOUT TO BE REMOVED


 Press SPACE to keep the form

 Press F10 to remove the form
```

Fig. 2-21. The warning message that is displayed before an individual record is removed.

```
Job #: 001               Job: Print depression pamphlets
Job description: Print 5000 "What is Depression" pamphlets.  Black on white.
Trifold.
Status: done
Act by (yy/mm/dd): 84/03/24

Date Began: 84/03/24                   Date Completed: 84/03/24
Time Began: 11:30                      Time Completed: 13:31

Service area: Public education
People benefiting: 5000 - # in stock.
Volunteer hours: 3
Volunteers: Lorraine Bearth (folding)


Notes:



--------------------------------------------------------------------------------
File: D-D-D                            FORM 1                             Page 1

F2-Print Form     F3-Remove Form     F5-Date      F6-Time            F10-Continue
```

Fig. 2-22. Completed form that has been automatically date and time stamped.

characters given in the Retrieve Specs must have an exact, one to one correspondence with the characters in the specified field of the form. Another example of a full item match would be using the word "Do" as a retrieve spec in the Status field. (Capital and small letters are treated identically, and match each other.) Only a full item match in the *first* field will yield instantaneous finding of forms. Otherwise, each page of the form will have to be rapidly scanned in order to find the ones that match the given criteria.

A partial item match utilizes the two periods (. .) or wildcard, as mentioned earlier, in front of the desired match to indicate "ignore everything in front of the desired letters." By using partial item matches, we can find all job descriptions that involve printing by indicating ". . print . ." (ignore everything before *and* after the word "print.") The same approach could be used to track all projects that included ". . Lorraine . ." as one of the volunteers. A partial match of "do . ." in the "Status" field should not be used because it would find all projects categorized as "Do," "Doing," or "Done." Since blanks, in this case "ing" or "ne," are ignored, all of these status categories would be a match.

Numeric item matches may be exact matches, or may utilize > (greater than) and < (less than) matches. The "Act by (yy/mm/dd)" field can be used as a tickler file because we are able to search dates that are treated numerically. If today is December 28, 1984, and I run one search of the D-D-D file specifying that I want to retrieve <84/12/29 I will be reminded of all of the projects that should receive action by this date. Any project I do not act on will keep cropping up every time the search is executed until they are completed, and the followup date is eliminated. "Volunteer hours >50" will recall all large events, while "jobs >210" will recall only the most recently logged jobs.

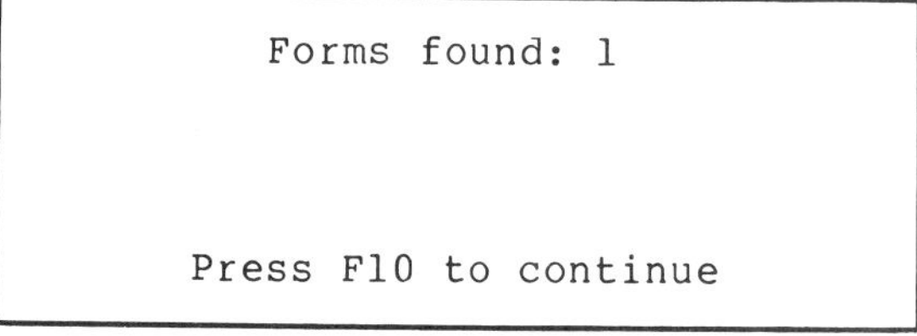
```
Forms found: 1


Press F10 to continue
```

Fig. 2-23. A summary of the number of forms found (that matched the Retrieve criteria specified).

Numeric Range searches are similar to numeric item matches, except that you are allowed to specify a beginning (or low) value and an ending (or high) value. For example a search criteria of =85/04/01 . . 85/06/30 in the "Date Completed" field will recall all projects completed in the second quarter of 1985. Retrieve specs of =10 . . 50 in the "Volunteer hours" field would recall projects with moderately high volunteer input.

The not match requires a slash in front of the retrieve specifications to indicate that all forms that do *not* meet the specified criteria are to be recalled. For example, "/Done" in the "Status" field will result in all projects "not done" (the "do" and "doing" projects). If we want to make sure that a field has had information entered into it for every page, we can use the "/. ." (not anything) search criteria. That way, we can check to make sure that all forms have been properly completed. For example, we might want to ensure that the "Service area" field has been completed before printing a summary of our organization's activities. This software helps you avoid a "how could I be so stupid" situation by allowing you to double check all entries. If we want to identify all of the projects begun in the first, third, and fourth quarters of the year, the retrieve specifications to enter in the appropriate field would be /=85/04/01 . . 85/06/30 (not equal to the second quarter).

Search criteria may be used alone or in combination. For example, we could identify well attended seminars with large volunteer involvement by retrieving "Volunteer hours >20" *and* "People benefiting >50." There are no limits to the number of fields that you can match to recall the form. However, combining criteria with *PFS:File* in a single pass is always an AND search. Remember, an AND search is an intersection of sets. (Review Fig. 2-1.)

Using the COPY Function

Searches intended to recap a union of sets, OR searches, require multiple passes (searches). For example, if we want to recall all events that benefitted at least 20 people OR that utilized at least 20 hours of volunteer time, we have to use two searches. One of the easiest ways would be to use the COPY function in the following manner:

1. Place a formatted disk into drive B.
2. Use option 1 COPY DESIGN ONLY of the Copy Function Menu to create a form identical to the one you are using.
3. Next use 2 COPY SELECTED FORMS of the Copy Function Menu.
4. For Retrieve specs of the forms to be copied, specify >20 in the "People benefiting" field. The number of forms copied will be displayed.
5. Use 2 COPY SELECTED FORMS again, only this time specify >20 in the "Volunteer hours" field item.
6. Now, there will be a single disk with all of the desired forms. Reports may now be generated, or the many projects that met those criteria may again be subdivided.

PRINTING FORMS

Being able to print information on a printer is tremendously helpful. We may want to print out the "Do" and "Doing" projects and be able to reference them during the day when the computer may be dedicated to other purposes. To obtain just such a printout, first select 5 PRINT and press the continue key. Apple *II*+/e/c versions operate differently at this point than IBM-type systems. Apple systems first present a PRINT MENU screen with two options: 1 PRINT FORMS and 2 DEFINE PRINT SPECS. The second option allows the user to store print specifications that will be used repeatedly, such as "labels." The first option, PRINT FORMS will bring the user to the RETRIEVE SPEC screen (that is identical to the RETRIEVE SPEC screen of the 4 SEARCH/UPDATE function).

When the RETRIEVE SPEC screen appears, type "/done" (not done) in the status field. That means that the "Do" and "Doing" projects will be selected. After pressing the continue key, the PRINT OPTIONS screen will appear. (See Fig. 2-24.) This figure compares the IBM version of the screen to the Apple *II*+/e/c version. The Apple *II*+/c/e is similar except for two prompts. Instead of Print to: LPT1 (print to line parallel printer) the

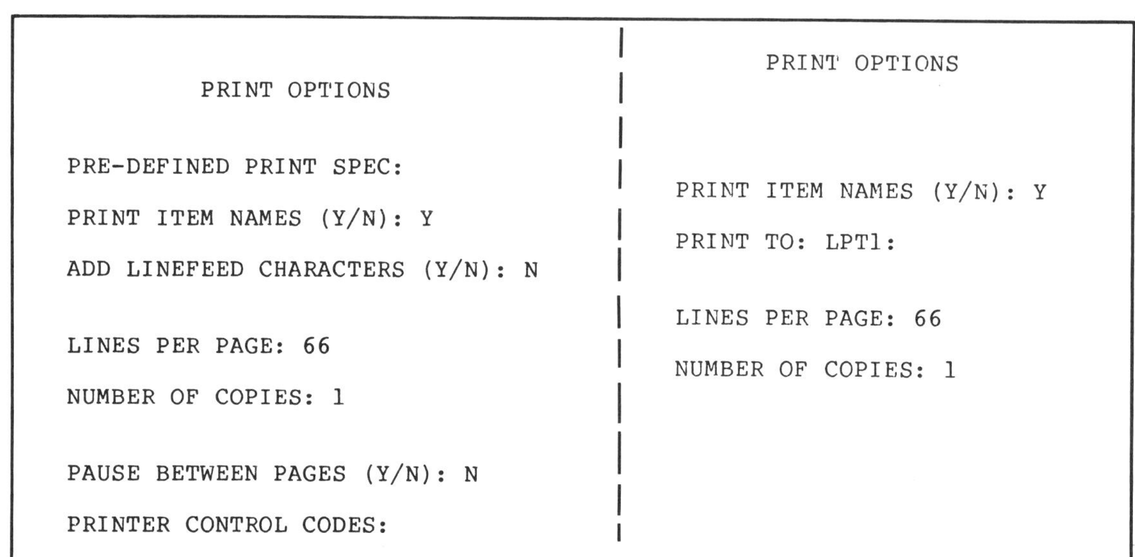
PRINT OPTIONS

PRE-DEFINED PRINT SPEC:

PRINT ITEM NAMES (Y/N): Y

ADD LINEFEED CHARACTERS (Y/N): N

LINES PER PAGE: 66

NUMBER OF COPIES: 1

PAUSE BETWEEN PAGES (Y/N): N

PRINTER CONTROL CODES:

PRINT OPTIONS

PRINT ITEM NAMES (Y/N): Y

PRINT TO: LPT1:

LINES PER PAGE: 66

NUMBER OF COPIES: 1

Fig. 2-24. Print Options of *PFS:File* for both Apple and IBM microcomputers.

Apple version has the prompt Output device (P/L):P. The "P" is used to signify a printer that uses an automatic line feed. "L" designates that a line feed be sent to the printer after each printed line (for double spacing or to supply one when there is not an automatic line feed). Don't wade through your printer manual to find out what yours requires. Try printing some information using the default value, "P." If the information prints over itself, change the value to "L" for all subsequent printings. There is also the opportunity (on the Apple only) to specify the name of a PRE-DEFINED PRINT SPC. In order to use that prompt, you would have to have previously defined print specs (such as "labels").

The blinking cursor flashes under the "Y" of PRINT ITEM NAMES, and all of the default values are provided. If you don't want the field item names (such as "Job") listed in the printout, you may change the response to the first prompt to an "N." The parallel printer value on IBM systems is given as LPT1. Serial printer users can change the value of COM1 or AUX. Lines per page may be changed to accommodate different paper sizes or compressed type fonts on the printer. Normally, mailing labels require only 6 lines. If the "number of copies" prompt is changed to a number other than one, *PFS:File* prints the specified number of copies of each selected form before selecting another form. Changes made in the values of the Print Options Menu will be stored by the program and supplied as the new default values the next time you use the print option.

Since, in this example, I only want a list of the projects not completed, I do not really need a page dedicated to each project, so I change the LINES PER PAGE to a value of 11. (To avoid the chance of printing on the perforations of the paper, I have choosen a number that divides into 66.) Old versions of *PFS:File* were somewhat limited in that there were no provisons for pausing between pages in the printing operation. A new Apple version of the program, and an expected new IBM version correct that limitation. Another enhancement is the ability to send control codes to the printer. After changing "66" to "11," I press the continue key.

Once again the D-D-D form is displayed. Only this time the status line on the bottom of the screen indicates PRINT SPEC. It is here that we tell the program what we want printed. *PFS:File* prints the items in the order they appear in the form. If you do not like that arrangement, you can utilize the sorting capability of *PFS:Report*, the merge capability of *PFS:Write*, or rearrange your form to reorganize the information.

There are three different print specifications that can be supplied:

- Placing an "X" beside the field item indicates that you want this item to be printed, and then a line feed sent to the printer.
- Placing a "+" beside a field item indicates that you want this item to be printed, but that no line feed should be sent to the printer (instead, two spaces will be skipped). It may be remembered as printing this item "plus" another item that will follow.
- An "S" following either an "X" or a "+" indicates the report items should be sorted on the basis this single item. An "S" used alone without an "X" or "+" will not cause the item to be printed. Only a single "S" (sort) function may be used in *PFS:File*.

To get a *hardcopy* printout (on paper) of our list of projects not yet completed, we will print the "Job #" and "Job" on the same line, followed by the "Job description." The "Status" will be printed on a separate line, and we have used "S" to indicate that we want the report sorted on this basis, that is, the "Do" projects should be listed before the "Doing" projects. Finally, our printout will include the "Act by" date for easy reference. The complete PRINT SPEC screen is shown in Fig. 2-25.

As the disk drive turns following the signal to continue, we see the screen display SELECTING and then SORTING, as it performs these functions. If we had not used the sort function, the program would begin immediately printing forms in sequential order from the most recent to oldest. The program informs us of the number of forms that have been printed. Maybe the printout will go onto our pegboard to remind us of our tasks at hand. A sample printout is shown in Fig. 2-26.

TRANSFERRING AND REMOVING FORMS

The sixth option on the Main Menu is 6 REMOVE. REMOVE allows you to remove forms that are no longer needed on your form. Let us suppose that we have been keeping our D-D-D file faithfully for several months. We note that there are several hundred forms on the disk and searches for items that cannot be identified by "Job #" are taking about 20 seconds to complete. An excellent way to avoid

```
Job #: +                  Job: X
Job description: X

Status: XS
Act by (yy/mm/dd): X

Date Began:                          Date Completed:
Time Began:                          Time Completed:

Service area:
People benefiting:
Volunteer hours:
Volunteers:



Notes:



-------------------------------------------------------------------------------
File: D-D-D                          PRINT SPEC                        Page 1

F5-Date     F6-Time                                              F10-Continue
```

Fig. 2-25. Completed print specifications that will result in a list of projects sorted by status.

```
Job #: 006  Job: telecommunicate with congressmen
Job description: send immediate communication supporting HB575
Status: do
Act by (yy/mm/dd): 84/05/12



Job #: 005  Job: Biofeedback Seminar
Job description: coordinate seminar activities
Status: do
Act by (yy/mm/dd): 84/07/17



Job #: 002  Job: Film & Speech
Job description: Present "Only Human" and lead discussion for H.S. seniors at
East High
Status: Do
Act by (yy/mm/dd): 84/04/30



Job #: 004  Job: Transitional Living meeting
Job description: Meet with Transitional living committee and consider budget for
next fiscal year.
Status: do
Act by (yy/mm/dd): 84/06/01



Job #: 003  Job: Prepare flyer
Job description: Develop, design and print flyer advertising the biofeedback
seminar to be held July 17, 1984
Status: doing
Act by (yy/mm/dd): 84/06/01
```

Fig. 2-26. A sample printout of "Do-Doing-Done" jobs not yet completed, with project catagorized as "Do" listed first.

crowded disks is to transfer all of the "Done" projects onto a new, "Done" data disk. Transferring them onto the new disk will ensure that the information can be recalled when needed. After the "Done" projects have been transferred, using the REMOVE command on the original disk will free more space on the disk, and shorten the time necessary for searches.

In order to subdivide a file into smaller files, the following procedure can be used:

1. Make a backup of the original data disk (in case something goes wrong).
2. Copy the design of the form, using 3 COPY from the Main Menu and then the 1 COPY DESIGN ONLY function from the Copy Function Menu.
3. Copy selected forms by using 3 COPY at the Main Menu and then 2 COPY SELECTED FORMS from the Copy Function Menu. The retrieve specs that you provide will select the forms that are to be copied. Make note of the number of forms that were copied.
4. Delete from the original file the forms that have been transferred to the new file by selecting option 6 REMOVE from the Main Menu. The retrieve specs that you provide will identify the forms that are to be removed. Note the number of forms that were removed.
5. If the retrieve specs that you provided for copying selected forms and removing forms were

```
Job #:                       Job:
Job description:

Status: done
Act by (yy/mm/dd):

Date Began:                                Date Completed:
Time Began:                                Time Completed:

Service area:
People benefiting:
Volunteer hours:
Volunteers:


Project (A/B):
Notes:


--------------------------------------------------------------------------------
File: D-D-D                    RETRIEVE SPEC                          Page 1

F5-Date     F6-Time                                            F10-Continue
```

Fig. 2-27. The screen that requests the "retrieve specs" of forms that are to be removed.

identical, the number of forms copied will equal the number of forms removed. If the numbers do not match, an error was made, and you should return to step 1. If the numbers of forms copied and removed match, proceed with use of the file and then backup the modified disks.

Choosing 6 REMOVE and pressing continue will bring you to the now familiar D-D-D form with a retrieve spec status line. (See Fig. 2-27.) The retrieve specs that you supply are the specifications for the forms that you want removed. Typing Done in the "Status" field and continuing will select all of the projects that are "Done" as pages that will be removed. *PFS:File* does not take this action lightly, and provides the user with one last warning as shown in Fig. 2-28.

Following this operation, the number of forms removed will be displayed. In this case the number of forms removed would equal the number of forms transferred. If the numbers are not equal, different retrieve specs were used for the two operations, and it is time to pull out the backup data disks.

CHANGING FORMS

The development of a form can be a trial and error process. After designing it, we find certain bits of needed information can't be put on the form, or circumstances change that require changing the form. Using the D-D-D form that we have developed, let us assume that we now remember that we have not left ample room for listing milestones. Let us make room for subdividing any project into four milestones. Also, imagine that our needs have just changed. A new service has come under the supervisory umbrella of our organization in order to save it from collapse. However, the funding source

```
 SELECTED FORMS ABOUT TO BE REMOVED


Press ESC to abandon this operation

       Press F10 to continue
```

Fig. 2-28. A last warning that selected forms are about to be removed.

```
DESIGN FILE MENU

1  CREATE FILE

2  CHANGE DESIGN

SELECTION NUMBER: 2

F10-Continue
```

Fig. 2-29. An illustration of the Design File Menu completed for modifying an existing form.

for the new service is different from ours, and we must be very careful to account for time spent in each service area as neither agency wants to fund the other's project. The existing "Time Began" and "Time Completed" field items could be very helpful in tracking our time commitment, if we had a convenient way of subdividing the time between the two projects. So, we need more fields in our form.

In order to modify an existing form, select DESIGN FILE. Again, the Design File Menu appears. This time, however, to change an existing file, 2 CHANGE DESIGN, will be selected as illustrated in Fig. 2-29. When it is selected, the serious looking warning in Fig. 2-30 appears. It admonishes us to make a backup before proceeding.

After ensuring that we have a backup we continue. The designated file, D-D-D appears, this time without the highlighted white background behind fieldnames and with DESIGN listed clearly on the status line. Anything may be changed or moved around at this point. Remember, however, that only the information that has IDENTICAL field item

```
W A R N I N G

THE CONTENTS OF THE FILE WILL BE CHANGED BY THIS OPERATION

MAKE A BACKUP OF THE FILE BEFORE CONTINUING

Press ESC to abandon this operation

Press F10 to continue
```

Fig. 2-30. Warning message given before modifying an existing form—to ensure that the user first makes a backup copy of his/her valuable data.

names will be transferred onto the revised form. With this form, since I still like the flexibility of using "Notes" as a free form field, I will use the cursor control keys to bring the flashing cursor to the beginning of "Notes" and type over it with a new field named "Project (A/B)" remembering to end it with a colon. On the next line, I will reeenter the field "Notes." Forms that already have data entered in the "Notes" field will have that information accurately transferred onto the revised form because the field "Notes" is named identically on both the old and revised forms. The new field, "Project (A/B)" will appear blank on every form. Next, we will use the PgDn or CTRL-N keys to move on to another area of work space and enter our "milestone" fields. After completeing the changes, we indicate our acceptance of the new form by pressing the continue key.

Most computers then involve a fair amount of time writing the information to a temporary file on the second disk drive and back to the revised form on the first disk drive. Figure 2-31 displays a completed form with the new fields present. Now each form has the capability of being classified into one of two categories. That will make it considerably easier to determine which "hat" the employees were wearing for what percentage of their work days.

Obviously, EXIT is a means of exit from the program. Again, I encourage taking the five extra seconds necessary to press 7 and F10. There is no better way to be sure you have properly closed all files than to properly exit a program. Also, there is no easier way to enter another program, such as

```
Job #: 006                    Job: Telecommunicate with congressmen
Job description: Send immediate communication supporting HB-575

Status: Done
Act by (yy/mm/dd): 84/05/12

Date Began: 84/05/12                Date Completed: 84/05/12
Time Began: 09:00                   Time Completed: 11:15

Service area: advocacy
People benefiting: 100,000
Volunteer hours: 12
Volunteers: Bacon, Schyler, & Wesley studied proposed changes.  Cole lobbied
directly on hill.


Project (A/B): A
Notes: HB-575 mandates adequate mental health coverage, including drug and
alcoholism services, on all group insurance policies sold in this state.

1st milestone: Draft letter explaining Association's position.
To be done by: 10:00
Actual date completed: 10:00

2nd milestone: Have content checked and proofed.
To be done by: 10:30
Actual date completed: 10:20

3rd milestone: Use PFS:Access to send 4 hour letter by MCI mail.
To be done by: 10:45
Actual date completed: 10:30

4th milestone: Confirm sending of communique to social action committee.
To be done by: 11:30
Actual date completed: 11:15
```

Fig. 2-31. A form that has had "milestone" fields completed for a telecommunications project.

```
Member #: 0031          Fname: Larry
Lname: Jackel           Ext(, Jr.):          Title(Dr.,Ms.): Mr.
L2:
L3: 123 Bellmont Circle
L4: Blue Grass, KY                 Zip: 25385
Telephone: 606 123-9876
Date Joined: 80/05/15              Date of last renewal: 84/05/15
Amount: $100.00                    Previous yr's amount: $100.00
General Membership (x): x          Newsletter  only (x):
Board of Directors (x):            Executive Board  (x):
Professional advisory board (x):
Committees: Finance

Types of Vol work: Investment, tax and accounting advice - as needed.

Mon   (x):      From:                    To:          Or:
Tues  (x):      From:                    To:          Or:
Wed   (x):      From:                    To:          Or:
Thurs(x):       From:                    To:          Or:
Fri   (x):      From:                    To:          Or:
Sat   (x):      From:                    To:          Or:

Sun   (x):      From:                    To:          Or:
Has own transportation (y/n):
Volunteer hours (current yr): 10
Other organizations: United Way, Green Peace

notes: Call secretary on Monday for week's schedule.


text:
```

Fig. 2-32. A completed "Members" file that will serve for mailing lists, track contributions, and schedule volunteer time.

PFS:Report, than to get the DOS> prompt and then type REPORT and press ENTER. To get the DOS> prompt, simply select 7 EXIT PFS:File.

EXAMPLES OF ADVANCED FORMS

Now that we've covered the mechanics of how *PFS:File* searches are done, we have a foundation for constructing useful forms. The capability of the system will be limited by the quality of the form design. Let's develop a *PFS:File* form that will be able to keep track of our membership, satisfy our mailing list needs, and track contributions to our organization.

First of all, the types of information that we want to record and be able to retrieve should be summarized. We want name, address, telephone number (s), dates of joining and renewing membership, amount contributed, committees and boards served, volunteer times available, types of volunteer work interested in, and total number of hours volunteered. That is a pretty ambitious form, but since we know that we will not be able to recall things that have not been planned for, let's try to include all possibilities. We certainly do not want to change forms unless we absolutely have to. All of the categories considered for the "Members" file is shown in Fig. 2-32, a form filled in with sample data.

The second consideration is to decide what will be our first item, the one that will allow instantaneous selection. My first inclination is to use "Last name." After all, that is how we are used to looking up names in telephone books and files. There would be little inconvenience to looking at the files of two or three members who have the same last name. However, the fact that *PFS:File* prints the fields in the order that they are presented on the form argues against that idea. If we choose to use the "Last name" as the first field, we will lose the ability to print address labels quickly without having to depend on the search and replace capability of *PFS:Write* to put the items into the proper sequence. (More about Write later.) *PFS:File* cannot reorder the sequence of fields in the printing operation. By using the sort feature, we could even have labels presorted by zip code.

An alternate approach is use "Member #" as the first field. I realize that a lot of people resent the use of numbers to represent people, but it is sometimes expedient. No one on the membership list will ever have to encounter a number. *PFS: Report* could easily produce an alphabetical listing and a numeric listing of the members that could provide quick cross reference for the computer operator. Another alternative that would enable the printing of address labels out of the *PFS:File* program would be to let the first field be used for "First name." That, however, has the distinct disadvantage of missing "Charles" when you look for "Chuck" or "Charlie."

Having decided on "Member #" as the first item, "Fname" suggests itself for the next field. Any middle initials or second names may be put into this field; for instance, "James B." or "Mary Lou." Next, we will have to account for names that have extensions after their names, such as "JR.," "III," "M.D.," or "Ph.D." It is not satisfactory to try to use an extension in the "Lname" field. Doing so would limit the flexibility of its use with the word processor, *PFS:Write*. For example, in the body of the letter, you may want to include, "Again, *Title* *Lname*, your support has been greatly appreciated." If you had not separated the extension from the name you could find that when the letter is printed, you have, "Again, Dr. King, Ph.D.", your support has been greatly appreciated." I chose to take care of that potential problem by naming a field "Ext (, Jr.)." That way, we have a built-in prompt for the kind of information we want, as well as the format we want it in. After all, more than one person may input information, and we will want it to be consistent.

Field items as prompts are useful until they become too long. For example, I once tried to name a field "Status (Contracted, Board, Submission, Waiting, Rejected)." When I tried to get a report for the data, *PFS:Report* typed the entire field name on the top of the report, and I had almost no room left for the rest of the report. I tried to remedy the situation by changing the form to "Status: (Contracted, Board, Submission, Waiting, Rejected)." That shortened the report heading, but caused problems in the transfer of data and required that I provide an "Identifier spec" at each time I used the next field because there was no colon (:) clearly marking it as a field item.

The field "Title(Dr. ,Ms.)" allows for the future writing of individualized form letters. It, too, prompts for the type and format of the data requested. It will be used to produce a "Dear Ms. Blake" salutation from a Dear *Title(Dr. ,Ms.)* *Lname* form letter. Some people may want to incorporate a separate field for "Salutation." That way, you have the flexibility of patching in a "Dear JeanneAnne" to one well known member, while maintaining the more formal, "Dear Ms. Casson," format in the next letter.

The next objective is to provide space for the members' addresses. Generally, I find that a simple "L2," "L3," "L4" does very nicely as a representation of the second through fourth lines of an address. Using such a format provides the flexibility needed for mailing to private addresses and to business addresses. Also, it avoids the squeeze in trying to fit some extremely long addresses onto a single line. For example, an address like "5241 Fish and Game Road, Apt. 3-G" might not fit into the space provided on a standard mailing label. It is convenient to have the option of moving the apartment number down to another line. Such formats also provide a form that is not limited in the handling of foreign address that may not be arranged in the standard "City-State-Zip" format.

We know that we are going to want to produce mailing labels and that we are going to want those mailing labels sorted by zip code, so we will provide a field "Zip" following the fourth line "L4" field. During the entry of information, we will just skip the "L2" field when there is only a three-line address. *PFS:File* will not print a blank line when the field is blank, so there will be no strange looking labels. Also, by designating that the second line be treated as text, there will be no difficulties later when we want to utilize the interactive capabilities of *PFS:Write* with *PFS:File* to produce individualized form letters. (More about that topic in Chapter 8.)

The way that *PFS:File* sorts numerically based on the first digit was mentioned as a limitation earlier in the chapter when we were discussing the necessity of entering job numbers in a standard format using the same number of digits. That limitation actually turns into an advantage in the treatment of zip codes. With some people using five digits and others using nine digits, it will be nice not to worry about entering the code in a standard format. *PFS:File* will sort according to each digit from left to right, thereby automatically sorting mail correctly. As a general rule, leave more room in each field than you think you will need. Remember that additional space will be required in the RETRIEVE SPECS phase if you need to designate a not search or a search for numbers within a range of values.

The "Telephone number" field is self explanatory. Plenty of room has been left so that numbers can be entered and designated with H (home) or W (work) tags. If your organization gets involved in heavy telephoning or wants to analyze data according to exchanges, separate space should be provided for each telephone listing. Grouping different numbers together causes the program to consider them as one huge number when treating a field numerically.

PFS:File should encompass every bit of information that is recorded anywhere on cards, histories, or personal memories. "Date joined" is an important piece of information to your organization. If someone was a founding member fifteen years ago and is now not responding to your membership drive, find out why. He or she may be able to point out some things you are doing wrong. Perhaps he/she is having financial problems and is unable to make a contribution right now, but you wouldn't want him/her to be removed from the mailing list. Computers can be used to make your organization more responsive and personal, not impersonal and dehumanizing.

"Date of last renewal" can become the criteria by which you select who will get second and third reminders of your membership drive. It can also serve as the criteria by which some forms are transferred onto a "Past members" file when, despite your best efforts, no renewal check has arrived. "Amount" is, after all, an important category for the future of your organization. A quick letter might begin as follows:

Dear *Title(Dr., Ms)* *Lname*:
Thank you for your contribution of
Amount(T) . . . . .

It will be appreciated by your members as a receipt for their tax records. Your treasurer will also appreciate the ability of *PFS:Report* to automatically add all of the contributions received. The statistician and analyst in the group can use the power of *PFS:File* to subtotal contributions from each zip code area to target redoubled effort in areas that are not well penetrated.

I know some contributors who only contribute to organizations every other year, doubling their normal contribution in their "giving" years in order to take advantage of tax benefits. In their honor, and in order to identify members who have made significant contributions, I have included the "Previous year's amount."

Next we have provided the opportunity to designate different subcategories of membership and committees that a person may be a part of. A single listing of name and address is all that is necessary. By placing an "X" in the retrieve spec beside "Board of Directors (X)," board meeting notices can be sent to only the 40 people who should receive them. A free form is left beside "Committees" in order to allow for the coming and going of *ad hoc* committees, without being locked into a useless form. In order to inform members of the Finance Committee of a meeting time and location, the retrieve spec can be given as ". . finance . ." after the "Committee" field.

The final part of the form has been dedicated to matching volunteer interests and times of availability. If your organization does not use volunteers to a great extent, it could be quite sufficient to have a free form "Days and times available" and then search for ". . Tues . ." for example. If the form does not make it very clear whether the person is available in the mornings or afternoons, the telephone number is always right there to call him/her and see.

In addition to the free form notes, I have included a field entitled "Text." It has no real function right now. However, you may find in writing individualized form letters that you want to write a sentence or two to only one person. In that case, "Text" can be inserted into the proper letter without interrupting the normal progress of the mass mailing.

The final stage for the development of a form is trying it out. Add a few forms to see if the input of information flows well. Are all field items very clear as to what should be entered? Is there ample room for all retrieve specs? Next try the print options. Are the fields in the correct order? After you master some of the other program modules, try printing out a few reports. Do any of the names of the fields have to be shortened? Graph a simple chart or two. Are you able to retrieve the information you need? Try merging the information from *PFS:File* into letters created with *PFS:Write*. Does it work? Can you write individualized form letters? Is it convenient to use?

MORE EXAMPLES OF ADVANCED FORMS

Now, we have the knowledge that will allow us to prepare as many forms as we can imagine. A few more forms will be developed for illustration of the many applications that are possible. Remember, *PFS:File* can be used to create as many different forms as you have a need for. In developing these forms, it is important to note a consistency of design that will allow you to transfer as much data as possible between forms. Once conventions are established, it will be best to follow those conventions consistently.

When I was employed with the Mental Health Association in Sedgwick County, Kansas, we cooperated with the Junior League in a project to distribute a series of parental educational newletters called "Pierre the Pelican." Volunteers visited area hospitals to leave the first issue with new mothers. Thereafter, Pierre could arrive, free of charge, once a month for the first year, every other month in the second year, four times a year during the third year, three times a year in the fourth year, twice the fifth year, and once, when the child turned six years of age. Needless to say, that was a huge mailing list problem that was destined to become worse and worse. Before computers became common, only the diligent efforts of volunteers and staff were able to maintain such a series of mailings.

Solving these kinds of problems are the kinds of things that computers and *PFS:File* do best. Another form can be easily designed (Fig. 2-33) while the *PFS:File* program is in the computer's memory by inserting another formatted or initialized data disk in the drive.

You will note that the format of lines for names, addresses, extensions, and titles are identical to that of the "Members" file. It does not matter whether the field names appear in the same order. As long as the field names are identical, the information that appears in those fields can be transferred onto another disk without any problems. For example, after some of the people who receive the "Pierre" newsletter join the organization, we will update the data base by entering "Y" after the "Membership (Y/N)" field. Then we will be able to transfer their information onto the membership file automatically by using retrieve specs of "Y" in the COPY SELECTED FORMS procedure. One key factor in optimal utilization of any database manager is to keep data entry and update procedures to a minimum.

The verification fields are to enable the

```
Child's d.o.b.(yy/mm/dd):
Title(Dr.,Ms.):
Fname:
Lname:
Ext(, Jr.):
L2:
L3:
L4:                           Zip:
Telephone:
6mo.verify (y/n):             lyr.verify (y/n):
2yr.verity (y/n):             3yr.verify (y/n):       4yr.verify (y/n):

Membership (y/n):
Date Joined:
Amount:
```

Fig. 2-33. A "Pierre" form for a periodic mail list that allows for periodic validation of addresses.

periodic updating and verification of the mailing list. New parents are a very mobile group, and letters in the dead letter office will do no one any good. If you select the appropriate year and month in the retrieve specs the program will select the appropriate address for each issue of Pierre. The sort option with the Print function can print out addresses in ascending order by zip code.

One of the most desired applications for computers is inventory control. There are some large programs dedicated to this area. Programs of that nature allow the user to indicate whether their inventory system uses the LIFO (Last In First Out) method or the FIFO (First In First Out) method. There are consumption histories and averages, order points, and a host of answers to questions that I don't even know how to ask. However, a little *PFS:File* called "Inventory" (Fig. 2-34) would

```
Product #:
Product Name:
Re-order point:              Normal order qty:
Price breaks:
Beginning qty:
1st order qty:               Date:                  Price:
2nd order qty:               Date:                  Price:
3rd order qty                Date:                  Price:
4th order qty:               Date:                  Price:
5th order qty:               Date:                  Price:
6th order qty:               Date:                  Price:

1st inv. count:              Date:
2nd inv. count:              Date:
3rd inv. count:              Date:
4th inv. count:              Date:
Suppliers:


Notes:
--------------------------------------------------------------------------------
File: INVENTORY                    DESIGN                             Page 1

F5-Date      F6-Time                                            F10-Continue
```

Fig. 2-34. An "Inventory" form designed to record the number of pamphlets printed and distributed.

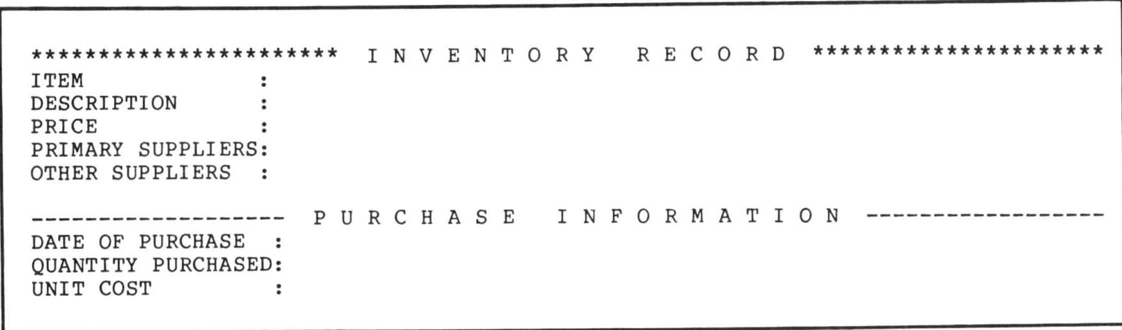

```
*********************** I N V E N T O R Y   R E C O R D ***********************
ITEM              :
DESCRIPTION       :
PRICE             :
PRIMARY SUPPLIERS:
OTHER SUPPLIERS   :

------------------- P U R C H A S E   I N F O R M A T I O N -----------------
DATE OF PURCHASE  :
QUANTITY PURCHASED:
UNIT COST         :
```

Fig. 2-35. An "Inventory" form designed by Software Publishing Corporation.

probably tell me everything I need to know about how many pamphlets I have used, and how many I should order to print.

The people at Software Publishing Corporation decided to make their own *PFS:Solutions* inventory template, a predesigned form you can purchase, a little more general. Its layout is revealed in Fig. 2-35. Stored right on that same disk are the means for generating pre-defined reports. Of course, these reports such as the sample shown in Fig. 2-36, must utilize *PFS:Report* to function.

In the next chapter, we will see how the *PFS:Report* companion program can manipulate numbers in fields. An obvious "quick fix" for determining what products to reorder would be to subtract "Reorder point" from the most recent inventory count. Any negative numbers displayed would indicate that the product has passed its reorder point.

Keeping track of our bills with PFS is no problem. As each group of bills arrives, they can be entered into the "payables" files of Fig. 2-37. Such a file will provide an extremely quick reference and be able to sort the paid from unpaid bills. Also, as

```
                    A Sample Printout of the MARGINS report

                DESCRIPTION              UNIT COST     PRICE      PROFIT MARGIN
        -------------------------        ---------     -----      -------------
        Garden Hoses                          2.89
                                              2.89
                                              2.89      5.79             100.35

        Garden rake - long prong              8.33
                                              8.33     12.99              55.94
                                              7.11

        Hammer                                2.14
                                              2.14
                                              2.14      8.99             320.09

--------------------------------                                  -------------
Average:                                                                 158.79
Count:                          3
--------------------------------                                  -------------
```

Fig. 2-36. A sample of the output of the PFS:Solutions "Invtry" form. This pre-defined report calculates profit margins.

```
Invoice no:                 Date received:
Description:
Amount:
Pay to:
L2:
L3:
L4:

Amount paid:                Date paid:

Check number:

Account category:
```

Fig. 2-37. A simple "Payables" form to keep track of paid and unpaid bills.

we shall see, *PFS:Report* can be used to calculate the total amount of payables or sort them from oldest to newest.

Another handy application of a database manager is to keep track of articles you have read and want stored. That is one area in which traditional filing methods fail miserably. Normally, recalling an article involves endless searching through tables of contents in numerous magazines. The keyword search capabilities of *PFS:File* provide a quick solution to that boondoggle.

The keyword file can be set up in pretty much the same manner as other database files. All of the articles can be indexed, and all of the pertinent information can be included in the form. Figure 2-38 illustrates one way a keyword file for magazine articles can be set up. The search phase of *PFS:Report* operates a little differently from other reports and is also slower to perform. We will discuss that in more detail in the next chapter.

PFS:SOLUTIONS

In an effort to make the process of getting started with computers as simple as possible, Software Publishing Corporation has begun to offer *PFS:Solutions*. *Solutions* are prepackaged templates (or files) similar to those we've just designed, that are intended to allow the user to "load and go" without having to participate in the time-consuming and tedious process of form design. In using these prepackaged forms there is a tradeoff in flexibility. Three commercially available "Solu-

```
Perodical:
Volume #:                   Issue #:
Date (yy/mm/dd):
Title:

Keywords:

Abstract:
```

Fig. 2-38. "Keyword" form for indexing and cross referencing magazine articles.

```
*********************** I N V E N T O R Y   R E C O R D **********************
ITEM             :
DESCRIPTION      :
PRICE            :
PRIMARY SUPPLIERS:
OTHER SUPPLIERS  :

------------------- P U R C H A S E   I N F O R M A T I O N -----------------
DATE OF PURCHASE  :
QUANTITY PURCHASED:
UNIT COST         :










-------------------------------------------------------------------------------
File: INVTRY                        RETRIEVE SPEC                    Page 1

F5-Date     F6-Time                                              F10-Continue
```

Fig. 2-39. PFS:Solutions "Invtry" template with screen prompts.

```
***************** T I C K L E R   F I L E / D A I L Y   L O G **************
DATE:                       DAY:
--------------------- T I C K L E R   F I L E   I T E M S -------------------
TIME          COMMENTS                                                      :




------------------------- A P P O I N T M E N T S ---------------------------
TIME          COMMENTS                                                      :




--------------------------- E X P E N S E   L O G ----------------------------
MEALS        :          LODGING         :           AIR FARE :
CAR/TAXI     :          MILEAGE/PARKING:            TELEPHONE:
ENTERTAINMENT:          OTHER           :
COMMENTS     :
-------------------------------------------------------------------------------
File: TICKLER                       RETRIEVE SPEC                    Page 1

F5-Date     F6-Time                                              F10-Continue
```

Fig. 2-40. PFS:Solutions "Tickler" template.

```
************************* P A Y R O L L   R E C O R D *************************
      NAME:
PAY PERIOD:
.
              GROSS PAY              :                  .
              REGULAR EARNINGS       :                  .
              OVERTIME EARNINGS      :                  .
              OTHER PAY              :                  .
              FEDERAL WITHHOLDING    :                  .
              FICA                   :                  .
              STATE WITHHOLDING      :                  .
              OTHER STATE TAX        :                  .
              OTHER DEDUCTIONS       :                  .
              OTHER DEDUCTIONS       :                  .
                                      -------------------
              NET PAY                :                  .
--------------------------------------------------------------------------------
SOCIAL SECURITY #        :           DEPARTMENT                :
REGULAR PAY RATE         :           OVERTIME PAY RATE         :
PERIOD 1 - REGULAR HOURS:            PERIOD 1 - OVERTIME HOURS:
PERIOD 2 - REGULAR HOURS:            PERIOD 2 - OVERTIME HOURS:
--------------------------------------------------------------------------------
File: PAYROLL                  RETRIEVE SPEC                      Page 1

F5-Date      F6-Time                                              F10-Continue
```

Fig. 2-41. PFS:Solutions "Payroll" template.

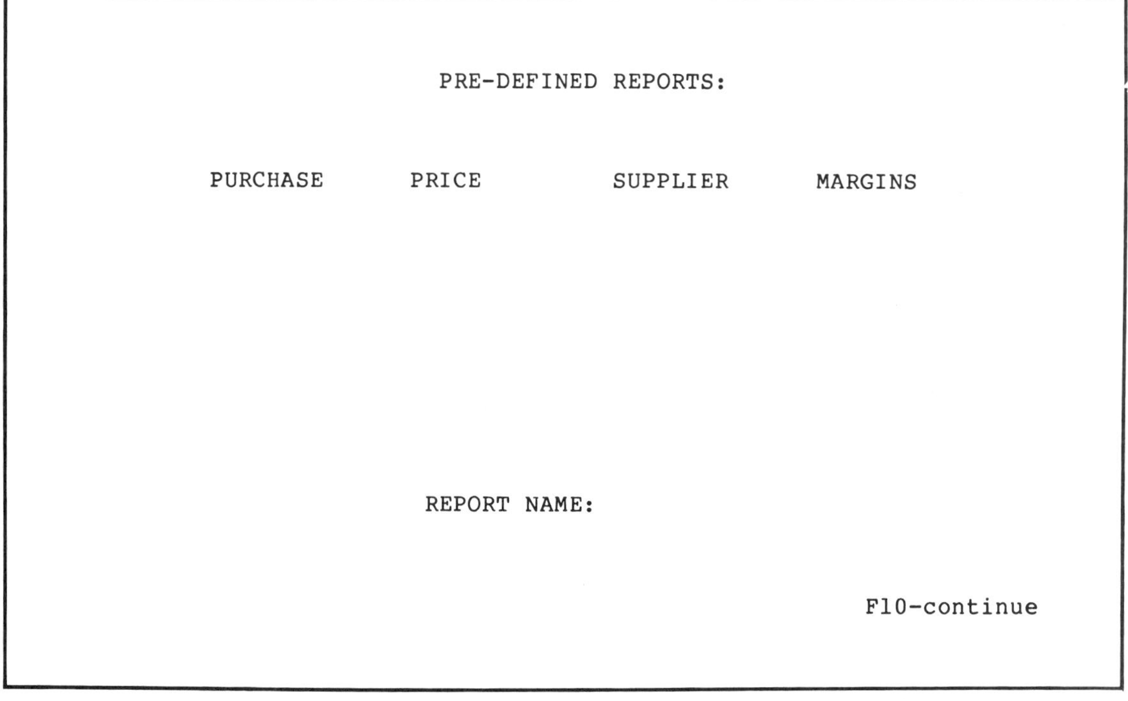

Fig. 2-42. A listing of the PFS:Solution "Invtry" reports that have been prepared and saved on disk.

PRE-DEFINED REPORTS:

TICKLER APPOINT EXPENSE

REPORT NAME:

F10-continue

Fig. 2-43. A listing of the PFS:Solution "Tickler" reports that have been prepared and saved on disk.

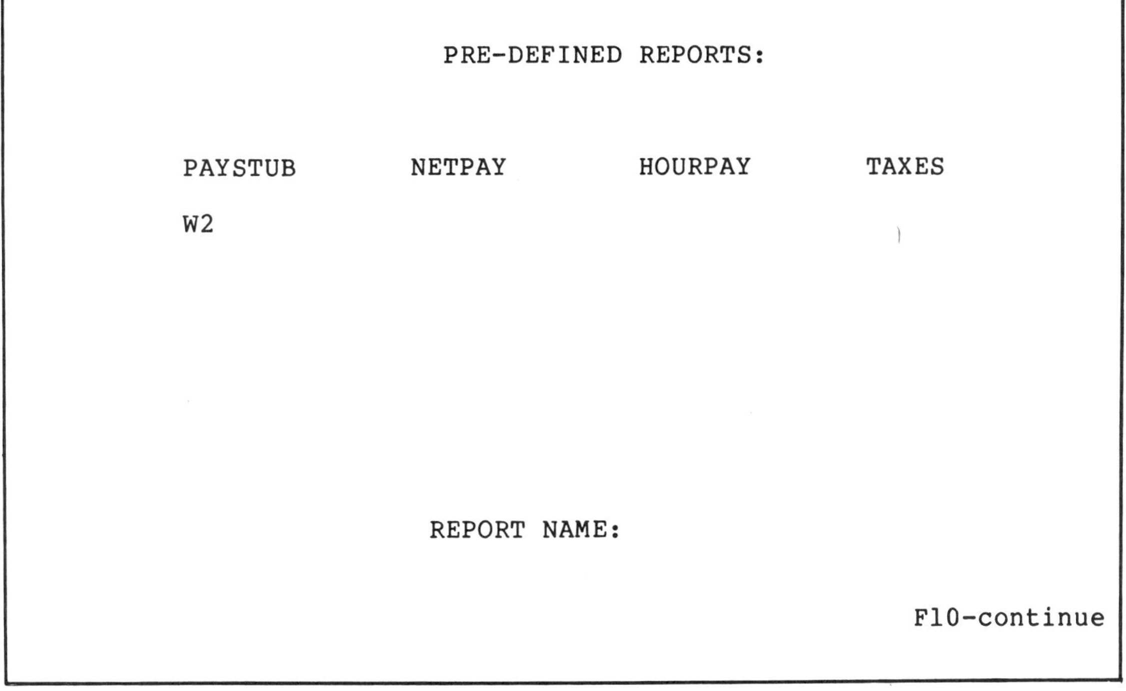

Fig. 2-44. A listing of the PFS:Solution "Payroll" reports that have been prepared and saved on disk.

tions" are displayed in Figures 2-39 through 2-41. They retail in the $20 to $25 price range. Other solutions, such as *PFS:School Recordkeeper* are much more complex and contain multiple forms, such as "Student Record Management," and "Room and Event Scheduling." *School Recordkeeper* retails for $150, or can be purchased in combination with *PFS:File* and *PFS:Report*.

In addition to the forms shown, predetermined reports are stored on the disk. They will be covered in the next chapter dealing with reports. A listing of the reports available from the *Solutions* packages above are summarized in Figures 2-42 through 2-44. For now, if any of the forms suit your needs, enter them in yourself. What is most likely is that you will use the parts of the forms that suit your needs, delete the parts that don't, and add useful items that are not on the forms. That is one of the main selling points of this database management system—its flexibility. Ease of use is important, but is secondary to getting the jobs done.

FILE STORAGE CAPACITY

Until now, we have taken the approach that if you need, or will ever need, another field, just put it in. This section will attempt to explain the overhead in terms of disk storage that is used when you expand the size of a form and thereby each file. Naturally the larger the files, the less of them you can have. Reasonable questions anyone contemplating the institution of an electronic filing system should want to ask include these: How many forms can I store on a disk? What is the capacity of the system? Reasonable answers are not always simple answers. To say "it depends" is not hedging. There are several factors that play an important part in determining the answers. First of all, the system you choose and the nature of the storage device is the single most important factor in the system's capacity. (You may want to refer back to the sections on types of disk formats in Chapter 1.) Second, the number of pages in a form, the number of items per page, and the amount of information entered into each item field determine the amount of space available on a disk.

A single sided, single density disk system, such as that found with an Apple *II*+/e/c will hold approximately 1000 simple forms. An IBM PC, IBM PCjr, TI Professional, or Tandy Model 2000 with double sided double density disks can hold approximately 2200 simple forms. However, the amount of time required to access information from huge forms can become a significant handicap.

Of course, the figures named here assume that only one type of form will be stored on any one disk. It is possible to store more than one type of form on any disk, but it is not a good practice. If two or more types are stored on the same disk, they will compete for space. There is also a much greater chance of operator error, saving the wrong file on top of another. Also, in the case of disk failure, there will be twice as much damage.

Before you reject the idea of using *PFS:File* on a moderately priced system because you want to handle more than a couple of thousand records on each form, reconsider. The ability to copy selected forms onto another disk allows you to constantly update and subdivide your forms. As some of your organization's members become inactive they can be transferred to another disk. That way your time will not be spent searching through pages of inactive members, nor will their names be lost when membership drives begin again.

Disk capacity is something you should be aware of, but don't let it get in your way. It's not really an overriding concern. With the ability to duplicate selected forms, it is possible to subdivide lists into smaller units that are more manageable. If subdivision is done with an eye toward future reports, the divisions can be made so as not to limit report cababilities.

PFS: FILE FOR MAILING LABELS

One of the most frequent uses for database managers is the production of mailing labels. In fact, a large number of programs have been sold exclusively for this purpose. *PFS:File* enables you to create mailing labels as a small part of its repertoire.

To illustrate the procedures followed in producing mailing labels, we will use an example

```
              PFS:FILE FUNCTION MENU
              ----------------------

     1  DESIGN FILE                 5  PRINT

     2  ADD                         6  REMOVE

     3  COPY                        7  EXIT PFS:FILE

     4  SEARCH/UPDATE


              SELECTION NUMBER: 5

              FILE NAME: MEMBERS


                                          F10-Continue
```

Fig. 2-45. PFS:File Function Menu completed to begin printing procedures for the "Members" file.

```
Member #:              Fname:
Lname:                 Ext(, Jr.):         Title(Dr.,Ms.):
L2:
L3:
L4:                              Zip:
Telephone:
Date Joined:                     Date of last renewal:
Amount:                          Previous yr's amount:
General Membership (x):          Newsletter  only (x):
Board of Directors (x):          Executive Board  (x): X
Professional advisory board (x):
Committees:

Types of Vol work:

Mon   (x):      From:                  To:             Or:
Tues  (x):      From:                  To:             Or:
Wed   (x):      From:                  To:             Or:
Thurs(x):       From:                  To:             Or:
Fri   (x):      From:                  To:             Or:
Sat   (x):      From:                  To:             Or:
--------------------------------------------------------------------------------
File: MEMBERS                      RETRIEVE SPEC                         Page 1

F5-Date     F6-Time                                                 F10-Continue
```

Fig. 2-46. Retrieve specifications of "Members" file designating than only members of the "Executive Board" be selected for printing purposes.

where we select members of our organization's Executive Board of Directors (the elected officers of the Board). Those peoples' addresses will be printed onto pregummed labels to be affixed to envelopes.

First of all, we will return to the Main Menu. If the program has already been in use, it is always possible to return to the Main Menu by pressing the ESC key. Figure 2-45 illustrates the responses to the prompts that will begin the PRINT sequence.

After the continue key has been pressed, the file designated will become active and be displayed in the RETRIEVE SPEC screen. Of our entire file of members, we want to select only those members who are on the Executive Board, so we will place an "X" beside the "Executive Board (X)" prompt, as illustrated in Fig. 2-46. Notice how convenient it is to be told that "X" is the designation that should be used to retrieve that group. If we had not designed the form to be self-prompting, it might be confusing as to whether we used "Y" for yes, "E" for executive, or some other key for the field. Pressing the continue key tells the program to search only for Executive Board members. Remember, we could have specified any combination of criteria to be met, such as Executive Board members whose zip code begins with "7."

Figure 2-47 shows the IBM version of the PRINT OPTIONS screen. Regardless of the system that you are using, you will want to answer "N" to the PRINT ITEM NAMES (Y/N) prompt. "N" will prevent the printing of the field designations, such as "Fname," so only the members' names and addresses will appear on the label. Also, the LINES PER PAGE must be adjusted to correspond to the size of the mailing label you are using.

Next, the PRINT SPEC screen will appear. Figure 2-48 displays the completed screen in a way

```
                PRINT OPTIONS


          PRINT ITEM NAMES (Y/N): n

          PRINT TO: LPT1:

          LINES PER PAGE: 6

          NUMBER OF COPIES: 1




                                        F10-Continue
```

Fig. 2-47. Print options completed to print on mailing labels one inch in width.

```
Member #:                    Fname: +
Lname: +                     Ext(, Jr.): X        Title(Dr.,Ms.):
L2: X
L3: X
L4: +                                  Zip: XS
Telephone:
Date Joined:                           Date of last renewal:
Amount:                                Previous yr's amount:
General Membership (x):                Newsletter  only (x):
Board of Directors (x):                Executive Board  (x):
Professional advisory board (x):
Committees:

Types of Vol work:

Mon   (x):       From:                    To:             Or:
Tues  (x):       From:                    To:             Or:
Wed   (x):       From:                    To:             Or:
Thurs(x):        From:                    To:             Or:
Fri   (x):       From:                    To:             Or:
Sat   (x):       From:                    To:             Or:
--------------------------------------------------------------------------------
File: MEMBERS                        PRINT SPEC                          Page 1

F5-Date     F6-Time                                              F10-Continue
```

Fig. 2-48. Print specification completed to produce mailing labels that will be sorted by zip code.

```
David J.  Wagner                    Kevin  Moran
582 Highland                        TAB BOOKS INC.
NY, NY  10012                       P.O. Box 40
                                    Blue Ridge Summit, PA  17214

JeanneAnne  Casson                  G. K.  Burton   , Jr.
#10 Lakeside Drive                  154 Dogwood Ave.
Skaneateles, NY  10153              Fairhope, AL  36532

Nell  VanDuzee                      Jerry W.  Cole   , C.L.U.
26 Ellwood Ave                      1234 Emporia Street
Cortland, NY  13152                 Wichita, KS  67214

Bobbie  Cyhanick                    Marc J.  Wagner
P.O. Box 142                        1184 Military Road
Afton, NY  13265                    Tacoma, WA  93523

Kathryn  Burton                     Sheri  Pictou
P.O. Box 164                        Box 2435
Blue Ridge Summit, PA  17214        Debert, N.S.
                                    CANADA  E0C 1Y0
```

Fig. 2-49. A sample of printed mailing labels ready to be attached to envelopes.

that will produce the labels we want. We want the first line of the label to include the "Fname" PLUS (+) the "Lname" PLUS (+) any "Ext" (extensions) before sending the printer a line feed (designated by an "X") to move onto the second line. The second line of the label will be the second line of the mailing label, and a line feed will be sent to the printer at the conclusion of the line. You will be able to see at the conclusion of this process that addresses that have no second line entered will begin printing the next line of the address without printing a blank line. However, addresses that include the full four lines print the second line before sending a line feed and moving onto the third line. The fourth line will include the fourth line of the address PLUS (+) the zip code. An "X" signifies that the printer should "move on" to another line after printing the zip code. The "S" following the "X" indicates that you want the labels sorted in ascending sequence based on the zip code. Notice that the sheet of labels printed in Fig. 2-49 sorts numeric zip codes before sorting alphanumeric postal codes. Those alphanumeric postal codes such as Canadian codes are sorted in alphabetical order.

SUMMARY

PFS:File provides the user with a useful and versatile tool. If you primarily need to keep track of information and generate mailing labels, it is all you will need. If you need more—to summarize and mathematically manipulate data—you will need to use *PFS:Report,* described in the next chapter. With the new enhancements to *PFS:File* that allows for pausing between printing pages you can even print addresses directly onto envelopes with letter quality printers. Older versions of the program made adhesive labels a must for mass mailings. *PFS:File* will integrate with *PFS:Write* to provide powerful individual form letter capabilities. *PFS:Graph* provides the means to graphically display information in your file. *PFS:File* is not the program for all needs, but it is more than a "bare bones" mail list. It is also an important component for creating an automated office.

PFS:Report–Selecting, Sorting, and Presenting Information

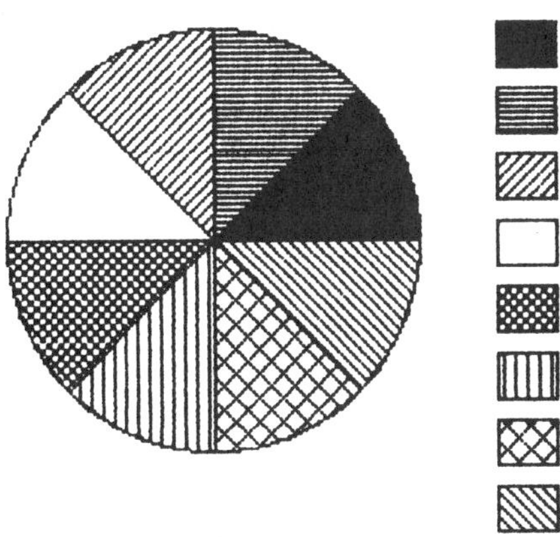

Chapter 3

PFS:Report is used to summarize the data that has been collected in *PFS:File*. *PFS:Report* will do just what its name implies—it will prepare reports. The information in *PFS:File* can be reported in a number of different ways. There is no need to change the data; the program can retrieve information according to your specifications. *PFS:Report* produces tabular reports of up to 16 vertical columns. There is no limit to the number of horizontal lines, or items, in your report, other than the limitation to the number of forms that can be saved on *PFS:File*.

PFS:Report can sort rows alphabetically or numerically. When a column has both numeric and alphabetic data, it sorts numerically first, then alphabetically. It can count the number of items in a column, and total or average numeric data. Subtotals, subaverages, and subcounts may be obtained. Finally, *PFS:Report* can even derive new columns by calculating numbers in existing columns. Up to three such *derived* columns may be used in a report.

Ease of use is the watchword for *PFS:Report*. It is organized in much the same way as *PFS:File*. Once you have mastered *PFS:File*, you will be able to begin using *PFS:Report* in a matter of minutes. The same search criteria and notations are used for both programs. For convenience, you may store report designs onto the data disk for repeated use. Eight such forms may be stored on a disk. That way, report specifications do not have to be entered each time you want a similar report.

GETTING STARTED WITH *PFS:REPORT*

As with all of the PFS programs, instructions are provided that allow users to begin using the programs with a minimum of delay. Apple systems only require that you provide a data disk created with *PFS:File*, insert the program disk, and turn on the machine. IBM and compatible systems that use MS-DOS or PC-DOS provide instructions so that you can make the disk self-booting. Again, I recommend against doing so and prefer using a DOS disk once on the initial power up. Simply using the same, most recent DOS, once on power up avoids any potential for incompatibilities. If you use this method, you can simply type REPORT at the DOS prompt after supplying the date and time. *PFS:Report*, of course, assumes that you have data on a data disk created with *PFS:File*. *PFS:Report* is useless without *PFS:File*.

When you have booted the *PFS:Report* disk, you will see the PFS:Report Main Menu displayed in Fig. 3-1. A summary of each of the commands available from the PFS:Report Main Menu follows:

1 PRINT A REPORT. Select this option to begin preparing a report. It is the beginning of a three part process. First, you will select the forms you want included in the report, then the printer that matches your system; then you will specify the items that will appear in the report, the order in which they will appear, and any special calculations to be used.

2 PRE-DEFINE A REPORT. This option allows the user to save the report specification that he/she is going to use on disk for future reference. If a report is going to be used periodically, this option allows the report to be printed in the same format every time without having to provide report specifications each time. Up to eight forms may be stored on a disk, and each form may have a name of up to 10 characters in length.

3 SET NEW HEADINGS. This option allows the user to change the name of the heading that appears in the report identifying a field item. This can be a handy feature for fitting all of a report onto a page. *PFS:Report* determines column width for the report by the number of characters in the field, or by the widest entry in a column, whichever is greater. The use of this option allows the user to shorten the length of the identifying field name.

4 EXIT. This option terminates the operation of

```
                    PFS:   R E P O R T
                    -----------------


                   1   PRINT A REPORT

                   2   PRE-DEFINE A REPORT

                   3   SET NEW HEADINGS

                   4   EXIT PFS:REPORT



                   SELECTION NUMBER:

                   FILE NAME:




                                             F10-continue
```

Fig. 3-1. PFS:Report Main Menu.

PFS:Report and returns the users of MS-DOS systems to the Disk Operating System. If there are corrections to be made in *PFS:File*, one could just type FILE and press ENTER with the program disk in the disk drive to modify the data disk. The Apple *II* versions of the program do not have the EXIT command, so users of those systems will have to remember to turn off the system only when the Main Menu is displayed.

Calculations Possible

A list of available calculations is summarized below. The calculation symbols should be placed in the fields in which they will be used. More than one calculation may be used in various combinations with other calculations.

T Total. The program will automatically treat the item column numerically, add all of the numbers, and print the total at the bottom of the column. For example, if we use the "Number benefiting" field of the Do-Doing-Done form specifying that we want to retrieve only events in a particular year, the total number of people served can be calculated by the program.

ST Subtotal. The program will provide subtotals for each item in column 1, and then supply a grand total at the end of the report. For example, if the first item sorted is "zip code," we can ask for a subtotal in the "contributions field" in order to find the amount of contributions received from each zip code area as well as a grand total of contributions received.

A Average. The program will treat the item numerically and automatically provide the average (average = total ÷ number of items).

SA Subaverage. The program will provide averages for each subcategory of the first report specification, and then provide an average for the grand total. In the example of sorting by zip code areas, "SA" entered after the report specifications for "Contributions" will analyze the average amount donated by each contributor within each zip code area as well as an average of all contributions.

C Count. A designation of "C" after the report specification will make the program count the number of different entries within a column and print the total at the bottom of the report.

SC Subcount. Subcount tells the program to count events within subclassifications. For example, if you wanted to count the number of each of several pamphlets distributed, the first report specification could be "Pamphlet name" while the "Number viewing" report specification could be designated with a "SC" to count the number of each type of pamphlet distributed during a given time as well as the total number of pamphlets distributed.

+ Add. Add numeric data to form derived columns.

- Subtract. Subtract numeric data in one column from another column or value.

*** Multiply.** Multiply numeric data in one column by another column value or constant.

/ Divide. Divide numeric data in one column by another column value or constant.

( ) Parentheses. Parentheses designate the proper order mathematical manipulation should follow in complex calculations. In order to add twice the amount of column #1 to the sum of columns #2 and #3, parentheses designate the order of operaas follows: (#1 * 2) + (#2 + #3).

N Numeric. The "N" designation after a retrieve specification will make the program treat information in a specific category as a numeric quantity. For example, a notation such as "3 hours" in a field can be treated numerically, that is, simply as a "3". The "3" may be added and averaged with other similar entries without having to go back to *PFS:File* to remove the word "hours" from the data.

A numeric designation also causes the column to be automatically aligned by the decimal point.

P Page break. To create a new page for each classification in column #1, the "P" designation is used following the first report specification.

K Keywords. The designation of "K" in the first column allows the program to sort information such as keywords in articles. With this designation, the same form is printed once for every occurrence of a selected keyword.

PREPARING TO PRINT THE REPORTS

A report that can be up to 16 columns wide can obviously take a lot of space. There are several different ways to accommodate different printers, and ways to manipulate printing to the screen or a disk file.

First of all, *PFS:Report*, like other modules in the PFS series, can print to parallel or serial printers. The default value on MS-DOS systems for OUTPUT TO is LPT1 to designate output to a parallel printer. Designations of COM1 or AUX are used to notify the program to send the information to the printer through the serial port. Apple II series system owners have the option of answering the PRINTER DEVICE prompt to adjust for printers, with and without automatic line feed mechanisms.

Occasionally, it will be advantageous to "print" the report to a disk file. Examples of times when that feature could be useful would be when you are going to send a report via telecommunications services through *PFS:Access* or when you are going to include a report within the body of a letter created with *PFS:Write*. This feature is not available on Apple *II* computers. In order to print to a disk file, answer the OUTPUT TO prompt with the name of the file, including the drive identifier, such as B:MEMBERS.RPT. If you want the report to be "printed" on the monitor console and not to the printer, respond CON (console) to the output prompt.

The default value for PAGE WIDTH for printer output is 80. However, the prompt may be answered with values between 40 and 255 characters. If the report takes more space than is available on the printer, the system will beep and tell you that the report is too wide. You will have the option to press the Space Bar to receive a *truncated* report, one that is "chopped off" where it runs out of room, or to make modifications, either to the page width or to the headings in order to try to make the report fit into the allotted space.

Printer control codes may be sent directly to the printer from within the *PFS:Report* program. For example, an Epson MX-80 responds with condensed print (132 characters in the normal space of 80 characters) when CTRL and 0 are pressed. Emphasized mode is achieved with ESC and E and double strike is selected by pressing ESC and G. Comparable commands may be sent to other dot matrix printers by referring to each printer's manual to learn the proper control codes for each function. Apple users have the opportunity of sending control codes by answering the PRINTER CONTROL CODES prompt in REPORT OPTIONS. To invoke the program that *talks* to the printer and enables the sending of control codes with MS-DOS, you type PRINTER at the DOS > prompt. For making permanent changes on the disk to accommodate a serial printer, type SETUP at the DOS > prompt. Additionally, with many systems, it is possible to print the current screen, or get a screen dump by utilizing the SHIFT and PrtSc (print screen) keys.

CREATING REPORTS

Printing reports with *PFS:Report* is really simple. To Print a report (you guessed it!) select PRINT A REPORT from the Main Menu. Use the TAB key or the RIGHT ARROW key on Apple *II*+ systems to move to the cursor beside the FILE NAME prompt. Insert the name of the file that you created with *PFS:File* in exactly the same way that it was named earlier. Spaces must be exact, letters must be exact, and extensions beyond a period must be exact.

Let us pretend for a moment that we have erred from good computing practices, and did not properly label our data disk. Nor can we remember the file name of the file. Try as we might, we cannot

```
PFS:  R E P O R T
-----------------

1  PRINT A REPORT

2  PRE-DEFINE A REPORT

3  SET NEW HEADINGS

4  EXIT PFS:REPORT


SELECTION NUMBER: 1

FILE NAME: DDD


  CAN'T FIND FILE

                         F10-continue
```

Fig. 3-2. The "Can't find file" message that appears on the PFS:Report Main Menu when the filename has not been properly specified.

come up with the right file name. All we get is a disgusting little beep and a CAN'T FIND FILE message (Fig. 3-2). What in the world can we do? Look at the disk (magnetically) of course. Select 4 EXIT PFS:REPORT and press the continue key. We don't have to have the right file name to do that. On IBM-like systems, we will see the DOS prompt. Type "DIR," which is short for "directory," and press Enter. The display on the screen will be similar to that of Fig. 3-3. There it is! MEMBERS is the file that is stored on the disk. Great! Now put in the *PFS:Report* disk, type REPORT and press ENTER. The next time that we need a filename, we will be ready. Please put a label on the disk so you won't have to go through the procedure again. Remember to use only soft felt tipped markers on disks so that there will be no damage to the disk. Now, too, you can see why it is not enough security just to leave your disks unlabeled. Apple users will not have such a simple time of reading data files. Since the program uses a Pascal format, a simple CATALOG command, or even BLOADing FID from the DOS 3.3 System Master will not do the trick. It will take a Pascal system to be able to read the file names on your disks.

After you have inserted your data disk into the drive, selected one of the available options, specified its filename as has been done in Fig. 3-4, and pressed the continue key, the form you inserted will be displayed. As a working illustration, we will use the Members file created in the last chapter. Suppose that our goal is to get an alphabetical listing of our members with a cross reference of "Member#." At the same time, we might as well list the member's telephone number. It should all fit on a standard size printout.

```
A>dir

 Volume in drive A has no label
 Directory of  A:/

MEMBERS          24576   6-07-84   1:25a
        1 File(s)    337920 bytes free

A>
```

Fig. 3-3. A display of a directory listing showing the "Members" file.

The status line on the bottom of the screen will indicate retrieve spec as it does in Fig. 3-5. At this point you will select the forms that you want to have included in the report. *PFS:Report* uses the same system of retrieving data that *PFS:File* used. There can be full item matches, partial item matches, numeric item matches, numeric range matches, not matches, or any combination of the above. If you want all of the forms in your data file to be included, just press the continue key when the RETRIEVE SPECS screen is displayed.

Perhaps we would have some people on our

```
                PFS:  R E P O R T
                -----------------

               1  PRINT A REPORT

               2  PRE-DEFINE A REPORT

               3  SET NEW HEADINGS

               4  EXIT PFS:REPORT


               SELECTION NUMBER: 1

               FILE NAME: members



(C) 1983 Software Publishing Corporation
                                             F10-continue
```

Fig. 3-4. A proper way to complete the PFS:Report Main Menu in order to begin generating a report.

```
Member #:               Fname:
Lname:                  Ext(, Jr.):          Title(Dr.,Ms.):
L2:
L3:
L4:                               Zip:
Telephone:
Date Joined:                      Date of last renewal:
Amount:                           Previous yr's amount:
General Membership (x):           Newsletter  only (x):
Board of Directors (x):           Executive Board  (x):
Professional advisory board (x):
Committees:

Types of Vol work:

Mon   (x):      From:             To:             Or:
Tues  (x):      From:             To:             Or:
Wed   (x):      From:             To:             Or:
Thurs(x):       From:             To:             Or:
Fri   (x):      From:             To:             Or:
Sat   (x):      From:             To:             Or:
-------------------------------------------------------------------
File: members                     RETRIEVE SPEC              Page 1

                                                       F10-continue
```

Fig. 3-5. A "RETRIEVE SPECS" screen will allow for the specification of the forms that you want included in the report.

file who are not members, who only receive the organization's newsletter, for example. We could choose to include only members in this report by placing an "X" beside the "Member (x)" field to indicate that we want to list all of the organization's members, but members only. If we wanted to include every record on the file, simply pressing the continue key at the RETRIEVE SPEC screen would select all forms on the file.

After specifying the forms that we want included in the report through indicating retrieve specs and pressing the continue key, there will appear a screen entitled REPORT OPTIONS (Fig. 3-6). The cursor will be blinking beside the TITLE prompt. You can name your report anything that you want, as long as you can keep it fairly brief (58 characters) and on one line. For our example, we will entitle the report, "List of Members, Member #, and telephone #s."

The next prompt to deal with is PRE-DEFINED REPORT NAME. The purpose of this function is to allow the user to use the reports that he/she has predefined using option 2 PRE-DEFINE A REPORT. Later, we will see how it is convenient to store report forms that will be used over and over again. Unless there are reports stored on the disk, this item will be left blank.

Tabbing on, we see OUTPUT TO on the IBM PC, or OUTPUT DEVICE (P/L) on Apple *II* systems. The same printer conventions applicable to *PFS:File* are applicable here.

LINES PER PAGE with a default value of 66, allows for different lengths of paper. Recent enhanced versions provide for the opportunity of pausing between pages, and will prompt you to insert each new page.

PAGE WIDTH allows reports to be printed to whatever width your printer allows. Remember, it is also possible to set dot matrix printers to the condensed mode, and then send 132 characters per line and still fit the report onto 8½ × 11-inch paper. Our small report will have no need for wide paper, so I will leave the value at the default value of 80 as shown in Fig. 3-7.

When the REPORT OPTIONS have been filled out to your satisfaction, and the continue key

```
                    REPORT OPTIONS


     TITLE:

     PRE-DEFINED REPORT NAME:


     OUTPUT TO: lptl:

     LINES PER PAGE: 66          PAGE WIDTH: 80




                                          F10-continue
```

Fig. 3-6. Blank REPORT OPTIONS screen that allows for customizing the format of reports.

```
                    REPORT OPTIONS


   TITLE: List of Members, Member #, and telephone #s

   PRE-DEFINED REPORT NAME:


   OUTPUT TO: lptl:

   LINES PER PAGE: 66          PAGE WIDTH: 80




                                          F10-continue
```

Fig. 3-7. Completed Report Options that will provide the title of the report on standard size paper.

pressed, the MEMBERs form will appear once again. This time the status line indicates REPORT SPEC. This is the section where you specify which items you want included in the report and in what order.

The first item that we want to have sorted is the "Lname" field. So, we place a numeric "1" in the space beside that prompt. Doing so will cause an alphabetical sorting of the "Lname" field. On the report we will want to see the member's first names next to their last names so we place a "2" beside the "FName" field. The second field is automatically sorted too. If we have more than one member with identical last names, say, "Jingleheimersmith," the second field, "FName," will determine the order of the listing of the members. "John J." will be listed before "Zelda." *PFS:Report* sorts only two columns, those designated "1" and "2". If you do not want any column sorted, you could make the first column designation a "3."

In order to provide our cross reference, we will designate the "Member#" field as our third column in the report. Placing a "C" after any of the selected columns will cause that total number of unique items in that column to be counted. It is natural to move the cursor to the first item, "Lname" to place our "C." However, remember that the program will count the number of ***unique*** items. Since the last name is not unique, it will only count the two Jingleheimersmiths as one unique name. Using the second field, "FName" is not any better a solution since similar first names will end up with a short membership count. Since there is a unique Member# for each individual member of the organization, we will place a "C" next to the "3" to count the number of members. Counting the "Member#" is preferable to counting last names that may be repeated, or telephone numbers that might not exist for some members. The count will be printed under the Member# column. As a cross check, you can note the number of forms selected, which will be displayed on the screen following the sort.

Finally, we will designate "Telephone" as the fourth column to be reported by placing a "4" beside the field. (See Fig. 3-8.) Remember, the width of

```
Member #: 3c               Fname: 2
Lname: 1                   Ext(, Jr.):          Title(Dr.,Ms.):
L2:
L3:
L4:                                   Zip:
Telephone: 4
Date Joined:                          Date of last renewal:
Amount:                               Previous yr's amount:
General Membership (x):               Newsletter  only (x):
Board of Directors (x):               Executive Board  (x):
Professional advisory board (x):
Committees:

Types of Vol work:

Mon   (x):       From:                    To:              Or:
Tues  (x):       From:                    To:              Or:
Wed   (x):       From:                    To:              Or:
Thurs(x):        From:                    To:              Or:
Fri   (x):       From:                    To:              Or:
Sat   (x):       From:                    To:              Or:
--------------------------------------------------------------------------------
File: members                      REPORT SPEC                        Page 1

F7-Derived Columns                                               F10-continue
```

Fig. 3-8. Completed Report Specs that will provide an alphabetized listing of members followed by "Member #" and "Telephone."

List of Members, Member #, and telephone #s

Lname	Fname	Member #	Telephone
Apa	Charity	0012	749-2435
Bacon	Bob	0015	203 534-3874
Bearth	Lorraine	0008	316 683-6739
Burton	Jonathan	0003	205 928-2063
	Kathryn	0026	947-2586
Casson	JeanneAnne	0010	315 687-2325 (w) 687-2784 (h)
Cole	Jerry W.	0001	315 685-1821 (w)
Condo	Trish	0016	603 873-1847
DeYoung	Christin	0020	617 935-2746
Grant	Lou	0017	212 356-news
Hanks	Dorothy	0009	343-3456 (h)
Jarvis	Al	0019	315 555-1212 (w) 236-4725 (h)
Johnson	Marilyn	0024	794-2191 (w) 974-0602 (h)
Krisukas	Gene	0022	794-2194
Laroucque	Roderick	0006	914 575-2345
Mohr	Rosemary	0014	685-1821
Moran	Kevin	0002	717 794-2191
Mustoe	Ruth	0023	787-3432
Pictou	Brent	0007	975-1531
	Shannon	0005	
	Sheri	0004	912 357-7823
Pierce	Eric	0011	614 834-2347
Sark	Connie	0025	674-2382
Smoot	Leroy	0013	814 834-1639 (d) 834-1939 (n)
VanDuzee	Nell	0018	315 969-3630
Wagner	David J.	0027	234 425-7274
	Marc J.	0028	515 913-3421
Yeary	Georgia	0021	209 384-8426

Count: 28

Fig. 3-9. Sample report sorted by last name and then first name.

the column will be equal to the longest entry listed.

When the report specifications have been entered, press the continue key. Apple users will have to have the sortwork disk in drive 2. IBM and compatible system users will have to have a formatted working disk in drive B. The second drive is a workspace for sorting forms. Soon the sorting will be done, and the report will be printed similarly to the one in Fig. 3-9.

At this time, we may want to provide a listing of the same members sorted according to "Member#." To print such a listing, we will proceed in a manner similar to that just completed. First of all, we should make sure to provide exactly the same retrieve specs supplied for the last report. Of course, counting the "Member# again will supply a check since both numbers from both reports will be equal if we supply the same retrieve specs and use the same data disk.

For this report, we will fill in the blanks of the

```
                         REPORT OPTIONS



        TITLE: Report with Member #, Names, and telephone #

        PRE-DEFINED REPORT NAME:


        OUTPUT TO: lptl:

        LINES PER PAGE: 66          PAGE WIDTH: 80






                                                    F10-continue
```

Fig. 3-10. Report options for a second report using the same data on file—a report sorted on the basis of "Member #."

```
Member #: lc            Fname: 3
Lname: 2                Ext(, Jr.):          Title(Dr.,Ms.):
L2:
L3:
L4:                              Zip:
Telephone: 4
Date Joined:                     Date of last renewal:
Amount:                          Previous yr's amount:
General Membership (x):          Newsletter  only (x):
Board of Directors (x):          Executive Board  (x):
Professional advisory board (x):
Committees:

Types of Vol work:

Mon   (x):      From:                   To:            Or:
Tues  (x):      From:                   To:            Or:
Wed   (x):      From:                   To:            Or:
Thurs(x):       From:                   To:            Or:
Fri   (x):      From:                   To:            Or:
Sat   (x):      From:                   To:            Or:
--------------------------------------------------------------------------------
File: members                    REPORT SPEC                       Page 1

F7-Derived Columns                                            F10-continue
```

Fig. 3-11. Report specifications for the "Member #" report.

REPORT OPTIONS in such a way as to clearly label the report. (See Fig. 3-10.) This time, in the REPORT SPEC display, we will make "Member#" the first column, followed by last and first names, and finally the telephone number. (See Fig. 3-11.) Please note that we will count the "Member#" entries again to provide the cross check of our accuracy. This time the report is nicely formatted according to an ascending order of the member's identification number. (See Fig. 3-12). The count for the occurrence of member numbers in each report is 28, so we can be assured that our two procedures were identical.

Flexibility and ease of use, again, are the watchwords for this program module. The only major limitations to being able to report the information that you want to gather is your own imagination. If the original *PFS:Report* data disk that you designed does not fill the need, it can be modified. The format of the report can be restructured. A little trial and error will result in a serviceable system for your data retrieval needs.

PRE-DEFINING A REPORT

Reports that have to be done periodically will be made easier by using option 2 PRE-DEFINE A REPORT from the Main Menu. When you predefine a report, you save the report criteria as a report name. Then, whenever you need to run that report, you have only to insert the report name in the space beside the PRE-DEFINED REPORT

```
                    Report with Member #, Names, and telephone #

        Member #         Lname          Fname              Telephone
        ---------      ---------      ----------    ------------------------------
        0001           Cole           Jerry W.      315 685-1821 (w)
        0002           Moran          Kevin         717 794-2191
        0003           Burton         Jonathan      205 928-2063
        0004           Pictou         Sheri         912 357-7823
        0005           Pictou         Shannon
        0006           Laroucque      Roderick      914 575-2345
        0007           Pictou         Brent         975-1531
        0008           Bearth         Lorraine      316 683-6739
        0009           Hanks          Dorothy       343-3456 (h)
        0010           Casson         JeanneAnne    315 687-2325 (w) 687-2784 (h)
        0011           Pierce         Eric          614 834-2347
        0012           Apa            Charity       749-2435
        0013           Smoot          Leroy         814 834-1639 (d) 834-1939 (n)
        0014           Mohr           Rosemary      685-1821
        0015           Bacon          Bob           203 534-3874
        0016           Condo          Trish         603 873-1847
        0017           Grant          Lou           212 356-news
        0018           VanDuzee       Nell          315 969-3630
        0019           Jarvis         Al            315 555-1212 (w) 236-4725 (h)
        0020           DeYoung        Christin      617 935-2746
        0021           Yeary          Georgia       209 384-8426
        0022           Krisukas       Gene          794-2194
        0023           Mustoe         Ruth          787-3432
        0024           Johnson        Marilyn       794-2191 (w) 974-0602 (h)
        0025           Sark           Connie        674-2382
        0026           Burton         Kathryn       947-2586
        0027           Wagner         David J.      234 425-7274
        0028           Wagner         Marc J.       515 913-3421

-----------------
Count:          28
-----------------
```

Fig. 3-12. A report using the modified Report criteria.

```
PFS:  R E P O R T
-----------------

1  PRINT A REPORT

2  PRE-DEFINE A REPORT

3  SET NEW HEADINGS

4  EXIT PFS:REPORT


SELECTION NUMBER: 2

FILE NAME: D-D-D


(C) 1983 Software Publishing Corporation
                                        F10-continue
```

Fig. 3-13. A example of PFS:Report Main Menu completed to begin the process of pre-defining a report.

NAME prompt instead of selecting each of the columns you want included in the report.

Let us say that we want to periodically track the number of people who have been serviced by our organization. About once a month we run the same report, so using the predefine option will save some time and avoid creating confusion by delivering reports that are formatted differently.

After selecting 2 PRE-DEFINE A REPORT, supplying the filename, D-D-D, as shown in Fig. 3-13, and then pressing the continue key, you will be presented with a new PRE-DEFINED REPORTS screen (Fig. 3-14) with the cursor blinking beside the REPORT NAME prompt. Also shown will be the other pre-defined report names that have been previously stored. Since this is the first report that we have stored, that will be indicated by displaying the word "none" in the space for saved reports. We shall give this report the name #SERVED (Fig. 3-15). It is wise to mark the report names saved onto the disk on the disk label with a felt tip marker so that you can remember the names of the reports you have saved. Normally, in the routine of printing a report you will not see the list of predefined reports saved. If you have forgotten the names of your reports it is possible to select 2 PRE-DEFINE A REPORT from the Main Menu to see the list. Once your memory has been jogged, you can press ESC to return to the Main Menu.

After giving the report its name and pressing the continue key, you will see the form that you designed with *PFS:File*. For this ongoing report of people served, we will want the name of the event, the date it was held, and the number of people attending. We could get that report easily by placing a "1" beside the "date completed" field (to sort chronologically), a "2" beside the "Job" field (to supply the name), and a "3T" beside the "People

```
                    PRE-DEFINED REPORTS:

                          (None)



                   REPORT NAME:

                                          F10-continue
```

Fig. 3-14. A display of the PRE-DEFINED REPORT screen when there has been no reports created.

```
                    PRE-DEFINED REPORTS:

                          (None)



                   REPORT NAME: #SERVED

                                          F10-continue
```

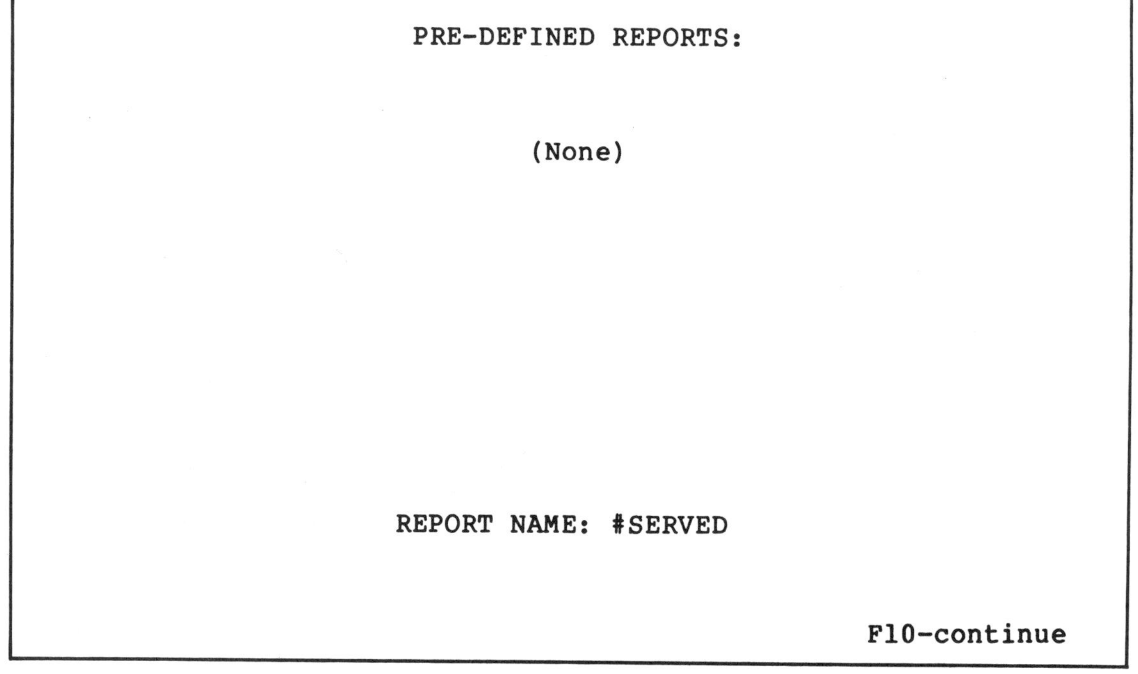

Fig. 3-15. Naming a pre-defined report "#Served."

benefiting" field in order to list the numbers served in each event and to provide a Total number of people served.

That would be simple, and simplicity has its advantages, but *PFS:Report* will give us much more information if we know how to maximize its effectiveness. First of all, let us sort the events we have engaged in according to "Service Area" by placing a "1" after that field. Second, let us place a "2" beside "Data Completed." The second column in *PFS:Report* is also sorted, so the result of this combination will be to provide a listing of each event in each service area from least recent to most recent. The third column will be dedicated to giving a listing of the job name, so we place a "3" after the "Job" field. Placing a "3SC" (Subcount) will automatically count the number of events within each service area (the first column designation) and then provide a total count of all of our jobs.

The purpose of our report is to total the number of people benefitting from our services. The fourth column we will manipulate is the field "People benefiting." Placing "4ST" (fourth column Subtotaled) will add the number of people within each of the service area groups as well as providing a grand total at the end of the report. Why should we be satisfied knowing the grand total when we can analyze the number of people we are effecting within each service area we are responsible for?

Finally, we will choose to designate "Job #" as the fifth column by placing a "5" beside that field. The purpose of that designation is to provide a printed cross reference so that if we need to update information about that job later, we will have the job number, which enables immediate access to the form because it is an exact first field match.

When the report specifications have been completed (Fig. 3-16), we press the continue key and the report will be automatically stored onto the disk for future use. We will then return to the Main Menu.

Now that we have predefined the #SERVED report, it becomes simple to generate that report. At the main menu select 1 PRINT A REPORT. The D-D-D filename will still be supplied after the FILE NAME prompt. For the RETRIEVE SPECS

```
Job #: 5                    Job: 3SC
Job description:

Status:
Act by (yy/mm/dd):

Date Began:                           Date Completed: 2
Time Began:                           Time Completed:

Service area: 1
People benefiting: 4ST
Volunteer hours:
Volunteers:


Project (A/B):
Notes:


-------------------------------------------------------------------
File: D-D-D                 REPORT '#SERVED'                Page 1

F3-Remove         F7-Derived Columns                    F10-continue
```

Fig. 3-16. Pre-defining a report so that jobs will be sorted by service area and date completed, jobs will be counted in each service area, and people benefiting will be totaled for each service area.

screen, specify that you want to select all forms in which "People Served" is >0—greater than zero. (See Fig. 3-17.) At the REPORT OPTIONS screen provide a title, such as, "Number of People served as of July 31, 1984." Then TAB or RIGHT ARROW to the PRE-DEFINED REPORT NAME prompt and respond #SERVED. With five columns, some of which are rather wide, I will modify my responses to the PAGE WIDTH and LINES PER PAGE prompts and prepare to turn the paper sideways in my printer so that there is room to fit all of the information. (See Fig. 3-18).

That is all there is to it. As long as we have a formatted work disk, or *sortwork disk*, in the second drive, the report will automatically select the proper forms, and print a nice summary in tabular form. (See Fig. 3-19.) Now, in a glance, we can see which areas we have been most involved in and which have been reaching the most people. Now, the power of *PFS:Report* is beginning to be demonstrated. As with all of the modules, its effectiveness is as great as your creativeness and imagination allows.

If you want to modify your predefined form, it is very easy to do. At the Main Menu, select 2 PRE-DEFINE A REPORT and define it in a manner similar to the original setup. This time, however, when the REPORT NAME prompt appears, type the name of the report that you want to modify, such as #SERVED. The existing report specifications will appear. They can be added to or modified in any way you want. When the report appears to meet your approval, press the continue key, and the modified report will be saved in place of the old report.

Pre-defined reports may also be removed from permanent storage on the disk. It may be handy to remove a report in order to make room for another report or to avoid accidently using an outdated report form. To remove a form, one may proceed in the same manner as for modifying a form. However, once the existing form is displayed, F3 or CTRL and R may be pressed to remove the form. There will be a warning that the form is about to be removed to avoid any accidental erasures.

At this point it may be important to go back to consider the RETRIEVE SPECS that we provided at the beginning of this report. We selected forms in which the number of people benefiting was greater than zero. That criteria could miss any of the forms that were not properly updated to include that information. A cross check for verification could be made by using "STATUS: done" as the retrieve specifications. Any discrepancies will quickly become apparent with the format of this printout.

Reports should always be predefined for the sake of generating consistent reports, especially if they are going to be used over and over again. Yes, they save time, but pre-defined reports save inaccuracies and confusion as well. After experimenting with and refining report specifications, you will have a report format that will serve you well for many reports to come. Reports do not have to be complicated to be effective. Figures 3-20 through 3-24 display pre-defined report specification from the two PFS Solutions packages discussed in the previous chapter, INVTRY and TICKLER. None of these five reports utilize any mathematical manipulations or derived columns, they just go about the task of keeping things in order.

SETTING NEW HEADINGS

Often times a report seems to take a few more spaces than you have available on the paper you normally use. *PFS:Report* gauges the width of each of its columns according to the widest single entry in the column. For example, in our #SERVED report the field name, "People benefiting," has 17 characters. Seventeen characters will be required for that column, even though none of our actual entries will exceed seven digits. Also, "Date Completed" currently uses fourteen Characters. Changing that to "Date" will save more room. If our report is a little too wide, we can avoid receiving the message REPORT TO WIDE; PRESS SPACE BAR FOR TRUNCATED REPORT by good planning and use of the SET NEW HEADINGS option.

To use the SET NEW HEADING option from the Main Menu, press 3, supply the proper filename, as shown in Fig. 3-25, and press continue. The file that you are working with will appear with

```
Job #:                          Job:
Job description:

Status:
Act by (yy/mm/dd):

Date Began:                               Date Completed:
Time Began:                               Time Completed:

Service area:
People benefiting: >0
Volunteer hours:
Volunteers:


Project (A/B):
Notes:


------------------------------------------------------------------------------
File: D-D-D                        RETRIEVE SPEC                        Page 1

                                                                  F10-continue
```

Fig. 3-17. Retrieve specifications that will consider only those jobs that benefitted at least one person.

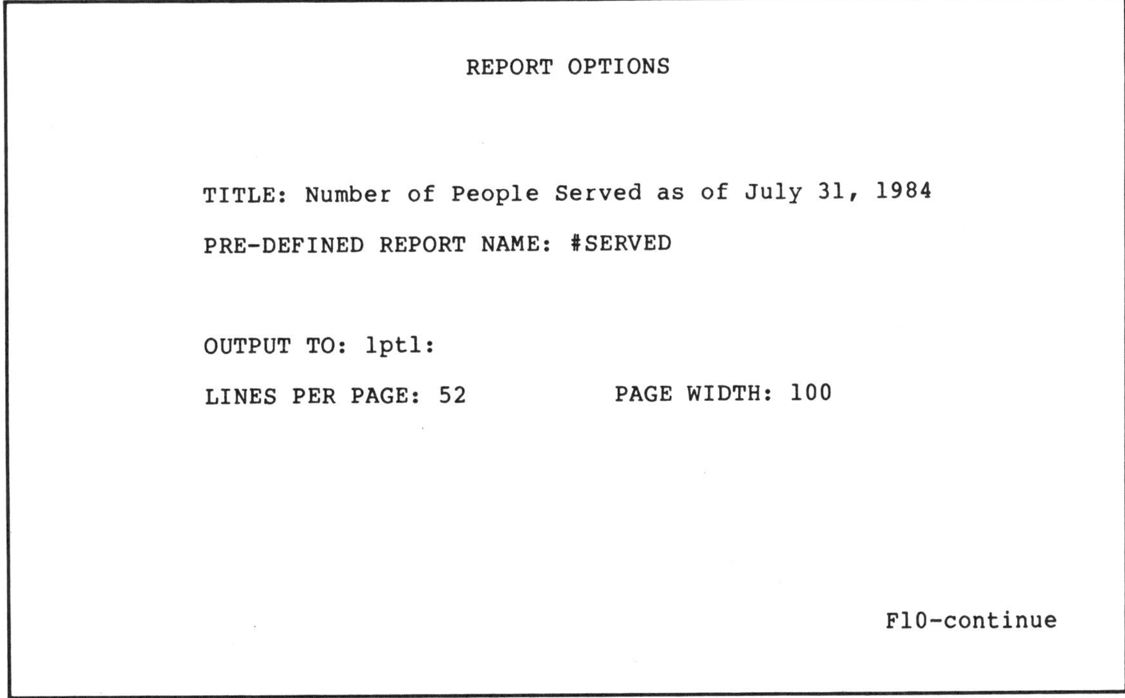

```
                              REPORT OPTIONS


          TITLE: Number of People Served as of July 31, 1984

          PRE-DEFINED REPORT NAME: #SERVED


          OUTPUT TO: lptl:

          LINES PER PAGE: 52          PAGE WIDTH: 100



                                                        F10-continue
```

Fig. 3-18. Screen of REPORT OPTIONS for modifying the print format for standard size paper turned sideways.

Number of People Served as of July 31, 1984

Service area	Date Completed		Job	People benefiting	Job #
Advocacy	84/05/11		Telecommunicate w/ congressmen	100,000	006
	84/07/01		Lobby for zone change	2,500	007
		Total:		102,500	
		Count:	2		
Community services	84/06/03		Biofeedback Seminar	45	005
	84/07/17		Prepare flyer	125	003
		Total:		170	
		Count:	2		
Direct services	84/05/12		SRS forms	25	008
	84/06/01		Transitional Living meeting	25	004
		Total:		50	
		Count:	2		
Public education	84/03/24		Print depression pamphlets	1,000	001
	84/04/30		Film & Speech	25	002
	84/07/02		Send Pierre mailing	6,450	009
		Total:		7,475	
		Count:	3		
		Total:		110,195	
		Count:	9		

Fig. 3-19. A sample report of "#Served" as printed from a "Do-Do-Done" form.

```
*********************** I N V E N T O R Y   R E C O R D *********************
ITEM              : 1C
DESCRIPTION       : 2
PRICE             :
PRIMARY SUPPLIERS:
OTHER SUPPLIERS   :

------------------- P U R C H A S E   I N F O R M A T I O N -----------------
DATE OF PURCHASE  : 3
QUANTITY PURCHASED: 4ST
UNIT COST         : 5SA









-------------------------------------------------------------------------------
File: invtry                    REPORT 'PURCHASE'                    Page 1

F3-Remove        F7-Derived Columns                              F10-continue
```

Fig. 3-20. Report specification from PFS:Solutions "INVTRY"—a report called "Purchase" that tracks the dates, quantities, and cost of each item ordered.

```
*********************** I N V E N T O R Y   R E C O R D *********************
ITEM              : 1C
DESCRIPTION       : 2
PRICE             : 3
PRIMARY SUPPLIERS:
OTHER SUPPLIERS   :

------------------- P U R C H A S E   I N F O R M A T I O N -----------------
DATE OF PURCHASE  :
QUANTITY PURCHASED:
UNIT COST         :









-------------------------------------------------------------------------------
File: invtry                    REPORT 'PRICE'                       Page 1

F3-Remove        F7-Derived Columns                              F10-continue
```

Fig. 3-21. Report specification from PFS:Solutions "INVTRY"—a report named "Price" that counts different items ordered, and gives their descriptions and price.

```
*********************** I N V E N T O R Y   R E C O R D **********************
ITEM                :
DESCRIPTION         : 1C
PRICE               :
PRIMARY SUPPLIERS: 2
OTHER SUPPLIERS   : 3

------------------- P U R C H A S E   I N F O R M A T I O N ----------------
DATE OF PURCHASE  :
QUANTITY PURCHASED:
UNIT COST         :









--------------------------------------------------------------------------------
File: invtry                    REPORT 'SUPPLIER'                        Page 1

F3-Remove        F7-Derived Columns                                F10-continue
```

Fig. 3-22. Report specification from PFS:Solutions "INVTRY"—this report, "Supplier" sorts inventory items by description, and then lists the primary and secondary suppliers for things.

```
***************** T I C K L E R   F I L E / D A I L Y   L O G **************
DATE: 1                     DAY: 2
--------------------- T I C K L E R   F I L E   I T E M S -------------------
TIME          COMMENTS                                                        :
3




-------------------------- A P P O I N T M E N T S --------------------------
TIME          COMMENTS                                                        :





--------------------------- E X P E N S E   L O G ---------------------------
MEALS          :         LODGING         :                AIR FARE :
CAR/TAXI       :         MILEAGE/PARKING:                 TELEPHONE:
ENTERTAINMENT:           OTHER           :
COMMENTS       :
--------------------------------------------------------------------------------
File: tickler                   REPORT 'TICKLER'                         Page 1

F3-Remove        F7-Derived Columns                                F10-continue
```

Fig. 3-23. Report specification from PFS:Solutions "TICKLER"—this report, also named "Tickler" will provide an ordered listing of file follow up items.

```
*****************  T I C K L E R   F I L E  /  D A I L Y   L O G  **************
DATE: 1                          DAY: 2
---------------------  T I C K L E R   F I L E   I T E M S  -------------------
TIME          COMMENTS                                                          :



--------------------------  A P P O I N T M E N T S  -------------------------
TIME          COMMENTS                                                          :
3



---------------------------  E X P E N S E   L O G  ---------------------------
MEALS          :       LODGING         :               AIR FARE :
CAR/TAXI       :       MILEAGE/PARKING:                TELEPHONE:
ENTERTAINMENT:         OTHER           :
COMMENTS       :
--------------------------------------------------------------------------------
File: tickler                   REPORT 'APPOINT'                      Page 1

F3-Remove        F7-Derived Columns                               F10-continue
```

Fig. 3-24. Report specification from PFS:Solutions "TICKLER"—the "Appoint" report will provide a listing of appointments.

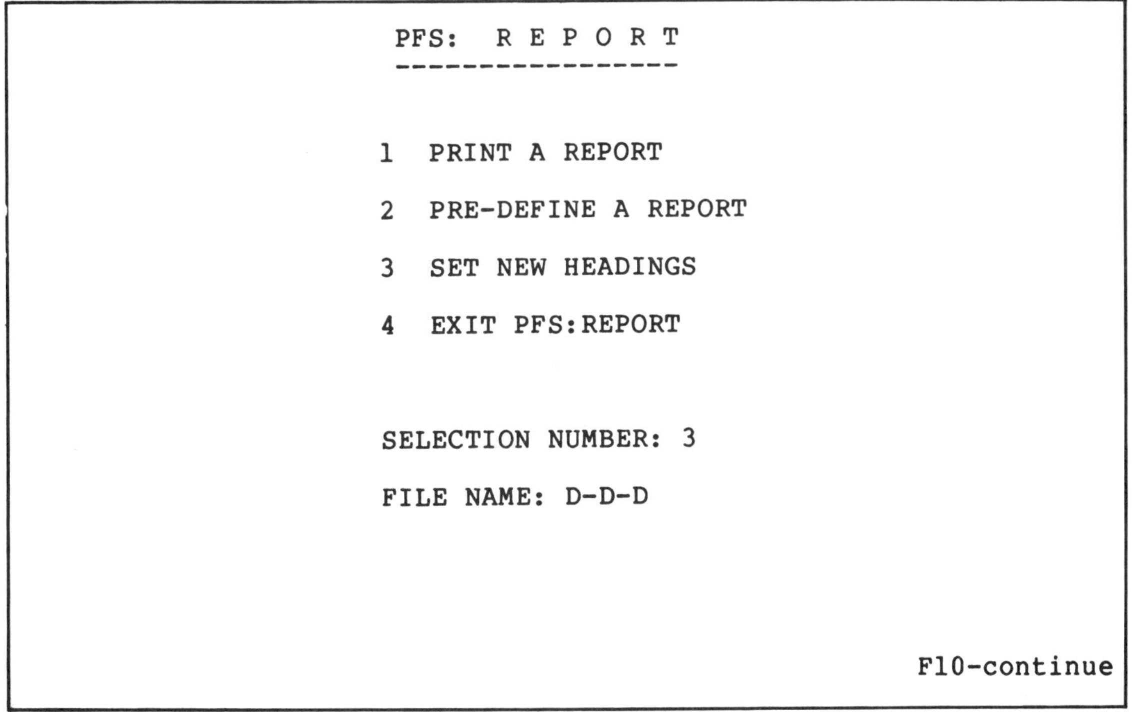

PFS: R E P O R T

1 PRINT A REPORT

2 PRE-DEFINE A REPORT

3 SET NEW HEADINGS

4 EXIT PFS:REPORT

SELECTION NUMBER: 3

FILE NAME: D-D-D

F10-continue

Fig. 3-25. Completed Main Menu for setting new headings for the item names listed on reports.

the status line on the bottom of the screen displaying HEADINGS (as in Fig. 3-26). Use the TAB key or the RIGHT ARROW key to move the cursor to the field item heading that you want to change in your reports. In our current example we will move to the "People benefiting" field in the D-D-D form Beside the field we type, #SERVED and press the continue key. Now, every time that particular field is used in a report, it will cause the heading to read "#Served," with a net savings of eight spaces in each report that uses that field. We will perform a similar operation by designating "Date Completed" as simply "Date." There might be the first impression that ten characters would be saved by substituting that different heading. Remember, though, that the actual data in the field will be in the YY/MM/DD format that takes eight spaces in that column, so our total savings will be six characters. Figure 3-27 illustrates the way the heading names can be modified.

Now when we want to print the report, we can utilize the standard size format of 80 columns wide and 66 lines long as illustrated in Fig. 3-28. The resulting printout of the #SERVED report is displayed in Fig. 3-29.

Setting new headings is not an irreversible procedure. If you want to modify any heading, you may simply duplicate the procedure just demonstrated to insert the headings you want. All new headings of a form may be removed at once by entering the operation 3 SET NEW HEADINGS and then pressing CTRL and H (for home) or F3.

REPORTS WITH DERIVED COLUMNS

PFS:Report has the ability to perform the four major arithmetic functions with any of the columns. Additionally, parentheses can be used to designate that one mathematical operation be done before another. That is an especially important feature since without any designations of operations, *PFS:Report* performs math from left to right.

There can be up to three derived columns in any *PFS:Report*. A report may even be sorted on the result of a computation, allowing the use of a derived column as the first column in the report specification. Derived column calculations may in-

```
Job #:                      Job:
Job description:

Status:
Act by (yy/mm/dd):

Date Began:                             Date Completed:
Time Began:                             Time Completed:

Service area:
People benefiting:
Volunteer hours:
Volunteers:



Project (A/B):
Notes:



--------------------------------------------------------------------------
File: D-D-D                             HEADINGS                    Page 1

                                                              F10-continue
```

Fig. 3-26. A display of the HEADINGS Screen.

```
Job #:                    Job:
Job description:

Status:
Act by (yy/mm/dd):

Date Began:                           Date Completed: Date
Time Began:                           Time Completed:

Service area:
People benefiting: # Served
Volunteer hours:
Volunteers:


Project (A/B):
Notes:


--------------------------------------------------------------------------------
File: D-D-D                           HEADINGS                           Page 1

                                                                    F10-continue
```

Fig. 3-27. A completed "HEADINGS" screen in which the title "# Served" will be substituted for "People benefiting" on all future reports, and "Date" will be substituted for "Date completed."

```
                              REPORT OPTIONS


          TITLE: Number of People Served as of July 31, 1984

          PRE-DEFINED REPORT NAME: #SERVED


          OUTPUT TO: lptl:

          LINES PER PAGE: 66          PAGE WIDTH: 80




                                                                    F10-continue
```

Fig. 3-28. The "# Served" report can now be printed on paper of a standard size as shown in these Report Options.

```
                 Number of People Served as of July 31, 1984

   Service area         Date                 Job                  # Served   Job #
------------------- --------- ------------------------------ ---------  -----
Advocacy             84/05/11  Telecommunicate w/ congressmen   100,000  006
                     84/07/01  Lobby for zone change              2,500  007

                        Total:                                  102,500
                        Count:                             2

Community services   84/06/03  Biofeedback Seminar                   45  005
                     84/07/17  Prepare flyer                        125  003

                        Total:                                      170
                        Count:                             2

Direct services      84/05/12  SRS forms                             25  008
                     84/06/01  Transitional Living meeting           25  004

                        Total:                                       50
                        Count:                             2

Public education     84/03/24  Print depression pamphlets         1,000  001
                     84/04/30  Film & Speech                         25  002
                     84/07/02  Send Pierre mailing                6,450  009

                        Total:                                    7,475
                        Count:                             3


                        --------------------------------------- ---------
                        Total:                                  110,195
                        Count:                             9
                        --------------------------------------- ---------
```

Fig. 3-29. An 80 column report printout of "# Served".

volve other derived column values as long as they are referred to from left to right. For example, column #4 may be a column that is derived as the sum of the first three columns. Column #5 can multiply .05 times column #4. Column #6 could be a derived column that is column #5 minused from column #4. However, column #4 could not be instructed to multiply .05 times column #5 since column #5 would not be calculated at that point.

A column may even include a reference to itself. For example, let's use the D-D-D form to illustrate. Suppose that we would like to keep a running tally of volunteer hours. Our retrieve specifications will be "Volunteer hours: >0." The first field to sort will be "Date Completed." We will end up producing a chronological listing of completed events. Our second report spec will be "Job," and we will designate it as such by placing a "2" beside that field. The third column of the report will be "Volunteer hours." Placing an "A" after the number 3 will produce a numeric average. The fourth column will be a derived column, the sum of column #3 and column #4. The value used for column #4 will be the value of column #4 in the previous row, beginning with a value of 0. See Figs. 3-30 and 3-31 to view a completed REPORT SPEC screen with a derived column. That report may provide more information by allowing us to see that by April we had only five volunteer hours. Otherwise, a "T" in a report column will allow the total to be shown, but only as a grand total. Figure 3-32 shows a sample report that has used the specifications described above.

The F7 key on IBM-style keyboards, and CTRL and D (for derived) on Apple style keyboards are used to set up derived columns when you are

```
Job #:                          Job: 2
Job description:

Status:
Act by (yy/mm/dd):

Date Began:                                Date Completed: 1
Time Began:                                Time Completed:

Service area:
People benefiting:
Volunteer hours: 3A
Volunteers:


Project (A/B):
Notes:


--------------------------------------------------------------------------------
File: d-d-d                          REPORT SPEC                          Page 1

F7-Derived Columns                                                  F10-continue
```

Fig. 3-30. The first screen of Report Specifications for a volunteer hours report that will sort projects by the date of their completion.

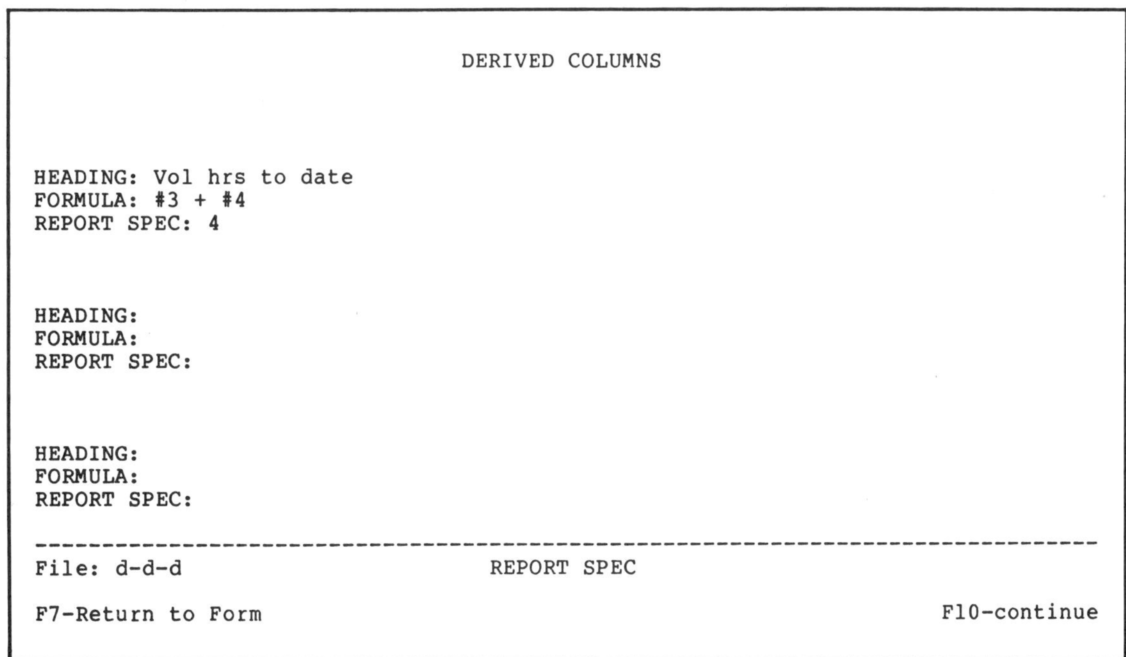

```
                                 DERIVED COLUMNS



HEADING: Vol hrs to date
FORMULA: #3 + #4
REPORT SPEC: 4



HEADING:
FORMULA:
REPORT SPEC:



HEADING:
FORMULA:
REPORT SPEC:
--------------------------------------------------------------------------------
File: d-d-d                          REPORT SPEC

F7-Return to Form                                                   F10-continue
```

Fig. 3-31. The second screen of a report of volunteer hours—the page of derived columns that uses the *PFS:Report* math functions to keep a running total of volunteer hours.

```
                    A report of volunteer hours

  Date               Job                       Volunteer hours   Vol hrs to date
---------  -------------------------------  ---------------   ---------------
84/03/24   Print depression pamphlets                     3                 3
84/04/30   Film & Speech                                  2                 5
84/05/11   Telecommunicate w/ congressmen                12                17
84/05/12   SRS forms                                      5                22
84/06/01   Transitional Living meeting                    8                30
84/07/01   Lobby for zone change                         25                55

                                  -----------------------
                                  Average:                9
                                  -----------------------
```

Fig. 3-32. A sample report of total volunteer hours.

designating report specifications. A good example of the usefulness of derived columns can be illustrated with the use of the "Payables" file.

We can create a report that will flag any unpaid invoices. Let's use "Date received" as the first report spec in order to get a chronological listing of invoices. (See Fig. 3-33.) The second column can be the "Pay to" field. Third in our report can be "Amount." Using a "T" in this field will total the amount of invoices received during the month. The fourth column can be "Amount paid." Again, a "T" will cause the column to be totaled. The fifth column can be a derived column, "Balance due," that will be the result of column #3 minus column #4. After designating the first four columns, we press the derived column key. Figure 3-34 shows the manner in which the report specs can be completed to create a column that will display the invoices

```
Invoice no:                 Date received: 1
Description:
Amount: 3T
Pay to: 2
L2:
L3:
L4:

Amount paid: 4T             Date paid:

Check number:

Account category:




----------------------------------------------------------------------------
File: payables                  REPORT SPEC                          Page 1

F7-Derived Columns                                              F10-continue
```

Fig. 3-33. The first screen of a "Payables" Report Spec that will sort bills by date received, list to whom the bills are due, and the total amount due and amount paid.

```
                         DERIVED COLUMNS



HEADING: DUE
FORMULA: #3 - #4
REPORT SPEC: 5T


HEADING:
FORMULA:
REPORT SPEC:


HEADING:
FORMULA:
REPORT SPEC:

--------------------------------------------------------------------------
File: payables                 REPORT SPEC

F7-Return to Form                                           F10-continue
```

Fig. 3-34. The second screen, one of a derived column that will subtract the amounts paid from the amounts due for the "Payables" report.

with a balance due. Placing a "T" after the "5" in the report spec will show our total of unpaid bill for the month.

Derived columns contain three different sets of prompts for each of the possible total of three derived columns.

HEADING is to specify the name of the column as you want it to appear on the report. In this example, we will enter, "Due." If you choose to leave this prompt blank, *PFS:Report* will print the formula for the column as the heading.

FORMULA is the area in which you designate the operation to be performed. Columns are identified with a "#" preceding the column number. We shall indicate #3–#4.

REPORT SPEC requires the same information as any field that you want to have included in your report. That information includes the number of the column as well as any of the column calculations, such a "T"otal, "S"ubtotal, or "C"ount. We will indicate "5T" in order to make "Balance due" our fifth column and have the total amount calculated. The primary sort may even take place on the first column as a derived column if you choose to place a "1" in the report spec of a derived column. However, such a sort is fairly complex and will take longer to complete than a normal report.

When we have completed the DERIVED COLUMNS screen, we press F7 or CTRL-<D> to return to the REPORT SPECS screen. As soon as the derived column key is pressed, you will return to the form in the REPORT SPEC phase. Pressing the continue key will cause the report to begin. Figure 3-35 illustrates a sample printout using the report specification shown in the previous two figures.

REPORTS WITH KEYWORDS

The ability to sort on the basis of keywords is a handy feature, particularly in those cases when you may want to reference and recall periodical articles

Date received	Pay to	Amount	Amount paid	DUE
	June Payables			
84/06/03	AB Dick	37.50		37.50
	R & J Properties	325.00	325.00	0.00
84/06/05	Bell telephone	98.12	98.12	0.00
84/06/08	Professional Administrator	25.00		25.00
84/06/13	The Learning Co.	275.00	275.00	0.00
	Total:	760.62	698.12	62.50

Fig. 3-35. A sample printout of "June Payables" using the "Payables" report specifications.

and similar entries. A typical *PFS:File* form to fulfill such a purpose may look something like the one shown in Fig. 3-36.

We will want a report that categorizes all of our articles in a meaningful way; one that lists each relevant article for each keyword listing we have supplied in *File*. To do so, we must specify "1K" after the "Keyword" field. Keyword sorts will only work on the first field, and because they produce a complex report, the process can take quite a bit longer than a normal report. Keywords are words that are important topic concepts of an article, such as "fundraising" or "MasterCharge." Keywords are identified as the set of characters between spaces, so in order to be considered as a single keyword, the word must not contain spaces. "MasterCharge" in a single keyword. "Master Charge" would be two different keywords, "Master" and "Charge." Keyword listings will appear alphabetically. Therefore if you mistakenly enter keywords in slightly different formats, such as "ad" and "advertising", they are likely to appear in close proximity.

The second column that we want in the report is "Date." Remember that only the first two columns of a report are sorted. By using "Date" as the second column, we will see the oldest to the most recent appearances of each of the selected keywords. We took care to prompt for dates to be entered in the standard YY/MM/DD format to enable such a sort. Forcing a publication date such as "Spring 1985" into 85/04/01 format is artificial, but effective.

The rest of the columns will consist of the Periodical (#3), Vol (#4), and Issue (#5). The abstract itself could also be printed, but not with regular width paper. Each entry will appear as many times as there are keywords for that abstract. In other words, if an article appears with three keywords, it will appear three times in the report. The keyword REPORT SPEC screen is illustrated in Fig. 3-37. The completed report is shown in Fig. 3-38.

```
Periodical:
Volume #:                  Issue #:
Date (yy/mm/dd):
Title:



Author:
Page:
Keywords:



Abstract:
```

Fig. 3-36. A keyword form for indexing articles.

```
Periodical: 3
Volume #: 4          Issue #: 5
Date (yy/mm/dd): 2
Title:

Author:
Page:
Keywords: 1K


Abstract:









--------------------------------------------------------------------------------
File: keywords                  REPORT SPEC                        Page 1

F7-Derived Columns                                           F10-continue
```

Fig. 3-37. Keyword report specifications that will sort by keyword and date and list periodical, volume, and issue.

Keyword Report

Keywords	Date (yy/mm/dd)	Periodical	Volume #	Issue #
3B2	84/04/03	PC WEEK	1	14
65C02	84/04/02	Computer + Software News	2	14
APL	83/09/01	PC	2	4
Apple	84/04/02	Computer + Software News	2	14
Assembler	83/09/01	PC	2	4
AT&T	84/04/03	PC WEEK	1	14
BASIC	83/09/01	PC	2	4
Bell	83/05/01	PC WORLD	1	3
C	83/09/01	PC	2	4
Cobol	83/09/01	PC	2	4
dBASEII	83/09/01	PC	2	4
DOS	83/05/01	PC WORLD	1	3
Fortran	83/09/01	PC	2	4
IIc	84/04/02	Computer + Software News	2	14
IIx	84/04/02	Computer + Software News	2	14
languages	83/09/01	PC	2	4
Pascal	83/09/01	PC	2	4
PL/1	83/09/01	PC	2	4
portable	84/04/02	Computer + Software News	2	14
programming	83/09/01	PC	2	4
supermicro	84/04/03	PC WEEK	1	14
Unix	83/05/01	PC WORLD	1	3

Fig. 3-38. A keywork report.

```
*********************** I N V E N T O R Y   R E C O R D *********************
ITEM              :
DESCRIPTION       : 1C
PRICE             : 3
PRIMARY SUPPLIERS:
OTHER SUPPLIERS   :

------------------- P U R C H A S E   I N F O R M A T I O N -----------------
DATE OF PURCHASE  :
QUANTITY PURCHASED:
UNIT COST         : 2









--------------------------------------------------------------------------------
File: invtry                     REPORT 'MARGINS'                        Page 1

F3-Remove        F7-Derived Columns                                F10-continue
```

```
                                 DERIVED COLUMNS



HEADING: PROFIT MARGIN
FORMULA: #3*(#3-#2)/(#2*#3)*100
REPORT SPEC: 4A


HEADING:
FORMULA:
REPORT SPEC:


HEADING:
FORMULA:
REPORT SPEC:
--------------------------------------------------------------------------------
File: invtry                     REPORT 'MARGINS'

F3-Remove        F7-Return to Form                                 F10-continue
```

Fig. 3-39. PFS:Solutions "INVTRY" report "Margins" that uses the derived column to calculate profit margins.

```
***************** T I C K L E R   F I L E / D A I L Y   L O G **************
DATE: 1C                          DAY:
--------------------- T I C K L E R   F I L E   I T E M S -------------------
TIME          COMMENTS                                                     :



-------------------------- A P P O I N T M E N T S -------------------------
TIME          COMMENTS                                                     :



--------------------------- E X P E N S E   L O G ---------------------------
MEALS         : 2TA     LODGING         : 3TA          AIR FARE : 4TA
CAR/TAXI      : 5TA     MILEAGE/PARKING: 6TA           TELEPHONE: 7TA
ENTERTAINMENT: 8TA      OTHER           : 9TA
COMMENTS      :
-------------------------------------------------------------------------------
File: tickler                  REPORT 'EXPENSE'                    Page 1

F3-Remove        F7-Derived Columns                              F10-continue



                               DERIVED COLUMNS



HEADING: TOTAL
FORMULA: #2+#3+#4+#5+#6+#7
REPORT SPEC: 8T


HEADING:
FORMULA:
REPORT SPEC:


HEADING:
FORMULA:
REPORT SPEC:

-------------------------------------------------------------------------------
File: TICKLER                  REPORT 'EXPENSE'

F3-Remove        F7-Return to Form                               F10-continue
```

Fig. 3-40. PFS:Solutions "TICKLER" report "Expense" that adds six columns to recap all business expenses for each day.

```
************************* P A Y R O L L   R E C O R D ************************
      NAME: 1P
PAY PERIOD: 2
.
              GROSS PAY              : 3ST              .
              REGULAR EARNINGS       :                  .
              OVERTIME EARNINGS      :                  .
              OTHER PAY              :                  .
              FEDERAL WITHHOLDING    : 4ST              .
              FICA                   : 5ST              .
              STATE WITHHOLDING      : 6ST              .
              OTHER STATE TAX        : 7ST              .
              OTHER DEDUCTIONS       : 8ST              .
              OTHER DEDUCTIONS       : 9ST              .
                                       ------------------
              NET PAY                :                  .
--------------------------------------------------------------------------------
SOCIAL SECURITY #       :               DEPARTMENT              :
REGULAR PAY RATE        :               OVERTIME PAY RATE       :
PERIOD 1 - REGULAR HOURS:               PERIOD 1 - OVERTIME HOURS:
PERIOD 2 - REGULAR HOURS:               PERIOD 2 - OVERTIME HOURS:
--------------------------------------------------------------------------------
File: payroll                   REPORT 'PAYSTUB'                        Page 1

F3-Remove        F7-Derived Columns                                F10-continue
```

Fig. 3-41. PFS:Solutions "PAYROLL" report "Paystub" that will print a payroll record for each employee on a separate piece of paper.

ADVANCED USES OF REPORTS

Figures 3-39 through 3-45 show the reports specifications of reports that use derived columns within computations. The examples will be drawn from reports that come prepackaged with two of the PFS:Solutions packages, *PFS:Payroll* and *PFS:Tickler*. There is probably no better way than to learn by doing, following the lead of the people at Software Publishing Corporation. Examining each of the sample report specifications and report examples will give you a pretty comprehensive understanding of the concepts involved. Particular attention should be paid to the ways in which "C," "T," "SC," "ST," "A," and "SA" are used, and the ways in which the derived columns play an integral part in the creation and retrieval of important data.

```
************************* P A Y R O L L   R E C O R D ************************
      NAME: 1C
PAY PERIOD:
.
              GROSS PAY              : 2T                 .
              REGULAR EARNINGS       :                    .
              OVERTIME EARNINGS      :                    .
              OTHER PAY              :                    .
              FEDERAL WITHHOLDING    : 3T                 .
              FICA                   : 4T                 .
              STATE WITHHOLDING      : 5T                 .
              OTHER STATE TAX        : 6T                 .
              OTHER DEDUCTIONS       : 7T                 .
              OTHER DEDUCTIONS       : 8T                 .
                                      -------------------
              NET PAY                :                    .
--------------------------------------------------------------------------------
SOCIAL SECURITY #        :           DEPARTMENT              :
REGULAR PAY RATE         :           OVERTIME PAY RATE       :
PERIOD 1 - REGULAR HOURS:            PERIOD 1 - OVERTIME HOURS:
PERIOD 2 - REGULAR HOURS:            PERIOD 2 - OVERTIME HOURS:
--------------------------------------------------------------------------------
File: payroll                   REPORT 'NETPAY'                    Page 1

F3-Remove        F7-Derived Columns                               F10-continue


                                DERIVED COLUMNS




HEADING: NET PAY
FORMULA: #2-#3-#4-#5-#6-#7-#8
REPORT SPEC: 9CT



HEADING:
FORMULA:
REPORT SPEC:



HEADING:
FORMULA:
REPORT SPEC:

--------------------------------------------------------------------------------
File: PAYROLL                   REPORT 'NETPAY'

F3-Remove        F7-Return to Form                                F10-continue
```

Fig. 3-42. PFS:Solutions "PAYROLL" report "Netpay" uses a derived column to calculate the payroll deductions that comprise the difference between gross and net pay.

```
************************  P A Y R O L L   R E C O R D  ************************
     NAME: 1C
PAY PERIOD:
.
              GROSS PAY               :                 .
              REGULAR EARNINGS        :                 .
              OVERTIME EARNINGS       :                 .
              OTHER PAY               :                 .
              FEDERAL WITHHOLDING     :                 .
              FICA                    :                 .
              STATE WITHHOLDING       :                 .
              OTHER STATE TAX         :                 .
              OTHER DEDUCTIONS        :                 .
              OTHER DEDUCTIONS        :                 .
                                       -------------------
              NET PAY                 :                 .
--------------------------------------------------------------------------------
SOCIAL SECURITY #        :             DEPARTMENT                :
REGULAR PAY RATE         : 2           OVERTIME PAY RATE         : 3
PERIOD 1 - REGULAR HOURS: 4T           PERIOD 1 - OVERTIME HOURS: 5T
PERIOD 2 - REGULAR HOURS: 6T           PERIOD 2 - OVERTIME HOURS: 7T
--------------------------------------------------------------------------------
File: payroll                    REPORT 'HOURPAY'                       Page 1

F3-Remove        F7-Derived Columns                                F10-continue


                                 DERIVED COLUMNS



HEADING: REGULAR $
FORMULA: #2*(#4+#6)
REPORT SPEC: 8CT


HEADING: OVERTIME $
FORMULA: #3*(#5+#7)
REPORT SPEC: 9CT


HEADING:
FORMULA:
REPORT SPEC:

--------------------------------------------------------------------------------
File: PAYROLL                    REPORT 'HOURPAY'

F3-Remove        F7-Return to Form                                 F10-continue
```

Fig. 3-43. PFS:Solutions "PAYROLL" report "Hourpay" uses two derived columns to calculate different rates of pay for regular and overtime hours.

```
************************ P A Y R O L L   R E C O R D ************************
     NAME:
PAY PERIOD:
.
             GROSS PAY                :                  .
             REGULAR EARNINGS         :                  .
             OVERTIME EARNINGS        :                  .
             OTHER PAY                :                  .
             FEDERAL WITHHOLDING      : 1T               .
             FICA                     : 2T               .
             STATE WITHHOLDING        : 3T               .
             OTHER STATE TAX          : 4T               .
             OTHER DEDUCTIONS         :                  .
             OTHER DEDUCTIONS         :                  .
                                        -----------------
             NET PAY                  :                  .
--------------------------------------------------------------------------------
SOCIAL SECURITY #        :            DEPARTMENT                 :
REGULAR PAY RATE         :            OVERTIME PAY RATE          :
PERIOD 1 - REGULAR HOURS:             PERIOD 1 - OVERTIME HOURS:
PERIOD 2 - REGULAR HOURS:             PERIOD 2 - OVERTIME HOURS:
--------------------------------------------------------------------------------
File: payroll                     REPORT 'TAXES'                     Page 1

F3-Remove         F7-Derived Columns                            F10-continue



                              DERIVED COLUMNS



HEADING: PAY TO FED
FORMULA: #1+(2*#2)
REPORT SPEC: 5CT


HEADING: PAY TO STATE
FORMULA: #3+#4
REPORT SPEC: 6CT


HEADING: TOTAL DUE
FORMULA: #5+#6
REPORT SPEC: 7CT
--------------------------------------------------------------------------------
File: PAYROLL                     REPORT 'TAXES'

F3-Remove         F7-Return to Form                             F10-continue
```

Fig. 3-44. Taxes are calculated using the maximum of three derived columns.

```
*************************  P A Y R O L L   R E C O R D  ************************
      NAME: 1C
PAY PERIOD:
.
              GROSS PAY                :                   .
              REGULAR EARNINGS         : 3ST               .
              OVERTIME EARNINGS        : 4ST               .
              OTHER PAY                :                   .
              FEDERAL WITHHOLDING      : 6ST               .
              FICA                     : 7ST               .
              STATE WITHHOLDING        : 8ST               .
              OTHER STATE TAX          : 9ST               .
              OTHER DEDUCTIONS         :                   .
              OTHER DEDUCTIONS         :                   .
                                        -------------------
              NET PAY                  :                   .
--------------------------------------------------------------------------------
SOCIAL SECURITY #         : 2          DEPARTMENT                :
REGULAR PAY RATE          :            OVERTIME PAY RATE         :
PERIOD 1 - REGULAR HOURS:              PERIOD 1 - OVERTIME HOURS:
PERIOD 2 - REGULAR HOURS:              PERIOD 2 - OVERTIME HOURS:
--------------------------------------------------------------------------------
File: payroll                     REPORT 'W2'                          Page 1

F3-Remove        F7-Derived Columns                                F10-continue

                                 DERIVED COLUMNS



HEADING: TAXABLE $
FORMULA: #3+#4
REPORT SPEC: 5ST



HEADING:
FORMULA:
REPORT SPEC:



HEADING:
FORMULA:
REPORT SPEC:

--------------------------------------------------------------------------------
File: payroll                     REPORT 'W2'

F3-Remove        F7-Return to Form                                 F10-continue
```

Fig. 3-45. W-2 forms can be easily generated using PFS:Solution "PAYROLL" and its "W2" report.

PFS:Graph—Worth a Thousand Data Points

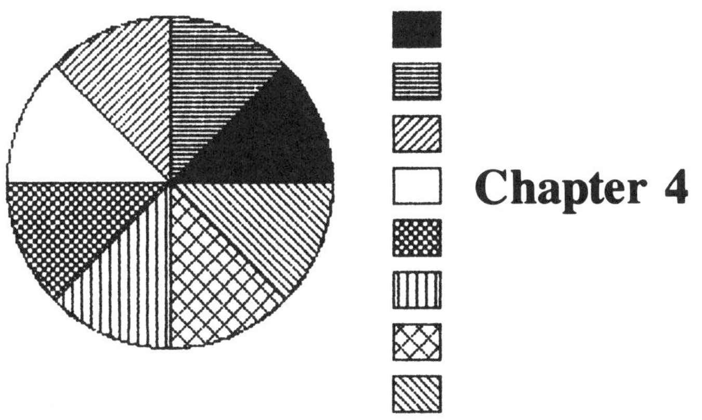

Chapter 4

There is no better way to transmit information about numbers than through the use of graphs. Numbers can be grouped and reported with *PFS: Report,* but if you want those numbers to be *understood,* they should be summarized in graphs. I recently heard of a Fortune 500 company that used *only* graphic displays in an annual report. The traditional multipage presentation of numbers and more numbers was available upon request, but the greatest portion of their message was carried entirely by graphs. We usually think of graphs as being a useful addition to our reports. Perhaps we should begin to think of numeric reports as an addition to our graphs.

PFS:Graph is perhaps the hardest of the PFS program modules to learn. There is not the almost intuitive understanding of its use found with the other modules. It is helpful that the menus and procedures are similar to the other PFS modules. However, much must be kept straight. X- and Y-axes must be remembered for orientation. Three different types of data to be entered on the X-axis (horizontal axis) must be differentiated: identifier, numeric, and date. There are eight different possible date formats. Three primary types of graphs are used, bar, line, and pie. Combinations of line and bar charts may be formed. Data may be displayed in a cumulative or noncumulative manner. Graphs may be stacked or treated separately. Line graphs may be stacked to create area charts. Grid lines may be shown or suppressed. In short, there are many options, and many skills that must be mastered. All of these concerns are about creating graphs. No one will help you to determine if it would be more appropriate to illustrate your data with a line chart or a stacked bar chart. You will need to spend some time with the program in order to use it effectively. Thankfully, it is fun to use, and becomes more fun as you become more proficient with it.

With all of its options and choices, *PFS:Graph* is "simple," that is, easy to use by comparison with some of the heavy-duty graphics programs on the market. To their credit, Software Publishing Corporation has managed to keep the task of learning to use the program as simple as possible while maintaining a fair amount of program power and flexibility. The package contains a Sampler disk that illustrates all of the various capabilities of the program. The sampler allows a certain amount of learning-by-doing and provides immediate rewards to the inquisitive user. The manual, the series' longest at about 100 pages, is more than adequate with clear illustrations of the major points and screen photographs to provide step by step instructions. The documentation usually "points the user in the right direction" rather than providing a complete tutorial for advancing to more complex applications.

Others will make the point that the term "simple" also applies to its capabilities and flexibility. The Fortune 500 company referred to above would not have created their entire report using *PFS: Graph*. Bar graphs, for example, can only be vertical, not horizontal. The colors and designs used are predetermined, and cannot be changed arbitrarily. There are no features for smoothing curves, and other amenities. We will not try to present *PFS: Graph* as the most sophisticated and powerful graphics system available. *PFS: Graph* maintains a philosophy consistent with the whole series of program modules. It provides a product that is adequate for most real-world applications, easy to use, user-friendly, and reasonably priced. Besides being adequate as a graphing program in its own right, its chief selling points are that it can graph data from *PFS:File* and *PFS:Plan* without requiring more data. It can also integrate with the *PFS:Write* word processor to print graphs within the body of a document.

GETTING STARTED WITH *PFS:GRAPH*

PFS:Graph maintains the consistent style of most of the PFS program modules. You may install the system onto the disk, or simply type GRAPH at the DOS A> prompt. Apple versions come complete with the Apple DOS and hello program and there is no need to do anything except turn on the computer with the disk in the disk drive.

```
                 PFS:GRAPH MAIN MENU
                 -------------------

      1  GET/EDIT DATA              5  PRINT CHART

      2  DEFINE CHART               6  PLOT CHART

      3  DISPLAY CHART              7  CLEAR CHART

      4  GET/SAVE/REMOVE            8  EXIT PFS:GRAPH


                  SELECTION NUMBER:


                                         F10-Continue
```

Fig. 4-1. A display of the PFS:Graph Main Menu.

PFS: Graph Functions Summarized

The Main Menu is displayed in Fig. 4-1. It works in a way similar to how the other PFS Main Menus do; that is, you select the option that you want by typing the number corresponding to your choice and press the continue key.

In the following descriptions and throughout the rest of the book, the word *chart* will be used to refer to a completed set of graphs, or the entire *picture* of the the set of graphs as they appear on the monitor. The word *graph* will be used to refer to the graphic representation of a set of data. There may be one to four graphs on any chart.

Each of the available menu options is described here:

1 GET/EDIT DATA. One of the main advantages of *PFS:Graph* is the many ways data may be entered. Graphs can be created from the immediate input on the keyboard or with information that comes from *PFS:File*. It can also graph information from the soon-to-be-released PFS spreadsheet module. Or it can graph information from VisiCalc or any spreadsheet that is able to utilize a DIF (Data Interchange Format) file. There are up to four graphs on each chart, and the data for each graph may come from different sources. For example, the information for Graph A may be entered from the keyboard, Graph B may be derived from *PFS:File*, Graph C from *PFS:Plan*, and Graph D from a VisiCalc file.

2 DEFINE CHART. This is the function that lets you select the way your graph is going to look. Each of the four possible charts may be defined as line, bar, or pie charts. (A pie chart takes up the entire screen and cannot be displayed in combination with other graphs.) Each of the graph bars, lines, or sections can be identified in the legend. The entire chart may be titled and the X- and Y-axes may be labeled. Cumulative, stacked or color displays may be designated. Maximum and minimum values may be declared and grid lines may be shown or hidden.

3 DISPLAY CHART. Pressing this option causes the chart to be displayed on the computer's monitor. A chart can be displayed as often as desired until it is "just right" to be printed or saved permanently on the disk.

4 GET/SAVE/REMOVE. This option allows charts that have been created to be saved on the disk, or retrieved or removed from the disk after they have been saved. This is the first option to use if you want to examine the charts saved on the "Sampler" disk. This option is similar in its operation to the same command used in *PFS:Write*. You may, for example, see the entire list of charts saved on a data disk by selecting 4 GET/SAVE/REMOVE from the Main Menu, and then 1 GET CHART at the Get/Save/Remove Menu without giving a Filename. In addition to simple file management, this option allows for the saving of charts in different formats. Saving a chart as a picture allows you to include it in a *PFS:Write* document at a reduced size that is appropriate for a single page document. Unwanted charts may be deleted by using the remove option.

5 PRINT CHART. The PRINT CHART option provides a way for printers with graphics capabilities to print the chart on paper. There are six printer types directly supported by *PFS:Graph* on IBM and MS-DOS systems: IBM Graphics, Epson, IDS Prism, Okidata 82A and 83A, NEC 8023, and C.Itoh printers. Any other printers that are compatible with the six printers listed will also work. *Compatible printers* are ones that utilize identical printer control codes. Apple *II* systems support the same printer codes except, of course, they support Apple printers rather than IBM printers. The print function includes options for printing charts in *normal* (3 × 4-inch) size, or in an *expanded* size that rotates the graph and fills an 8.5 × 11-inch page. Data points may also be listed or omitted according to the user's preference. Once a printer choice has been indicated, that printer setup will be stored on the disk as the assumed printer until it is changed.

6 PLOT CHART. This option allows output to one of four standard plotters. Plotters produce high quality graphics on paper or on transparencies for overhead projection. The four types of plotters supported are the Hewlett-Packard series (7470A, 7220C, 7220T, and 7225), the HIPLOT DMP-29 or DMP-40, the Strobe 100, or the Sweet-P Plotter. Options are also provided for choosing between paper and transparencies and for plotting continuously or pausing for pen changes (for different color pens). Charts can be plotted using solid colors or patterns.

7 CLEAR CHART. CLEAR CHART is used to zero all information on the current chart that is being worked on. It is a "Let's start all over" option. There is a warning message that appears before a chart is cleared and an option to cancel the command. This command affects only the chart being worked on and does not affect any charts stored on the disk.

8 EXIT PFS:GRAPH. The EXIT command allows the termination of the Graph program. If this option is chosen before the chart being worked on has been saved, an appropriate warning message will remind you to save the chart or forever part with it.

USING *PFS:GRAPH*

Let us create a graph that uses information that entered directly from the keyboard. Suppose we find in our organization's history that five years ago when the membership contributions amounted to $1000, an ambitious goal was set to double the membership contributions each year for five years. We will use that information to create the first graph on our chart, entitled "goal." Later we will enter actual membership figures for each of those years in order to compare actual figures with the objective.

At the Main Menu (refer back to Fig. 4-1), pressing 1 GET/EDIT DATA and the continue key will bring the user to the Get/Edit Data Menu shown in Fig. 4-2. The cursor will be blinking beside the SELECTION NUMBER prompt. We must indicate the source of the data. In this case we will type 1 ENTER/EDIT DATA for keyboard data entry. Pressing the TAB key will bring the cursor to the GRAPH (A/B/C/D) prompt. Information may be entered for only one graph at a time, so we type A and tab onto the next prompt, MERGE (Y/N). We are beginning from scratch, so we will leave the default value at N. The MERGE prompt allows for combining from a *PFS:File*, PFS:Plan spreadsheet, or VisiCalc file with information already entered for a graph. The final prompt on the screen, DIRECTORY OR FILE NAME, is for capturing data from a PFS or VisiCalc file. It may be left blank when data is being entered from the keyboard. When the screen has been completed to our specifications, we press the continue key.

The next screen that appears is shown in Fig. 4-3. There are essentially three elements to this screen. Two columns represent the values for the X-axis (horizontal) and Y-axis (vertical). There are 18 lines that may be shown on any screen, but PgDn (page down) allows for the inclusion of more data points. The third element of this screen, the X DATA FORMAT prompt is the most confusing. It is the prompt we must answer to indicate the type of data that is going to be entered, whether date, identifer, or numeric. I would like there to be a reminder that appears with that prompt, but realize that stringing about eight different possible codes could be as confusing as no prompt at all.

DESIGNATING DATA FORMATS

PFS:Graph limits itself to the amount of information that can fit on the screen. Extended charts where only parts of the screen are visible are not allowed. There are a maximum of 36 horizontal data points per graph (144 per chart) allowed with this program. "N" designates a numeric data format for the X-axis (horizontal). The Y (vertical) value is assumed to be a numeric quantity. If the Y value is designated as a numeric value, there will be a scattering of data points, and the only type of graph possible with both X and Y values as numeric is a line graph. The values of allowable numbers that may be entered range from 10^{29} to 10^{-29} (very large and very small numbers).

There are a number of different possibilities for date formats as types of data format. "D" designates that X values will consist of Days, and the

```
GET/EDIT DATA MENU

1  ENTER/EDIT DATA

2  GET VISICALC FILE

3  GET PFS FILE

 SELECTION NUMBER:

 GRAPH (A/B/C/D):

 MERGE (Y/N): N

 DIRECTORY OR FILE NAME:

                                   F10-Continue
```

Fig. 4-2. The PFS:Graph Get/Edit Data Menu that appears after selecting 1. GET/EDIT DATA.

horizontal axis may have values of 1 through 31. "Y" is the designation for Year. Years should generally be entered in two digit formats, such as 84 or 85. If data is entered as 1980, for example, it will be displayed as "80" and no harm will be done. However, if you later want to supply some information from *PFS:File*, the date format will only contain two digits, and there will be different values on the chart, such as "19" and "80." The example that we are using will use Year at the X DATA FORMAT prompt. "M" designates Months and can have values 1 through 12. Months may also be used in combination with "Y" in the formats of "YM" or "MY" for months of more than one year (to a 36-month limit). Q is used to designate that the data format will be in Quarters of the year. Q may be used alone and entered as 1, 2, 3, and 4, or in combination with (Y)ear as "QY" or "YQ" for graphs that will display quarters of more than one year. Values in the various date formats do not have to be entered in any particular order, the program will automatically sort and order dates from the earliest to latest dates.

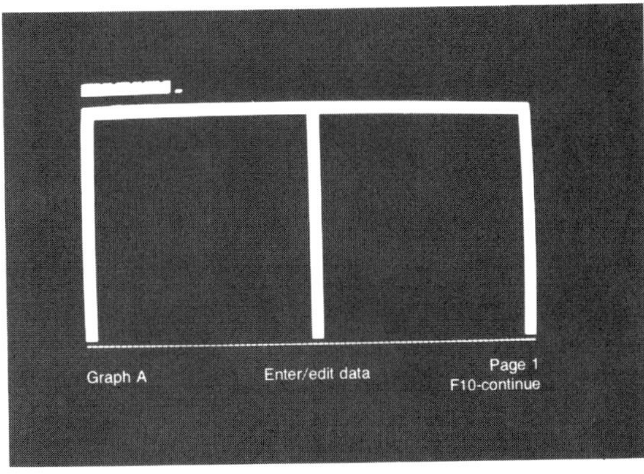

Fig. 4-3. A blank ENTER/EDIT DATA screen for keyboard input of data.

The third type of X data format that may be used is "I" for identifier. An identifier specification allows for a great amount of flexibility. An Identifier may consist of one to 15 characters. A bar chart showing the number of projects in each service area, for example, could list the X data format as "Education." Or, in order to avoid a crowded display, we might want to abbreviate the format as "Ed." Pie charts that use identifiers do not have any space problems even if the whole 15 characters are used for each item. However, pie charts can be used to display only data with two to eight different data points.

Summary of X DATA FORMAT designations

Code	Meaning	Sample Data Entry
I	IDENTIFIER	EDUCATION
N	NUMERIC	55
D	DAY	18
M	MONTH	9
Y	YEAR	1984
Q	QUARTER	3
YM	YEAR/MONTH	84/9
MY	MONTH/YEAR	9/84
QY	QUARTER/YEAR	3/84
YQ	YEAR/QUARTER	84/3

ENTERING DATA FROM THE KEYBOARD

To continue with our example, we enter Year as the X DATA FORMAT and then press the TAB key. The cursor will not be positioned in the X DATA column. We type 80 and then press the (TAB) key again. The cursor will move to the right, Y DATA, column. We enter 1000 and tab onto the X column, and so on until all of the information has been entered. If you make a mistake, simply move the cursor to the data to be changed and type over the incorrect entry. Press the continue key when the information is complete. (See Fig. 4-4). *Do not* press ESC. If you pressed ESC instead of the continue key the program would escape to the Main Menu, and all of the data that had been input would be lost. Pressing the continue key will store the information and then return you to the Main Menu.

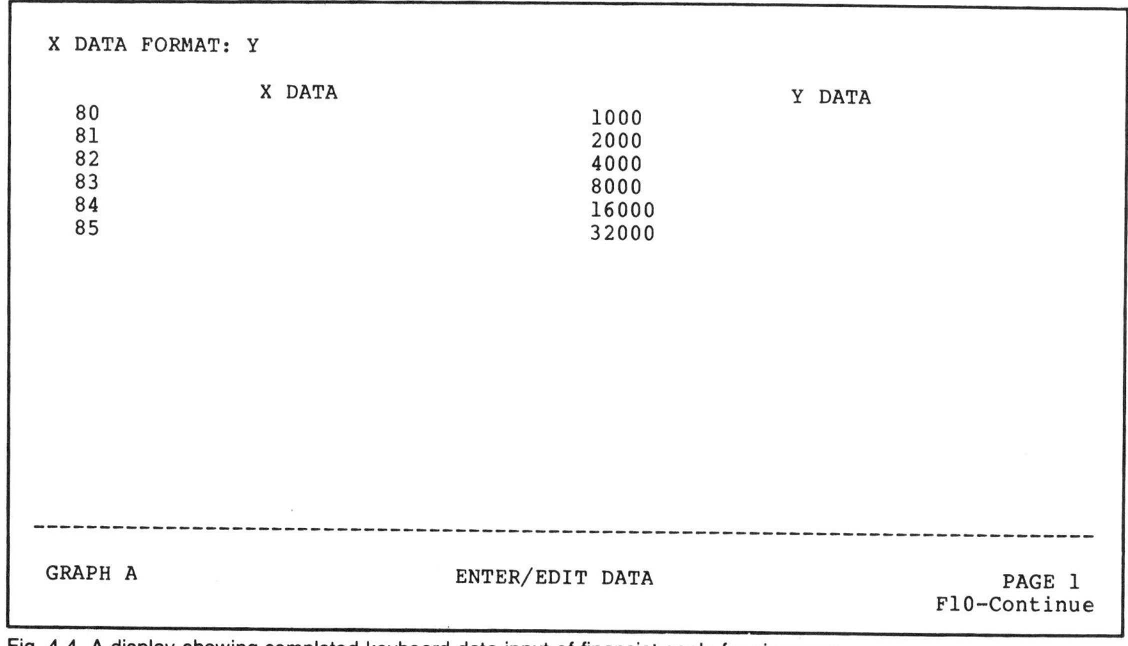

Fig. 4-4. A display showing completed keyboard data input of financial goals for six years.

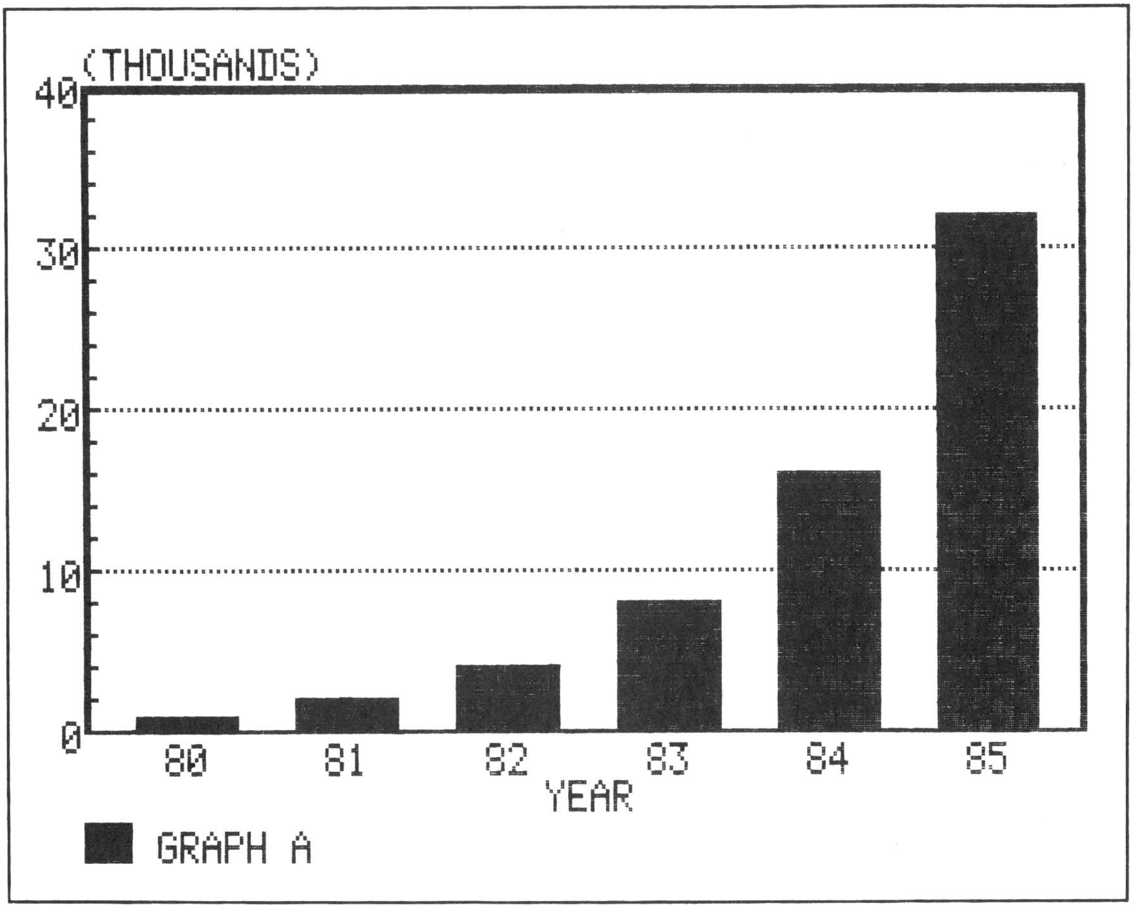

Fig. 4-5. An unlabeled bar chart showing financial goals.

CREATING THE CHART

The next logical step in the creation of a chart is to use the second option on the Main Menu, DEFINE CHART. We don't have to be completely logical. We can peek at the chart in progress by pressing 3 DISPLAY CHART and the continue key. The resulting display is presented in Fig. 4-5. *PFS: Graph* has already assigned a designation of BAR chart based on the X data format being in the date format. A Bar Chart is the default setting when the X data format is date or identifier. A line chart is the default value when the X data format is numeric. We can see that neither of the axes have been labeled, nor has the chart been named. The only legend is "Graph A." The display is also in monochrome. All of these things may be modified in the DEFINE

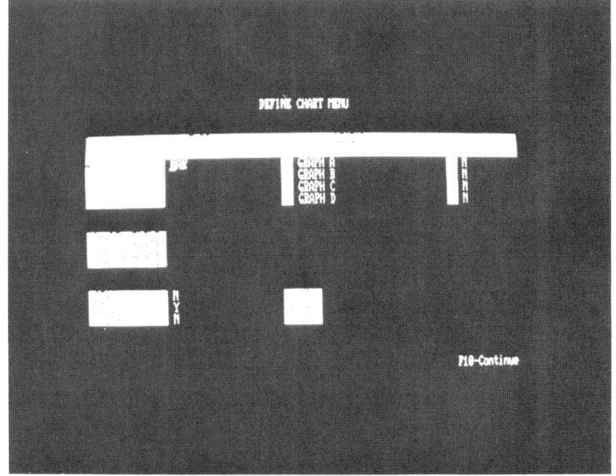

Fig. 4-6. A DEFINE CHART screen that shows Graph A contains data and that it will be shown as a bar chart.

CHART option. Pressing ESC will return to the Main Menu.

Pressing 2 DEFINE CHART and the continue key brings us to the Define Chart Menu of Fig. 4-6. The following explanations summarize each of the prompts in the DEFINE CHART screen:

TYPE. Bar, Line, or Pie may be entered to specify the type of graph desired.

LEGEND. The legend identifies each of the four possible graphs in a chart. Up to 18 characters may be entered to demarcate a graph.

CUM. Cumulative treatment of the vertical (Y) data adds each amount to the previous one to create a "running total" effect. The default value, N causes the data to be graphed at their actual value. Typing Y for the CUM prompt causes that graph to be represented cumulatively.

CHART TITLE. A title of up to forty characters can be given to the entire chart. The title is prominently displayed at the top of the chart.

X-AXIS TITLE. A title for the X-axis (horizontal) may be designated using up to thirty characters.

Y-AXIS TITLE. The Y-axis (vertical) may also be labeled with up to thirty characters.

STACK (Y/N). Using the default value N for the STACK prompt causes the X-axis to be used for the base of all graphs. Answering "Y" for yes causes the graphs in a chart to be stacked on top of each other. That is, the base of the second graph will be the top of the first graph. An example of a stack graph is the one where we compared the cost of microcomputers in Chapter 1 (Fig. 1-4).

GRID (Y/N). Answering "Y" will draw horizontal grid reference lines across the chart. N will suppress the appearance of any grid lines.

COLOR (Y/N). Answer Y and the charts and graphs appear in color if you have a color monitor. Answer "N" and the program uses different shapes and shading to distinguish between different data in different graphs. The program chooses the shading and color, and they may not be changed by the user. A "Y" answer will make plotters plot solid colors, while an "N" will direct the plotter to create patterns.

Y MIN, Y MAX, AND Y DIV. These options allow for the user to set the maximum and minimum values that will appear on the chart as well as the number of divisions on the Y-axis. If these values are left blank, *PFS:Graph* will automatically scale the chart in accordance with the data entered.

An asterisk will appear to the left of Graph A, B, C, and D if that particular graph contains data. So far, in our chart, there is only one asterisk—the one beside Graph A.

A bar graph will be all right for our purposes, so we tab over to the Legend column. In place of "Graph A," we will supply our own legend, GOAL. The CUM default of N will be left alone because we want to view yearly totals, not grand totals for all of the years. Next, we tab down until the cursor is beside the CHART TITLE prompt. We will entitle the chart. "Actual Contributions Compared to Goal." Whew! We just made our forty character limit. X-AXIS can be entitled "Year" and the Y-AXIS "Contributions." The rest of the default values are fine, I guess, except the COLOR one. Since I have a color monitor, I'll choose to see the chart in color by changing the COLOR (Y/N) designation to "Y." A summary of the new values chosen is displayed in Fig. 4-7.

Pressing the continue key implants the new values, and returns us to the Main Menu. Now, using option 3 DISPLAY CHART, Fig. 4-8 shows a more fully developed chart than the last one. We can modify the chart at any time. For example, we can use 2 DEFINE CHART and change the type of graph from a bar graph to a line graph (Fig. 4-9) or into a stacked line graph (Fig. 4-10).

If we used a stacked line chart in this example, it would obliterate part of the information we are yet to add, so we change the response to STACK (Y/N) back to "N." Let's start by using a line graph

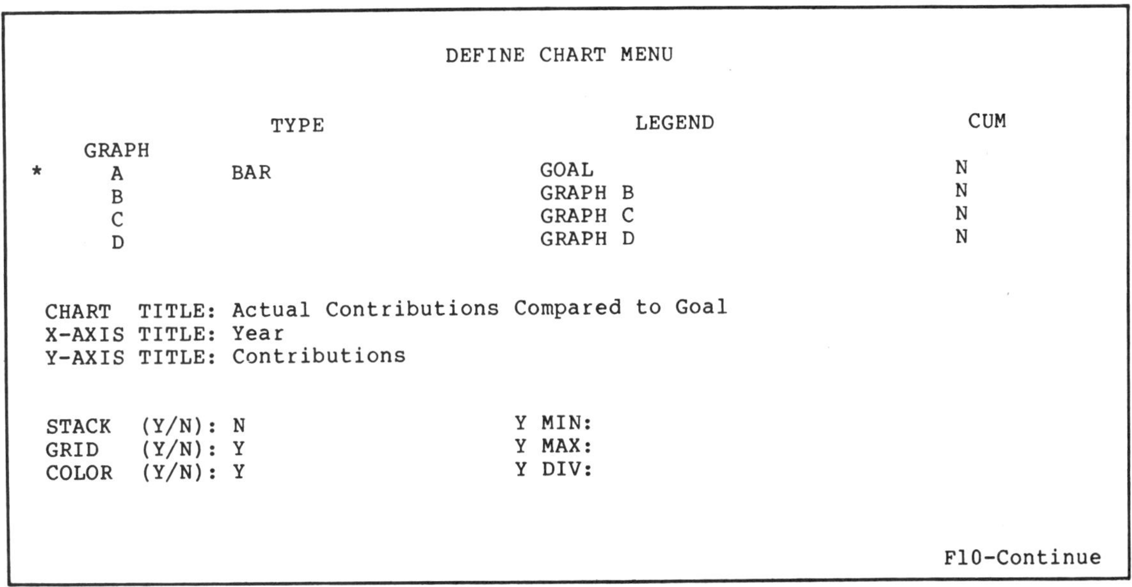

```
                              DEFINE CHART MENU

                 TYPE                       LEGEND                   CUM
    GRAPH
*     A       BAR                     GOAL                         N
      B                               GRAPH B                      N
      C                               GRAPH C                      N
      D                               GRAPH D                      N


  CHART  TITLE: Actual Contributions Compared to Goal
  X-AXIS TITLE: Year
  Y-AXIS TITLE: Contributions


  STACK  (Y/N): N                    Y MIN:
  GRID   (Y/N): Y                    Y MAX:
  COLOR  (Y/N): Y                    Y DIV:


                                                              F10-Continue
```

Fig. 4-7. The modified values for DEFINE CHART will cause the chart to be labeled.

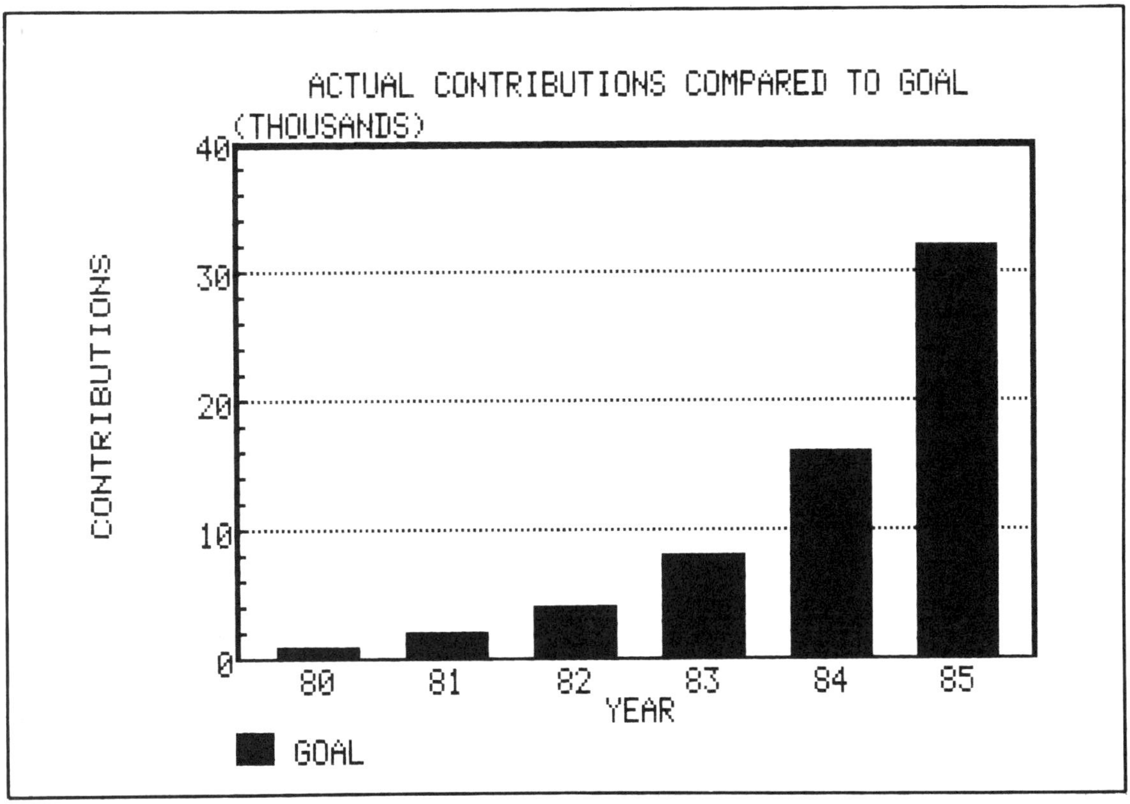

Fig. 4-8. The labeled chart display in progress.

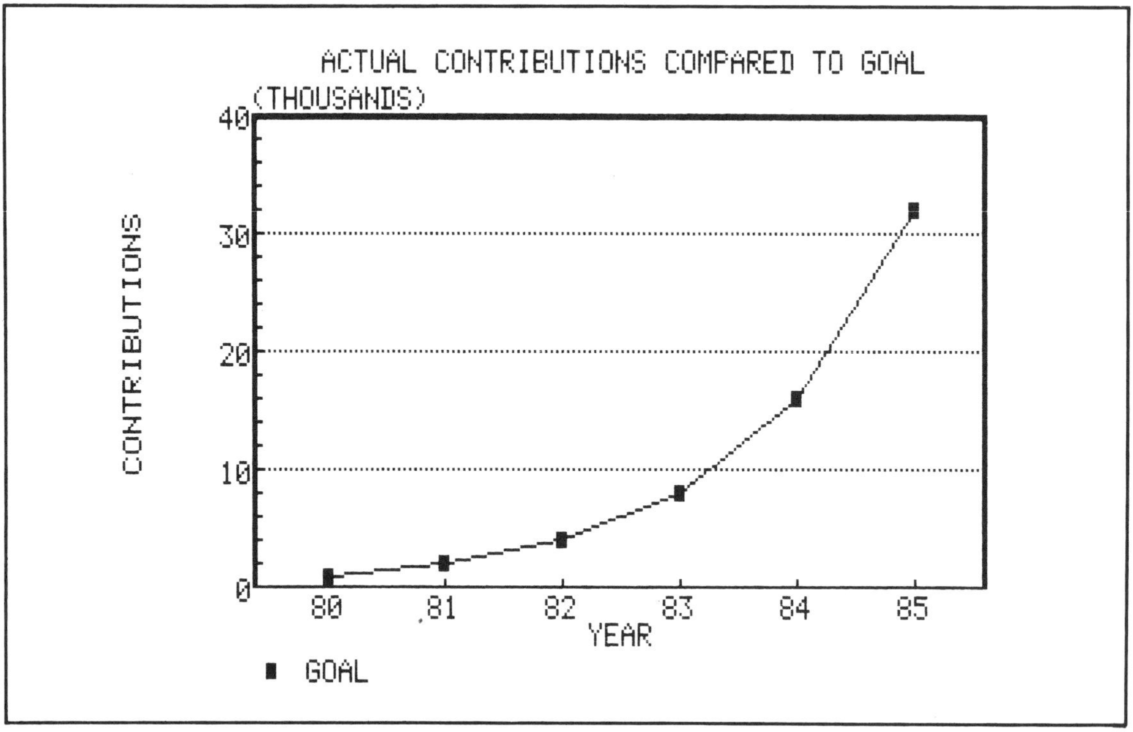

Fig. 4-9. The chart that results from changing the type of graph from bar to line graph.

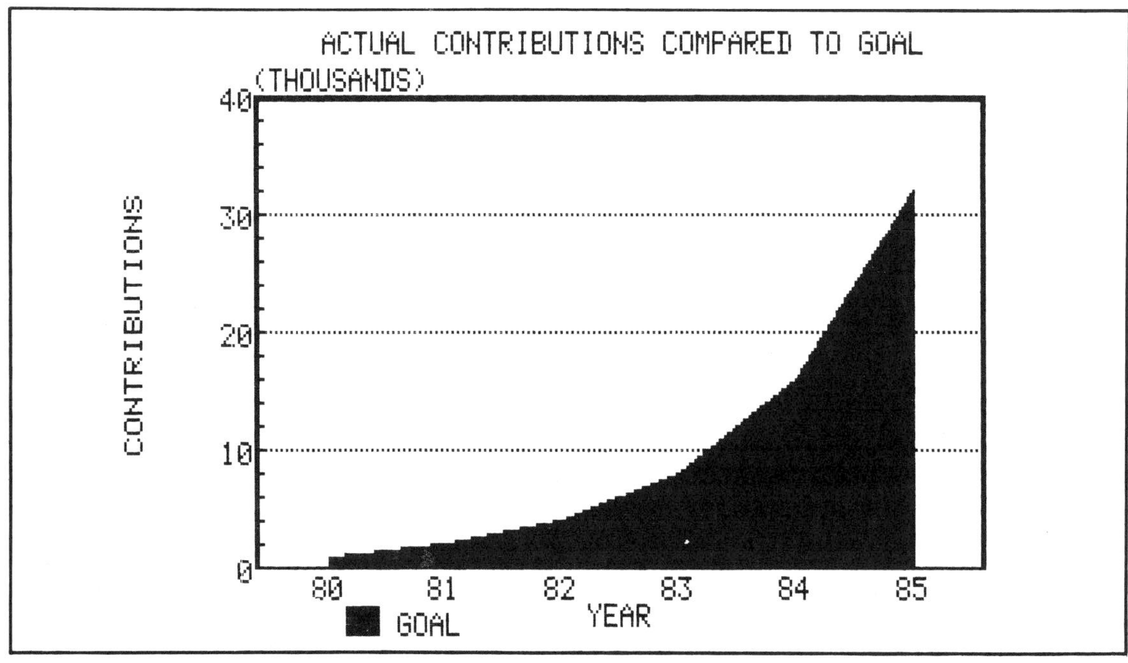

Fig. 4-10. The chart that results from changing the "STACK (Y/N) prompt from "N" to "Y" in the DEFINE CHART MENU.

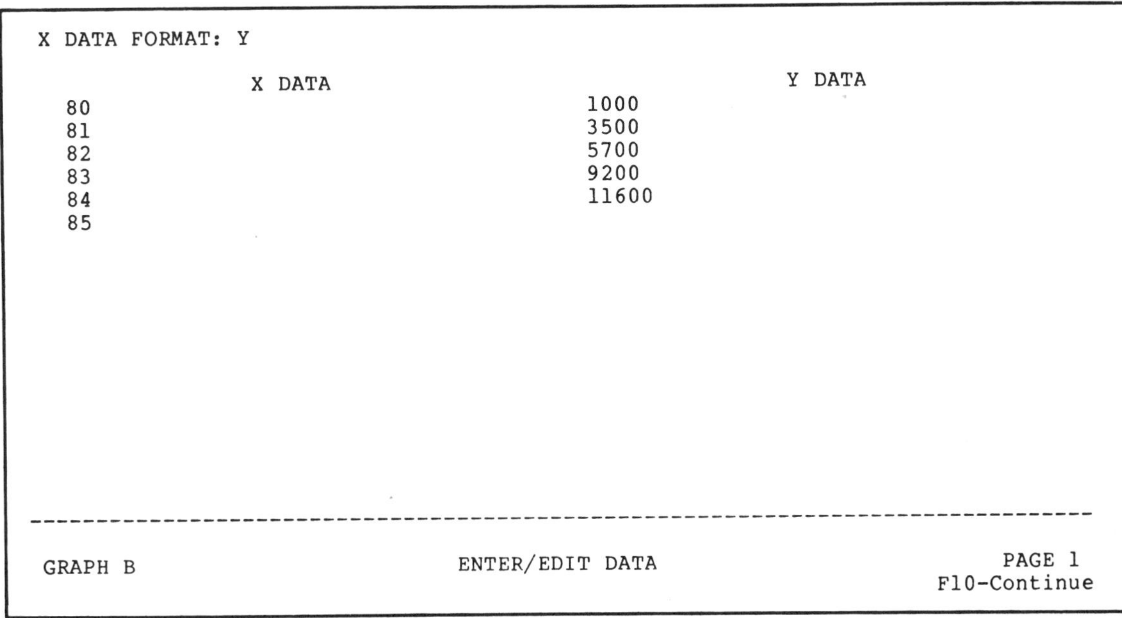

X DATA FORMAT: Y

X DATA	Y DATA
80	1000
81	3500
82	5700
83	9200
84	11600
85	

GRAPH B ENTER/EDIT DATA PAGE 1
F10-Continue

Fig. 4-11. Manually entered data for graph B reflects the organization's actual historic fundraising.

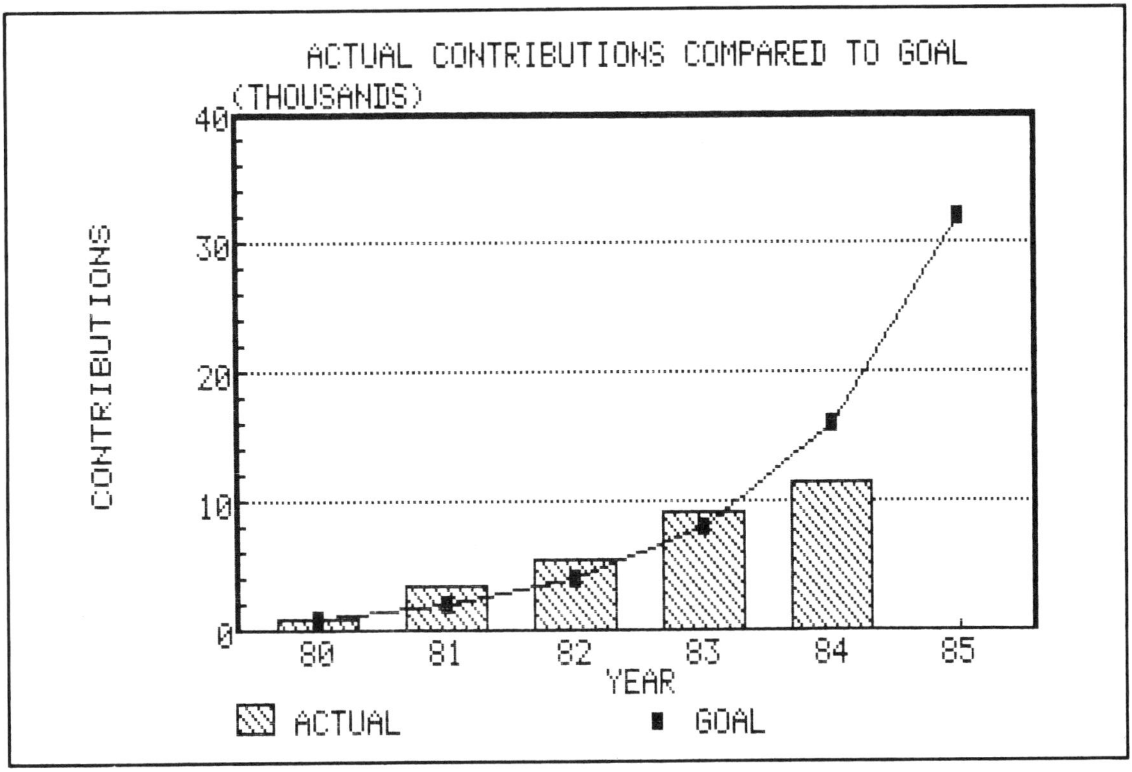

ACTUAL CONTRIBUTIONS COMPARED TO GOAL
(THOUSANDS)
CONTRIBUTIONS
40
30
20
10
0
80 81 82 83 84 85
YEAR
ACTUAL
GOAL

Fig. 4-12. A chart that shows actual figures as bar graphs and goal amounts as a line graph.

to represent our goal and a bar graph to represent actual contributions. We will assign ACTUAL as the legend for Graph B. Of course, any of these values may be changed at any time. We begin to enter actual historic figures. We will enter the data for the first five years from the keyboard, and then use data that collected with *PFS:File* to determine the actual figures for the current year.

The procedures for entering data for actual contributions will be identical to goal figures, except after selecting 1 GET/EDIT DATA from the Main Menu the GRAPH (A/B/C/D) prompt will have B entered. You will notice that the next ENTER/EDIT DATA screen already has the X Data format specified as "Y" for year and the X Data already contains 80 through 85. The historic figures from our records will be entered in the Y column in the spaces corresponding to the appropriate dates as shown in Fig. 4-11. The progress of the chart is now displayed in Fig. 4-12.

GRAPHING DATA FROM *PFS:FILE*

We will now be able to retrieve our actual, to-date figures for 1985 contributions from our *PFS:File* "MEMBERS." At the Main Menu, we will once again choose 1 GET/EDIT DATA and then press continue. The Get/Edit Data Menu should be filled out as illustrated in Fig. 4-13. The SELECTION NUMBER will be 3 GET PFS:FILE, the GRAPH (A/B/C/D) is B to indicate that the information will be used in Graph B (actual contributions). MERGE (Y/N) is answered "Y" since we will be combining information that we have entered from the keyboard with information that will be supplied from *PFS:File*. If the MERGE (Y/N) prompt were to be left with the default value

```
GET/EDIT DATA MENU

1  ENTER/EDIT DATA
2  GET VISICALC FILE
3  GET PFS FILE

 SELECTION NUMBER: 3
 GRAPH (A/B/C/D): B
 MERGE (Y/N): Y
 DIRECTORY OR FILE NAME: B:MEMBERS

                                   F10-Continue
```

Fig. 4-13. A completed Get/Edit Data Menu for use w/PFS:File. Information will be sent to the actual figures of Graph B.

```
Member #:                  Fname:
Lname:                     Ext(, Jr.):          Title(Dr.,Ms.):
L2:
L3:
L4:                                  Zip:
Telephone:
Date Joined:                         Date of last renewal: 85..
Amount:                              Previous yr's amount:
General Membership (x):              Newsletter  only (x):
Board of Directors (x):              Executive Board  (x):
Professional advisory board (x):
Committees:

Types of Vol work:

Mon  (x):      From:                     To:             Or:
Tues (x):      From:                     To:             Or:
Wed  (x):      From:                     To:             Or:
Thurs(x):      From:                     To:             Or:
Fri  (x):      From:                     To:             Or:
Sat  (x):      From:                     To:             Or:
--------------------------------------------------------------------------------
File: B:MEMBERS                    Retrieve Spec                   Page 1

                                                                F10-Continue
```

Fig. 4-14. Retrieve specs specify that we want to consider data for 1985 contributions.

of "N," the information derived from *PFS:File* would replace any values currently in the graph. If you have forgotten the name of the *PFS:File* data file, simply designating the desired disk drive, such as B:, will display a directory of the files on the disk.

As soon as the continue key has been pressed, the computer will look to the second drive, find the referenced file, display it, and ask for retrieve specs. Since we want only 1985 contributions, we supply the search criteria of 85.. in the "Date of last renewal" field. (See Fig. 4-14.) If we had wanted to consider every form, we would have pressed the continue key without specifying any retrieve criteria.

After the retrieve specs have been supplied, the form will appear once again, this time with GRAPH SPECS across the bottom line. It is here that you will indicate which items comprise X and Y values. The format of the X data—identifier, numeric, or date—must also be specified. In the case of date formats such as this, you must specify not only the appropriate combination of "D"ay, "M"onth, "Y"ear, and "Q"uarter, but you must also specify the way those dates will appear. In the example (Fig. 4-15) XY-- is entered in the "Date of last renewal" field to indicate that the data is to be read into the X value, that the type of X data is "Y"ear, and that the key numbers will appear first. The "--" after "Y"ear indicates that the next two groups of numbers (month and day) should be ignored. The "Y" following the "Amount" field indicates that the numbers in that field are to supply the Y data for the graph. This procedure clarifies the absolute necessity of entering date information in a consistent manner. Had there been inconsistent entries, there would be no possibility of this kind of data retrieval.

Pressing the continue key will initiate the reading and recording process. READING FORMS will be displayed while this information is being processed. Following its completion, a message telling the number of FORMS READ will be supplied along with a message to press the continue key. Pressing the continue key again will return you to the Main Menu. Figure 4-16 illustrates that the values have been read in from the program and merged with the existing information entered via the keyboard. The way to view the data that was entered from the data file is to press 1 GET/EDIT

```
Lname:
Fname:                  Ext(, Jr.):          Title(Dr.,Ms.):
Company name:
Address:
City:                          St:                Zip:
Telephone:
Date Joined:                      Date of last renewal: XY--
Amount: Y                         Previous yr's amount:
General Membership (x):           Newsletter  only (x):
Board of Directors (x):           Executive Board  (x):
Professional advisory board (x):
Committees:

Types of Vol work:

Mon   (x):      From:                    To:            Or:
Tues  (x):      From:                    To:            Or:
Wed   (x):      From:                    To:            Or:
Thurs(x):       From:                    To:            Or:
Fri   (x):      From:                    To:            Or:
Sat   (x):      From:                    To:            Or:
--------------------------------------------------------------------------------
File: B:MEMBERS                    Graph Spec                          Page 1

                                                                  F10-Continue
```

Fig. 4-15. The graph specs for graphing 1985 contributions will consider "Date of last renewal" as X axis data (on a yearly basis) and "Amount" as Y axis data.

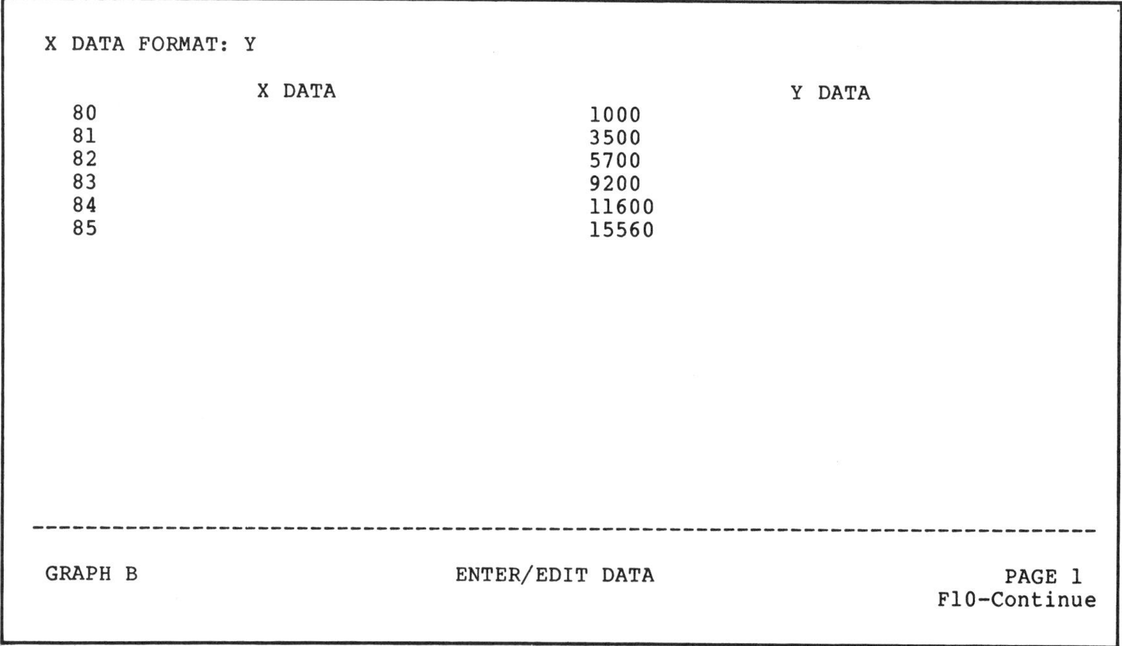

```
X DATA FORMAT: Y

               X DATA                                  Y DATA
  80                                  1000
  81                                  3500
  82                                  5700
  83                                  9200
  84                                  11600
  85                                  15560

--------------------------------------------------------------------------------
GRAPH B                      ENTER/EDIT DATA                          PAGE 1
                                                                  F10-Continue
```

Fig. 4-16. Merged data from the *PFS:File* "Members" file shows actual contribution for 1985 of $15,560.

DATA at the Main Menu, and then complete the Get/Edit Data Menu with SELECTION NUMBER: 3 and GRAPH: B. You can see that the values have been properly placed in the appropriate data columns. Any printings or displays of the graph will automatically include the new data. (See Fig. 4-17).

By using the DEFINE CHART option and changing the "Goal" graph to a line graph, the same figures can be displayed as a comparison of a bar graph and a line graph. (See Fig. 4-18.) The line format seems to convey the disparity between goal and actual figures more clearly than through the comparison of two bar graphs. Either way that the chart is displayed, we can come to an immediate conclusion that we should either revise our goals or intensify our fund raising efforts.

COUNTING THE OCCURRENCE OF VALUES

It is possible to count the number of occurrences of a particular value by leaving the Y value in the GRAPH SPECS screen blank. The result of doing so is to count the occurrences of the X value, and to assign the number of items counted as the Y value. For example, suppose we would want to create a chart to show the relative number of projects in each of the organization's service areas.

Any existing information that you are working with should be stored and the chart cleared by using 7 CLEAR CHART on the Main Menu. Data may be entered in a manner similar to the way the information from the membership file was entered. This time, however, the DIRECTORY OR FILE NAME

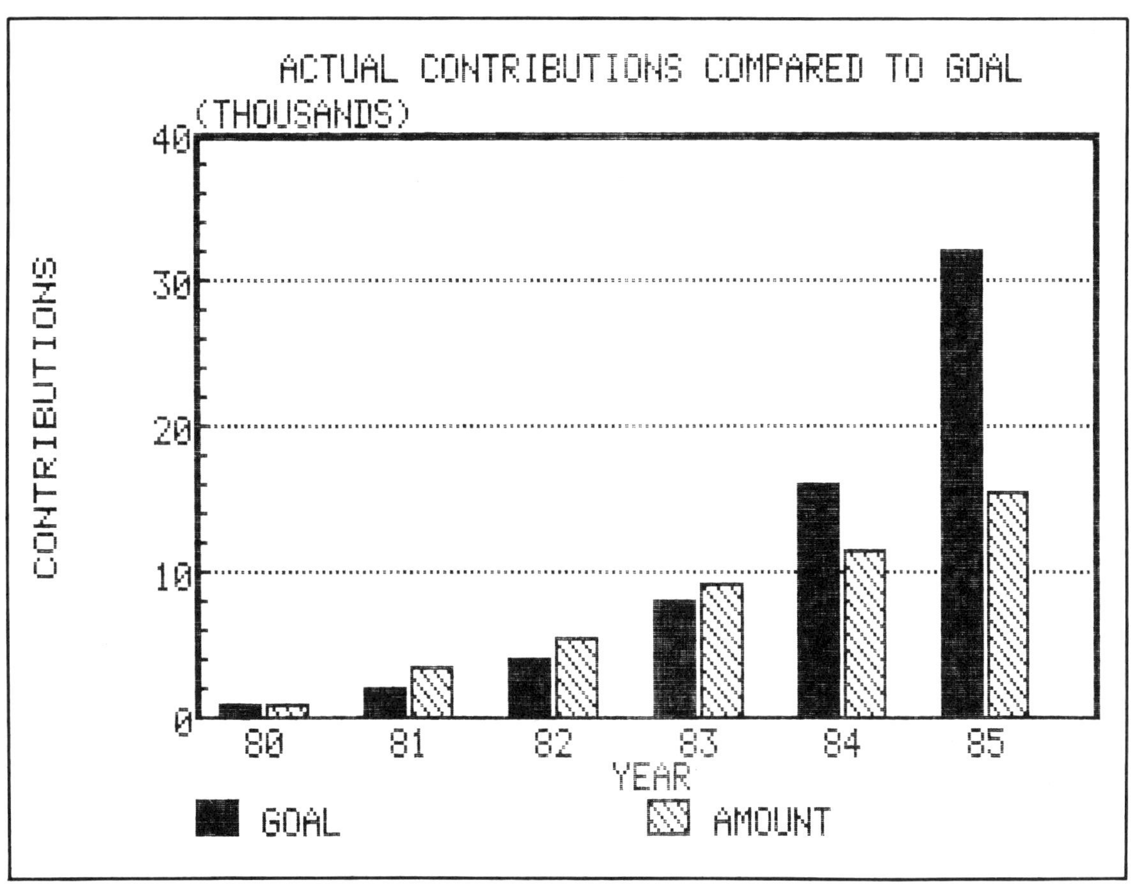

Fig. 4-17. Comparative bar chart of actual vs. goal.

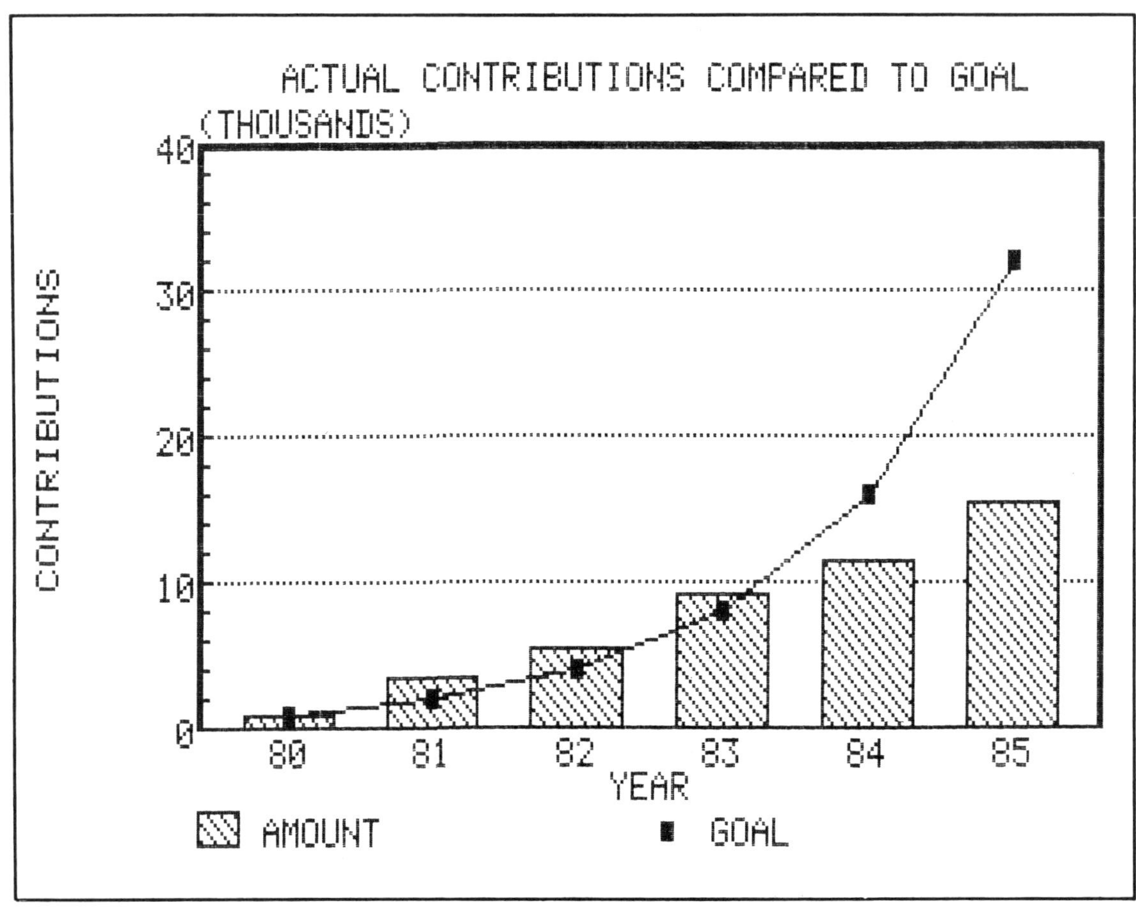

Fig. 4-18. Comparative chart with bar and line graphs.

prompt will be answered B:D-D-D and the MERGE (Y/N) prompt will be left at "N" as illustrated in Fig. 4-19. We want to consider every project, so we just press the continue key at the RETRIEVE SPEC screen. At the GRAPH SPEC screen, we tab to the "Service area" prompt, and place an "X" beside it to specify that this field will comprise the X DATA. We also place an "I" to signify that the data format will be an identifier. Since we do not specify a Y DATA field, the program will count the occurrence of each of the service areas. The completed screen is shown in Fig. 4-20. The number of occurrences of each job that was categorized as "Public Education" for example within the "Service area" field will be counted. A sample of this kind of input is displayed in Fig. 4-21.

AN EXAMPLE: DISPLAYING VOLUNTEER HOURS

We are now prepared to gather some more information for graphic display from our *PFS:File*, D-D-D. Let's assume that we are eventually going to include some laudatory remarks in the newletter about the rising volunteer spirit found among our membership. We will not have to speak in generalities. We will not have to be vague or make up figures. We can *show* the representation of those efforts directly with *PFS:Graph's* ability to retrieve information from *PFS:File*.

In order to begin this process, we will first select 7 CLEAR CHART to insure that we start with a clean slate. Next, from the Main Menu, we will once again choose 1 GET/EDIT DATA and

```
GET/EDIT DATA MENU


1  ENTER/EDIT DATA

2  GET VISICALC FILE

3  GET PFS FILE

 SELECTION NUMBER: 3

 GRAPH (A/B/C/D): A

 MERGE (Y/N): N

 DIRECTORY OR FILE NAME: B:D-D-D

                                          F10-Continue
```

Fig. 4-19. After clearing chart new information may be gathered from another *PFS:File* data disk.

```
Job #:                   Job:
Job description:

Status:
Act by (yy/mm/dd):

Date Began:                         Date Completed:
Time Began:                         Time Completed:

Service area: XI
People benefiting:
Volunteer hours:
Volunteers:



Project (A/B):
Notes:



-----------------------------------------------------------------
File: B:D-D-D                       Graph Spec          Page 1

                                                   F10-Continue
```

Fig. 4-20. X axis data is to be in the form of an "identifier" Y data will be an item count.

```
X DATA FORMAT: I

              X DATA                                    Y DATA
  PUBLIC EDUCATIO                       3
  DIRECT SERVICES                       2
  ADVOCACY                              2
  COMMUNITY SERVI                       2
















--------------------------------------------------------------------------------

GRAPH A                        ENTER/EDIT DATA                            PAGE 1
                                                                     F10-Continue
```

Fig. 4-21. A sample run "counts" occurrences of each job within a service area.

```
Job #:                   Job:
Job description:

Status:
Act by (yy/mm/dd):

Date Began:                        Date Completed:
Time Began:                        Time Completed:

Service area: XI
People benefiting:
Volunteer hours: Y
Volunteers:



Project (A/B):
Notes:


--------------------------------------------------------------------------------
File: B:D-D-D                      Graph Spec                        Page 1

                                                                F10-Continue
```

Fig. 4-22. Different Graph Specs will total volunteer hours, not just count the number of jobs.

then press the continue key. The Get/Edit Data Menu should be filled out just as it was in Fig. 4-19.

In this case we want to consider only those projects that had volunteer input, so we will specify ">0" (greater than 0) after the "Volunteer hours" field. If we had wanted to consider every form, we would have pressed the continue key without specifying any retrieve criteria. For the graph specs we want to identify the volunteer hours associated with each service area. We will therefore complete the graph specs in the manner shown in Fig. 4-22. Notice that the "Service area" field has had an "XI" inserted after it as was done for the "counting" example. Following the "Volunteer hours" field, a "Y" has been inserted. Our Y value on the chart will be the number of volunteer hours in each service area.

The data will automatically be inserted and added. In order to assure yourself that the values have been properly placed in the appropriate data columns, it is possible to press 1 GET/EDIT DATA at the Main Menu and complete the Get/Edit Data Menu (as shown in Fig. 4-23) to view the data areas. Figure 4-24 illustrates the format and layout of information gathered in this process.

Since we know that bar charts have room for only nine characters as identifiers in the X axis, we will abbreviate those identifiers to comply with those restrictions. (See Fig. 4-25.) Again, I must caution the user to press the continue key rather than the ESC key. The continue key will record the changes, while the ESC key will escape to the previous status.

PRINTING AND PLOTTING CHARTS

Being curious people, I am sure that we would like to see the progress of our work. Pressing 5 PRINT CHART will bring us to the Printer Menu as shown in Fig. 4-26. The SELECTION NUMBER

```
                GET/EDIT DATA MENU


                1  ENTER/EDIT DATA

                2  GET VISICALC FILE

                3  GET PFS FILE

                 SELECTION NUMBER: 1

                 GRAPH (A/B/C/D): A

                 MERGE (Y/N): N

                 DIRECTORY OR FILE NAME:



                                               F10-Continue
```

Fig. 4-23. Answering the Get/Edit Data Menu prompts will allow for "manually" entering into data areas.

```
X DATA FORMAT: I

              X DATA                                     Y DATA
  PUBLIC EDUCATIO                         57
  DIRECT SERVICES                         13
  ADVOCACY                                37
  COMMUNITY SERVI                         35

--------------------------------------------------------------------------------

GRAPH A                    ENTER/EDIT DATA                      PAGE 1
                                                          F10-Continue
```

Fig. 4-24. GET/EDIT DATA screen displays volunteer hours found recorded in "Do-Doing-Done" file.

```
X DATA FORMAT: I

              X DATA                                     Y DATA
  PUBLIC ED                               57
  DIRECT                                  13
  ADVOCACY                                37
  COMMUNITY                               35

--------------------------------------------------------------------------------

GRAPH A                    ENTER/EDIT DATA                      PAGE 1
                                                          F10-Continue
```

Fig. 4-25. Labels can be modified to make them fit into chart.

```
PRINTER MENU

1  IBM GRAPHICS          4  IDS

2  EPSON                 5  NEC

3  OKIDATA               6  C.ITOH


        SELECTION NUMBER: 1

        EXPANDED SIZE(Y/N): N

        PRINT DATA(Y/N): N

        PRINT TO: LPT1:


                                    F10-Continue
```

Fig. 4-26. Printer Menu provides a number of options.

means the number corresponding to the prompt printer that you are using. EXPANDED SIZE (Y/N) allows for two different size charts. "N," the assumed value, results in a chart approximately 3×4 inches. "Y" rotates the graph and fills an entire 8½×11-inch piece of paper. Figure 4-27 is a sample that has been expanded to the 8½×11-inch size. PRINT DATA (Y/N) allows for the printing of all of the data points before the chart is printed. PRINT TO allows for the selection of the port to which your printer is attached. Apple printer menus will be identical except for the substitution of Apple printers for IBM Graphics printers.

At this point you have only to match the printer selection with the equipment and decide whether to print a small or expanded chart. After making those selections, the program will check that the printer status is ready and then inform you that the chart is about to be printed. Now, you may escape or continue. Continuing will produce the graph illustrated in Fig. 4-27. Notice that the Y-axis has been automatically scaled and that grid lines have been inserted. Also notice that the legend for the graph has taken the name from the *PFS:File* field from where the information came, "Volunteer hours."

Following the printing of the chart, the Main Menu will reappear. Selecting 2 DEFINE CHART will allow us to dress it up and, perhaps, to modify it. Figure 4-28 shows the current status of the Define Chart Menu. The asterisk beside Graph A indicates that it is the only graph with information in it. Simply typing over BAR with the letters PIE will produce the chart in Fig. 4-29 when 3 DISPLAY CHART or 5 PRINT CHART is selected. Notice that the pie is automatically divided in descending size proportions. The largest section is automati-

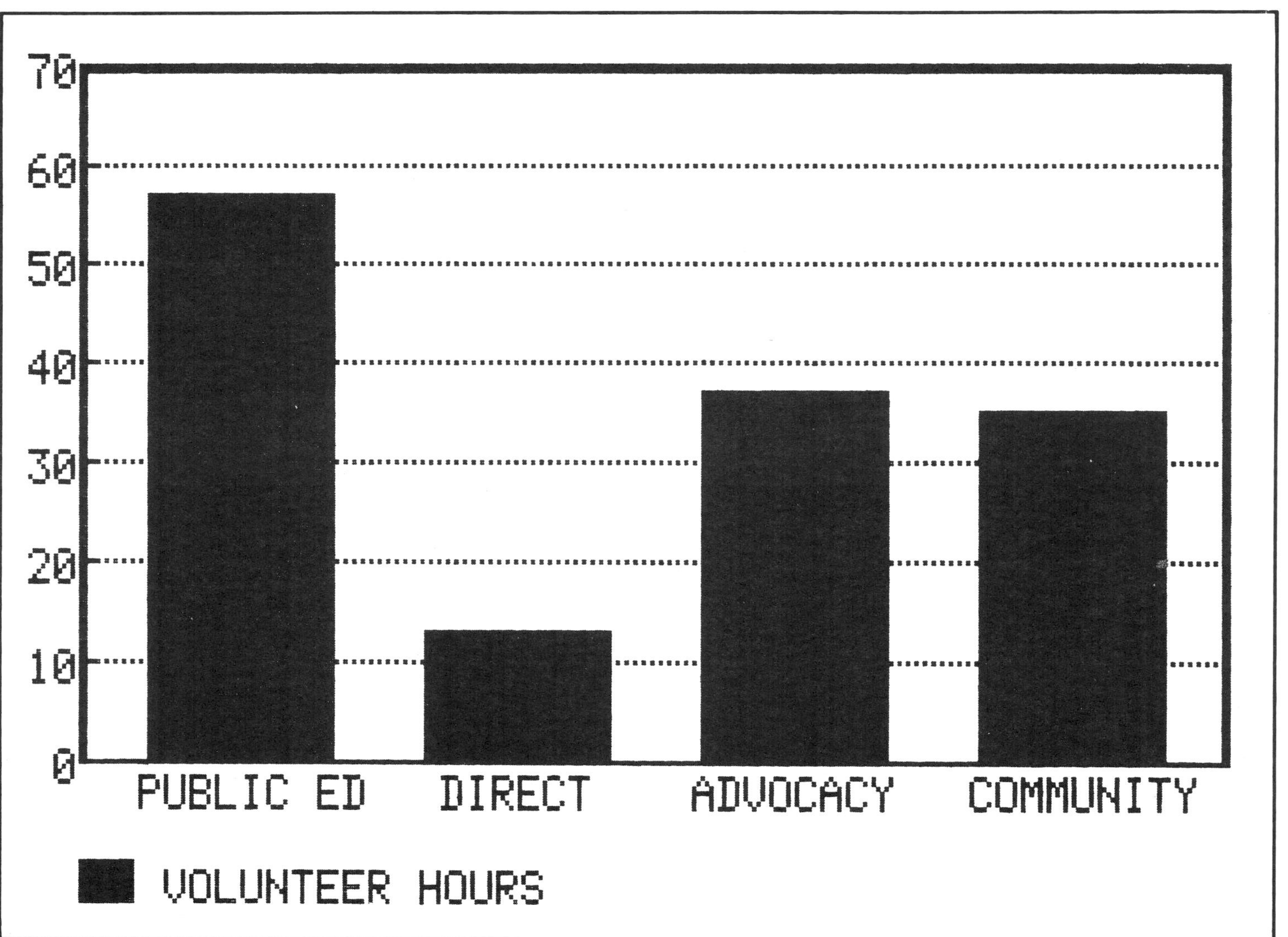

Fig. 4-27. A simple bar chart depicts volunteer hours.

```
                         DEFINE CHART MENU

                   TYPE                    LEGEND              CUM
     GRAPH
*      A        BAR                   VOLUNTEER HOURS           N
       B                              GRAPH B                   N
       C                              GRAPH C                   N
       D                              GRAPH D                   N


  CHART  TITLE:
  X-AXIS TITLE:
  Y-AXIS TITLE:


  STACK  (Y/N): N                   Y MIN:
  GRID   (Y/N): Y                   Y MAX:
  COLOR  (Y/N): N                   Y DIV:


                                                         F10-Continue
```

Fig. 4-28. A display of the default values for DEFINE CHART.

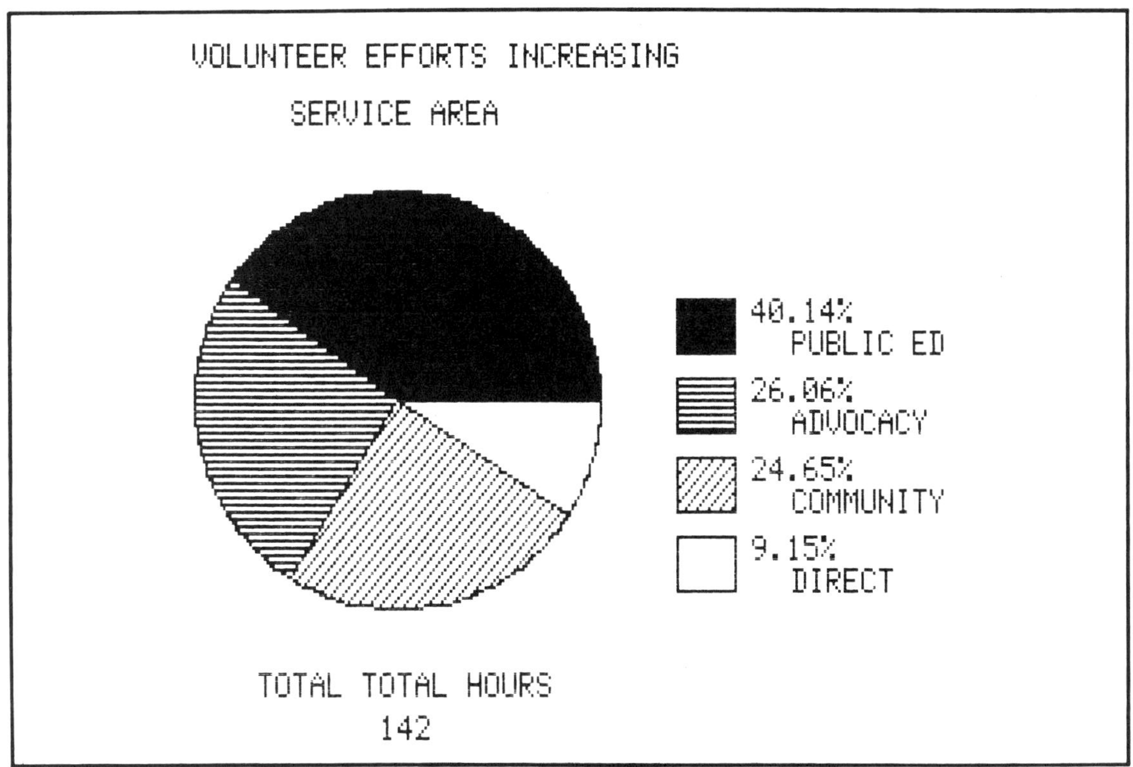

Fig. 4-29. Substituting "PIE" for "BAR" results in a pie chart of volunteer hours.

cally displayed first with the solid shading, and so on, in a predescribed manner that the user has no control over.

There are other ways information from different sources may be displayed simultaneously in the same chart. For example, we could change the designation of the type of chart back to BAR and proceed to enter data from the keyboard as described earlier. This time, we will supply information for Graph B. In so doing, we will note that the identifiers used in Graph A are automatically supplied for Graph B. In this case, we will enter volunteer hours from a previous period of time, and supply it with a legend of "Last Mo. Hrs." Since these hours can be thought of as part of a cumulative volunteer effort, it makes good sense to stack the graphs by answering "Y" to the STACK (Y/N) prompt in the Define Chart Menu. The resulting stacked graphs are presented in the chart of Fig. 4-30.

Each microcomputer system comes with its own default values for the types of printers and plotters that are most frequently used. Those default values can be changed to any of the options on the menus by running the SETGRAPH program at the DOS > prompt. If that is done, the default values will be permanently stored on disk to match your equipment configuration.

The plotting command, 6 PLOT CHART, on the Main Menu operates in a manner similar to how the Print command does. The PLOT CHART command can only be used if you have a plotter connected to your computer. Figure 4-31 shows the Plotter Menu screen. Obviously, you select the plotter by typing the proper number beside the SELECTION NUMBER prompt. If you select the TRANSPARENCY (Y/N) prompt, it slows down the speed of the plotter so that there will be no slippage on the slicker transparency paper used for creating overhead projection displays. Also, pie charts are "exploded" or separated so that none of the colors overlap. PAUSE FOR PEN CHANGE (Y/N) allows for changing the colors of pens on plotters with a single pen holder and the capability

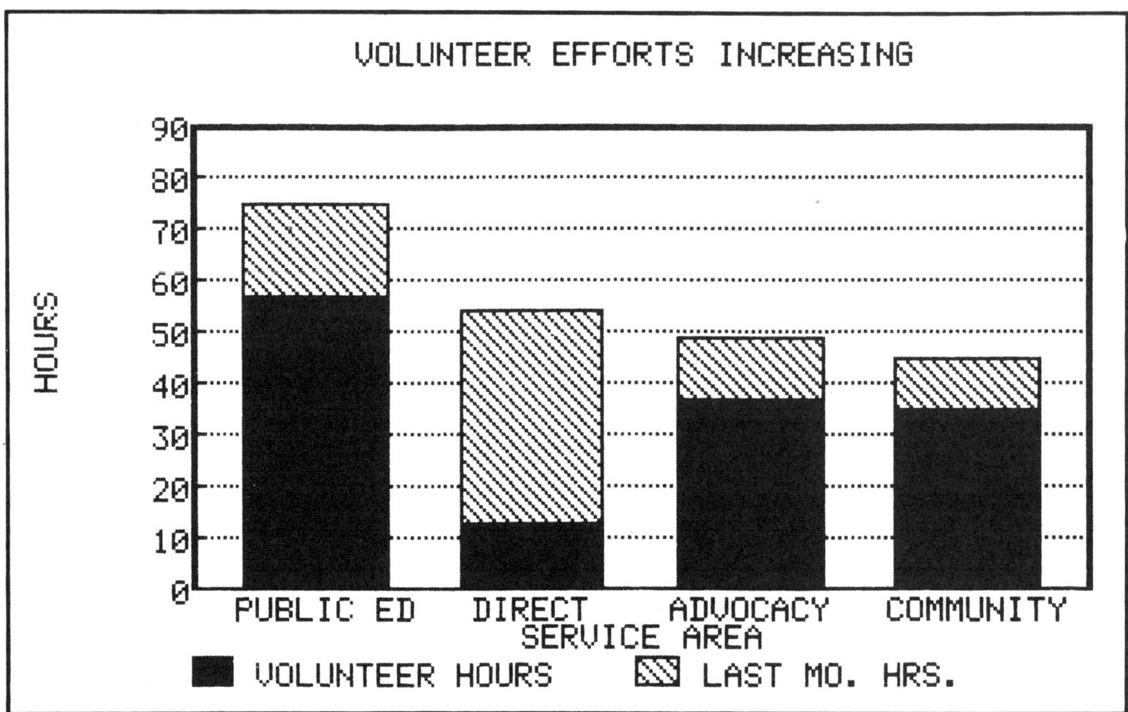

Fig. 4-30. A chart showing last month's volunteer hours "stacked" on top of last month's hours.

```
                    PLOTTER MENU

        1  HP                  3  STROBE

        2  HIPLOT              4  SWEET-P


            SELECTION NUMBER: 1

            TRANSPARENCY(Y/N): N

            PAUSE FOR PEN CHANGE(Y/N): N

            PLOT TO: COM1:




                                        F10-Continue
```

Fig. 4-31. Plotter Menu provides for using different plotters for various purposes.

of plotting in multiple colors. PLOT TO specifies the output port from the computer to the plotter. Any values you put in any of the printer or plotter prompts remains the default value until it is changed.

SAVING AND REMOVING GRAPHS

After pressing 4 GET/SAVE/REMOVE and continue on the Main Menu, the Get/Save/Remove Menu of Fig. 4-32 appears. Getting and saving charts requires almost no explanation. Those commands save and retrieve charts onto and from the disk. Pressing any of the menu selections except 5 PRINT PICTURE without a directory or file name specified will result in a listing of the disk files. Appropriate warnings are supplied if you begin to save a chart with an identical filename on top of another, previously saved chart.

The third option, 3 SAVE PICTURE, saves your chart as a dot image, 320 dots wide and 200 dots high. The purpose of this command is to save charts in picture form so that they may be used directly in *PFS:Write* documents. Pictures saved in this manner cannot be edited, only displayed on the screen with 4 DISPLAY PICTURE or printed from with *PFS:Write* (or from any program that can call up images that have been BSAVED). Selection 4 DISPLAY PICTURE displays the picture on the screen while 5 PRINT PICTURE sends the dot image to the printer.

Selection 6 REMOVE FILE operates in a manner similar to all of the other PFS modules. There is a beep and a warning that appears on the screen before the removal action is actually taken.

Figure 4-33 demonstrates saving a chart and Fig. 4-34 demonstrates saving a picture. It will be handy to designate the picture files with an extension of ".PIC". That way it will be easily identified

```
                GET/SAVE/REMOVE MENU

     1  GET CHART                4  DISPLAY PICTURE
     2  SAVE CHART               5  PRINT PICTURE
     3  SAVE PICTURE             6  REMOVE FILE

            SELECTION NUMBER:
            DIRECTORY OR FILE NAME:

                                          F10-Continue
```

Fig. 4-32. An illustration of the PFS:Graph Get/Save/Remove Menu.

```
                GET/SAVE/REMOVE MENU

     1  GET CHART                4  DISPLAY PICTURE
     2  SAVE CHART               5  PRINT PICTURE
     3  SAVE PICTURE             6  REMOVE FILE

            SELECTION NUMBER: 2
            DIRECTORY OR FILE NAME: VOL.HRS

                                          F10-Continue
```

Fig. 4-33. Responses for saving a chart.

```
                    GET/SAVE/REMOVE MENU

    1  GET CHART                  4  DISPLAY PICTURE

    2  SAVE CHART                 5  PRINT PICTURE

    3  SAVE PICTURE               6  REMOVE FILE


              SELECTION NUMBER: 3

              DIRECTORY OR FILE NAME: VOL.PIC



                                              F10-Continue
```

Fig. 4-34. Response for saving a "picture" of the chart.

when, later, we will merge the picture into a word processed document.

CLEARING AND EXITING PFS:GRAPH

Option 7 CLEAR CHART wipes out the existing chart, and begins anew. There is a beep and a warning that the chart is about to be cleared. You may ESC or continue to clear it. There is no check to see if you have saved the chart that you have been working on. BE CAREFUL and be sure to save your work. Clearing a graph that you have been working on, of course, has no effect on the permanent storage of the chart on the disk if it has been previously saved.

Option 8 EXIT PFS:GRAPH is the most potentially devastating, unchecked option in *any* of the PFS modules. Error checking and user-friendliness got shortchanged with this one. There is no beep. There is no opportunity to ESC. There is no check to see if your most recent changes have been saved. There is just the immediate loss of your chart and an exit to the DOS > prompt. BE CAREFUL, BE CAREFUL, BE CAREFUL! Make sure you have saved your important work *before* you choose to exit.

SHORTCOMINGS AND LIMITATIONS

Of all of the PFS modules, *PFS:Graph* has the most serious limitations. One of the most surprising is its inability to utilize derived columns in its data. For instance, if we wanted to create a pie chart showing the number of people who had increased their giving, decreased their giving, or given the same amount, there would be no way to do it directly using the information stored on *PFS:File*. *PFS:Report* can subtract last year's contributions from this year's, but *PFS:Graph* cannot handle the derived figures. To solve this problem, *Report* would first have to be run, counting and totaling the appropriate columns, and then the information would have to be manually entered into *Graph* through the keyboard. That is not exactly what I call *integrated* software.

Another major limitation of *PFS:Graph* is that

the format of the X *data* cannot be changed without losing the data. For an example, suppose that we want to create a pie chart showing the relative number of members who have joined our organization during each of the years of its existence. The field of the Members file that we want to key in on is "Date Joined." In the graph specifications, we designate that field as the X *data* and then must specify "Y--" to tell the program that we want only the years, and not the months and days to be sorted. We only want to count the numbers at this point, so no Y value will be specified. The numbers sort themselves properly into the X and Y columns. However, the X DATA FORMAT is "Y"ear, a kind of a date format. Pie charts can only be created using identifier formats, so we are locked out. There is no way to retrieve that information as Identifiers, and no way to change its format once it is retrieved. One would have to print out the information, and then, once again, resort to manually inputting the data in the only acceptable format.

Still another limitation is that there is no capability of transferring data between charts. Graph A, and only Graph A, is able to be used to create a pie chart. If you have been working on a chart with two, three, or four graphs that you suddenly realize would be better displayed as separate charts, you are out of luck. You cannot transfer the data from Graph B, C, or D to form a new chart, and you can never make one of them into a pie chart without manually reentering the information. Similarly, you cannot take information from separate charts and merge it into one chart for comparison purposes.

The three limitations mentioned previously, and other similar problems, are substantial, but they are mostly matters of convenience. Usually you can get around them by using manual input. Other limitations are not often of great importance, but neither can they be "gotten around." If for example, you were comparing computer systems, and you wanted Apple products to always be represented by red and IBM products to be represented by blue, you can't do it with *PFS:Graph.* Graph priorities the appearance of colors and designs according to its agenda, not yours. Horizontal bar charts, rather than vertical is another example of a *PFS:Graph* "can't do." There are others.

Many considerations and trade offs are made in the creation of any software package. In dealing with graphics, memory requirements are often a large consideration. *PFS:Graph* will operate with a minimum of 128K of RAM for the IBM PC and 64K for the Apple II systems. Many of the more powerful graphics systems require more memory. Some limitations could easily be overcome if the required amount of RAM were shifted to 256K, but that would limit the market. As the cost of additional memory continues to plummet, it is feasible that improved versions of the program, with more "horsepower," will be made available. For now, *PFS:Graph* offers a relatively simple, relatively complete way of producing graphics for presentations and for letters. For the future? Fill out the User Group Enrollment Card and see what happens.

PFS:Write–Writing Without Drudgery

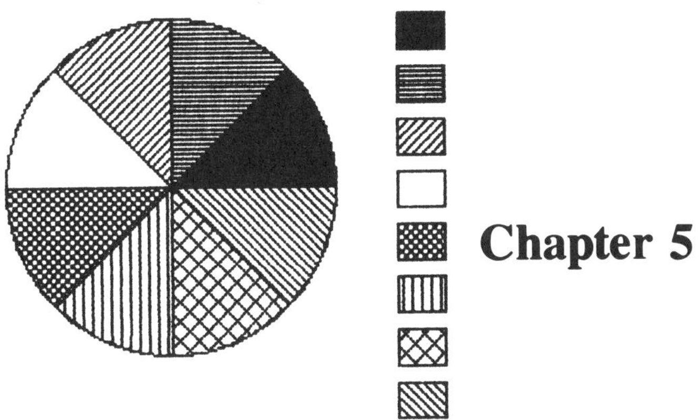

Chapter 5

Word processing is one of my favorite productivity tools for a microcomputor. Not only does it save time, keep accurate records of correspondence, and avoid repetitive tasks, word processing also allows the user to concentrate on the creative process and temporarily ignore the mundane aspects of writing. A mistyped character is no longer a big deal. Revising drafts is easy, even fun. When the words are no longer in "black and white," you are no longer irrevocably tied to what you have written. A flow of consciousness results; the process of refining becomes more thorough, and the quality of writing improves.

Are you one of the people who have had difficulty typing on a manual typewriter after becoming accustomed to an electric one? The introduction to word processing will create a corresponding reluctance to ever use a typewriter again. Consider whether you often have to fill in the blanks on prepared forms. If you do, keep the typewriter. If not, have a yard sale, but keep the price of the old typewriter low—you are not the only one experiencing this revolution. When you are cleaning drawers and find stray sheets and bottles of correct type, give them the old heave ho. You are about to become liberated!

PFS:Write will depend primarily on its ease of use to establish its position in the market. You will not have to learn hundreds of commands in order to use it. It has been designed so that its operation is almost as easy as choosing selections from a menu. The *almost* is what scares the person who believes that a computer may help him or her to become more productive, but does not want to invest a great amount of time and money learning how to use a new machine. The preliminaries for *PFS:Write* are as painless as any word processor and quickly absorbed. Until very recently people believed that they had to know how to program in order to use a computer. Now we know that ready-made software packages bypass the need to be able to program. It is, however, necessary to grasp the concepts of how to get your program running and how and where your letters are going to be stored.

One of the chief advantages of word processing over traditional typing is the ability to store your work on magnetic media form for reuse or modification at a later time. If the purpose were just to see words on a screen before seeing them printed on paper, word processing would be a giant flop. Besides saving a tremendous number of repetitive tasks, keeping letters and documents on disk can save a lot of time spent searching through papers to find a filed letter. It can be a kind of filing cabinet for outgoing mail as well.

GETTING STARTED WITH *PFS:WRITE*

To start word processing with *PFS:Write*, type WRITE at the DOS > prompt on IBM-type systems or start the computer with the disks inserted on Apple systems. It will also be necessary to have formatted disks in the disk drive in order to save the information we create. Chapter 1 contains a more detailed explanation of the startup procedure. We will be presented with the PFS:Write Main Menu shown in Fig. 5-1.

Listed here is an overview of the items on the menu:

1 TYPE/EDIT. This option allows you to enter your documents or modify the documents already entered. Within this command it is possible to enter, delete, insert, and move text. You can set tabs, search for and replace words and phrases, and use underlining and boldface. You can even count the words in the document.

2 DEFINE PAGE. This option accommodates your need to change top, bottom, left or right margins, to enter headers or footers on each page of your document, or to change the page length you are going to work with.

3 PRINT. PRINT is the command used to send your letter to a printer. Included are options to join *PFS:Graphs*, merge with *PFS:Files*, specify printing parameters such as number of pages, single or double spacing, and indenting or not indenting the entire document. Also included is a handy option for automatically addressing envelopes using the information from a completed letter.

4 GET/SAVE/REMOVE. This selection allows for the easy saving and retrieving of letters and documents. By "saving" we mean that the letters and documents will be recorded onto the disk in the disk drive. All procedures are checked by the computer and warning messages are given in order to

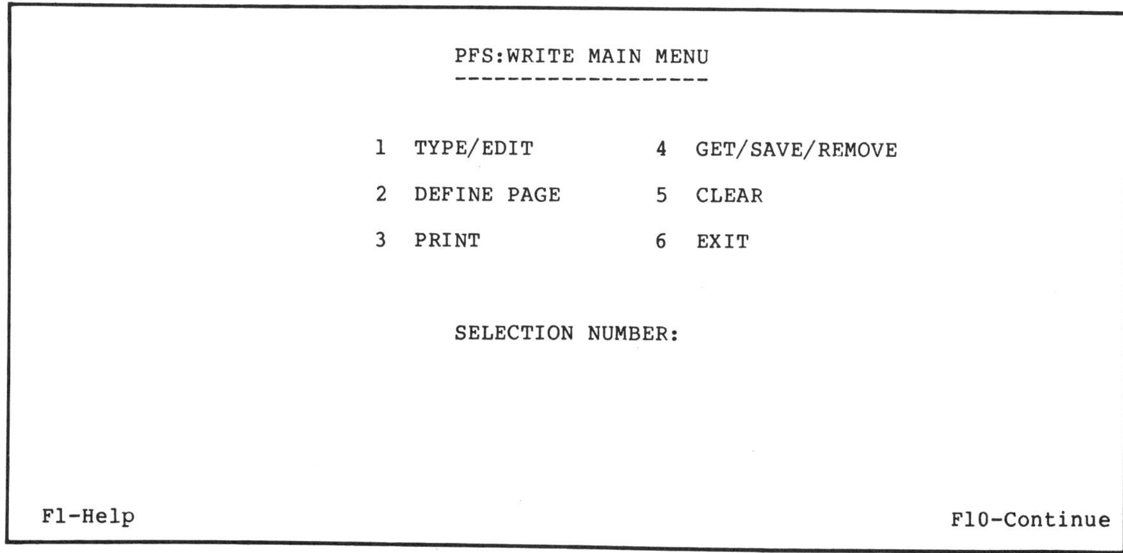

Fig. 5-1. PFS:Write Main Menu.

Option	To Do
TYPE/EDIT	Type in a new document or edit the text in the working copy.
DEFINE PAGE	Change left, right, top and bottom margins. Enter new page headings and footings.
PRINT	Print the working copy.
GET/SAVE/REMOVE	Retrieve a document from disk, save the working copy to disk, or remove a file. GET/SAVE/REMOVE also provides a listing of files on each disk.
CLEAR	Erase the working copy in preparation for typing a new document.
EXIT	Leave PFS:WRITE.

PFS:WRITE Main Menu Options (screen title); Press F10 to continue

Fig. 5-2. Main Menu HELP screen.

avoid unintended actions and mistakes. For example the following message will appear if you try to exit without saving your work:

WARNING. ABOUT TO EXIT
PROGRAM LATEST CHANGES NOT SAVED.
Press ESC to abandon this operation.
Press F10 to continue.

This option can also be used to review the programs already saved onto your disk.

5 CLEAR. CLEAR is the menu option that allows you to start with a clean "sheet," or screen, for a new document.

6 EXIT. EXIT provides a means for terminating the word processing program. It returns you to the system's DOS. Apple II systems do not have the EXIT command.

A selection from the menu is made by pressing the number associated with your choice, and then pressing the continue key.

You will also notice that on the bottom of the screen F1-HELP or "PRESS OPEN APPLE H FOR HELP. In order to use the "help" screens, the program disk must be in the disk drive. If you have replaced the program disk with a data disk, and later attempt to use a help function, the program will prompt you to enter your *PFS:Write* program disk into the disk drive. Pressing the help key at the Main Menu will result in the presentation of the following screen in order to remind you of the functions of each menu selection. The HELP screen is illustrated in Fig. 5-2.

From the Main Menu we select 1 TYPE/EDIT to get started, and then press the continue key. We are now presented with the screen shown in Fig. 5-3.

Note that there is a rectangle 80 columns wide with space for 22 vertical lines. Across the bottom of the screen is a "ruler," which is reminiscent of the pica markings on a typewriter. Ten marks from the left and from the right are brackets ([and]) that are margin indicators. As you can quickly determine, these are standard 60 columns margins that

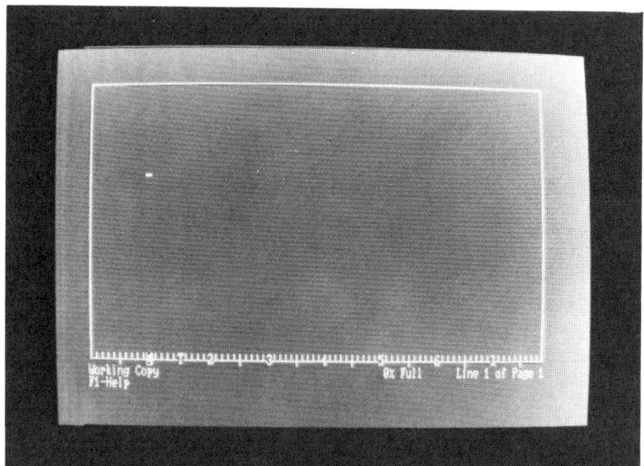

Fig. 5-3. Illustration of working space after selecting 1. TYPE/EDIT.

are the default margins. They may be changed at any time by selecting 2 DEFINE PAGE from the Main Menu. However, you are limited to one set of margins for each document. Later on we will see how you can utilize the *JOIN* function if you require that the margins of the document change within the body of the text.

If you look carefully, you will also see that the "[" is highlighted with a small block. This block is a pointer and indicates your position on the page. It will move as you type across the screen. Five spaces from the left margin ([) you see a "T." This indicates the position of the default typewriter tab. Tab setting may be changed while you are the TYPE/EDIT mode. If you choose to enter another tab, you will have the option of using either typewriter tabs or decimal tabs. Decimal tabs are convenient for handling the tabulation of numeric data, because the data will automatically be aligned according to the position of the decimal.

Immediately below the ruler you will see "Working Copy." This is actually the filename location and will show the name of the file that you are working on if you have previously saved it on the disk.

Beneath the filename on IBM and compatible systems is the reminder F1-Help. Apple systems can also utilize the help function by pressing the OPEN APPLE and H keys. The HELP screen from within the TYPE/EDIT function is different from the HELP screen at the Main Menu. When you ask for help, the program disk will be accessed, and a screen reminding you of the special editing keystrokes will be displayed. A sample of the TYPE/EDIT help screen from the IBM version is shown in Fig. 5-4.

Systems with special function keys available on the keyboard have a definite edge in convenience because it is not necessary to remember special control key sequences. *PFS:Write* supplies a cardboard insert that fits around the 10 function keys of an IBM PC that lists the sixteen editing functions shown on the HELP screen. (See Fig. 5-4 again.) The editing functions shown on the top of the line are invoked by pressing SHIFT and the function key; editing functions shown on the bottom of the line are called upon by pressing the function key alone. For example, pressing F4 will take your cursor to the next word. Pressing the SHIFT and F4 keys will take the cursor to the end of the line. Apple II system users would have to press OPEN APPLE and RIGHT ARROW keys to move to the next word and the CLOSED APPLE and RIGHT ARROW to move to the end of the line. Keys such as Ins (insert) and Del (delete) are also a lot easier to use than CTRL and Y (ynsert?) and CTRL and R for remove.

To avoid unnecessary repetition and confusion, the majority of references in this manuscript will refer to keyboards that have function keys, such as the IBM PC and TI Professional Computer. Some keyboards, such as the IBM PCjr are a com-

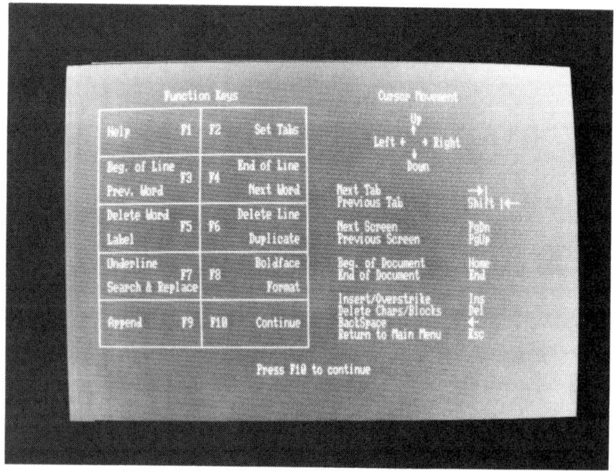

Fig. 5-4. A display of the IBM PC TYPE/EDIT HELP Screen.

bination of keyboard types in which one would first press a generalized function key (almost like a shift) while pressing a number key corresponding to a particular function on a larger keyboard. Keyboards without function keys are able to derive the same performance from the PFS programs, only somewhat more awkwardly.

STATUS LINES

The remainder of the space on the screen beneath the ruler is dedicated to status lines. Status lines can be very helpful, and paying attention to them will guarantee no sudden and unwanted surprises occurring after you have completed your letter. The amount of working space that has been used is displayed, and begins with, 0% Full. It will be continually updated to ensure that you will never have a document that exceeds the computer's ability to store it on disk. When it reaches 100% Full you will be presented with an audible beep, and be informed of that fact with a document full message. No further text can be typed beyond that point. If you tried to append another document that would surpass its capacity, the same DOCUMENT FULL message would be seen. In this case the working document would have to be saved, and another document started with a different name. It takes about 24 pages of text to fill up a document. Extremely long documents will have to be divided into smaller sections. If that situation is ever faced, it is possible to use the program's ability to join documents by inserting the command:

JOIN document name

Line 1 of Page 1 in the lower right screen is the first report of the status for *line number* and *page number* that keeps you updated on the position of your cursor. This update is extremely useful and an important part of the *PFS:Write* "what you see is what you get" approach. If, for example, you see that your letter has exceeded a page length by only one or two lines, you could use option 2 DEFINE PAGE to change top or bottom margins in an attempt to fit the letter onto one page. However, "what you see" isn't always "What you get;" you will only see the single spaced layout on the screen. You cannot see double spacing until you print the letter.

When you begin, those are all of the status reports that you see. However, there are several other status reports that will be given as different circumstances arise. They are as follows:

Inserting. Informs you that text entered will push all of the text below that point down automatically. When you are *not* inserting, you overwrite any letters already typed rather than inserting text between them. The cursor becomes a blinking block when you are in the insert mode as opposed to a blinking line when you are not. To begin inserting, press Ins or CTRL and Y. To terminate the insert mode, simply press the same key or keys to toggle out of the insert mode.

Underlined. If you use the keyboard's arrow keys to move the cursor to a position on top of a letter that is underlined, you will see the message "underlined" appear on the status line. On a color display, the letters will also appear in a cream color. With *PFS:Write's* original release, there have been no provisions made for removing the underlining except by deleting and then reentering the underlined text or by typing over it. To underline a word on an IBM, move the cursor to the characters you want underlined, and press SHIFT and F7. Apple systems press CTRL, SHIFT and the underline key (–) with the cursor on the appropriate characters.

Boldface. If the cursor is moved over a letter that has been marked "bold" it will also be reflected in the status line. "Bold" characters are ones that are overstriked several times by the printer to create a darker appearance. Additionally, the letter will appear in a bold white color on the monitor. It is also possible for the message "Underlined Boldface" to appear when a letter has been both underlined and marked for bold. In that case, the letter or letters will appear green on a color display. As is the case with underlining, there is no easy way to remove a boldface mark. Characters are made to appear in boldface type by pressing SHIFT and F8 or CTRL and B (for boldface) when the cursor appears on top of the characters you want to emphasize.

Labeling. *PFS:Write* has the ability to label text in order to either move it to another position in your letter or store it for uses in other documents. The keys F5 or CTRL and L begin the labeling process. Using the arrow keys to move the cursor will highlight all of the text being labeled. Moving the arrow cursor controls up or down marks entire lines. After the text is labeled, the Delete function (Del or CTRL and R) is then used, and the text will disappear from the screen. It is however, stored in a memory *buffer*, or holding place, and can be duplicated in any place at any time by using the Duplicate function (F6) or CTRL and D. Be cautioned, however, that only one item can be stored at a time. Only the last block of text labeled is stored in the memory buffer. Labeling a new body of text removes any previously labeled text from memory. This label function, while handy, is not as complete as the ones offered in some other word processors that, for instance, allow you to save several labeled groups of text and insert them anywhere at any time.

Name of Document to Append. This message appears when you want to append a document that you have previously saved on a disk. Append is used by pressing F9 or CTRL and A. A CAN'T FIND FILE message will appear on the status line if there is no document on disk with the name you have indicated.

Left Center Right (L/C/R). This message will appear on the status line when you have used the FORMAT LINE command (F8) or CTRL and F. The user presses C to center the line, L to bring the text on the line flush left, and R to bring the last letter of the line to the right margin. Formatting of lines is done on a line by line basis. No commands available will center all lines until you change it. Also, pressing R to bring the text to the right margin should not be confused with a justify command that automatically aligns the text in columns and on both left and right margins as if it had been typeset. There is no such function in this word processor, which can be a serious disadvantage to someone who wants to prepare columns for newsletters and other purposes. The only alternative with *PFS:Write's* current release is to manually insert spaces into each line to adjust the margins.

Selecting the Search function will also display new prompts on the status line. SEARCH FOR REPLACE WITH, and MANUAL OR AUTOMATIC (M/A) will appear, asking for the *string*, or group, of characters to be searched for, the replacement for that string, and whether the replacement should be done manually or automatically. Manual replacement means that the replacement is to be verified on each occurrence of the string of characters, while automatic replacement means that it will be replaced on each and every occurrence of the string. To move from prompt to prompt, simply use the TAB key. The cursor must be brought to the place where you want the search to begin. Usually, that means bringing the cursor to the beginning of the document by pressing the Home key on IBM keyboards or CTRL, G (for go) and B (for beginning) on keyboards without function keys. The search function is invoked by pressing F7 or CTRL and S.

Replace (Yes/No/Quit). The REPLACE message is displayed for every occurrence of the string of characters in the manual replacement. Pressing Y implements the replacement; pressing N causes the search to proceed to the next match; pressing Q quits the search and replace and returns you to your document in the TYPE/EDIT mode. Partial searches can take place using two periods (. .) as wildcards. For example SEARCH FOR: str . . will locate all words that begin with "str," such as string, strings, and straw. Wildcards may be used at the beginning, end, or the beginning and end of any group of letters. A handy way of counting the words in a document is to SEARCH FOR . . . (wildcard), REPLACE WITH: (leave blank), and do it "A"utomatically. The number of matches will be the total number of words. The search and replace function is limited in that underlined or bold characters cannot be put into the replacement blank.

When working with extrememly long documents, such as this manuscript, the SEARCH FOR function provides an invaluable tool. Often in editing, a printout is marked up for future corrections. Several pages may separate editing marks. Rather than having to search line by line for the next occurrence, it is possible to invoke the SEARCH FOR function by pressing F7 and enter a keyword from the area you want to edit. Leaving the REPLACE WITH space blank will take the cursor to the next occurrence of that keyword and automatically return you to the TYPE/EDIT mode with the cursor at that position in the text.

INSERT AND STRIKEOVER MODES

In my early days of personal computing, I remember discussing the relative merits of two of the early word processors. One of the programs was always in the insert mode while one was always in the strikeover mode. It was my opinion that the insert mode system was superior, and I would argue that, except in the few cases where there were equal numbers of letters being substituted or replaced, the insert mode always required fewer keystrokes.

In the heat of the "either-or" argument, no one ever considered that it would soon be possible to have both and to be able to select either of the two modes within the same word processor. This is one of the amenities of *PFS:Write*. Not only do you have the choice, you have the opportunity to switch back and forth between the modes as frequently as you desire by toggling the Ins key on IBM PC keyboard and CTRL-Y keys on Apple II keyboards.

There can be unexpected side effects of selecting the insert or strikeover mode of *PFS:Write*. Primarily, the difference appears in using the destructive BACK ARROW and Del keys. When you use the commands to delete characters in the insert mode, all of the text beyond that point will be dragged up to the final position of the cursor. When you are not in the insert mode, the text below the cursor remains stationary. The effect can be especially dramatic around the end of a line.

ENTERING TEXT

Now, let us assume that we are going to send a quick letter of thanks to several people who have made contributions to our organization.

We simply begin to type. Each letter we type appears on the screen. The flashing line cursor blinks continuously as if the computer has its meter running and is going to bill us after its use. Along with the cursor moves its shadow, the highlighted pointer on the ruler at the bottom of the screen. Some computer keyboards take a little getting used to. The SHIFT keys on the IBM PC, for example, are represented by arrows pointing up, and are positioned slightly farther away than you may expect. The TAB key is marked with two horizontal arrows pointing in opposite directions. The largest difference between computer keyboards and typewriter keyboards is that computer keyboards either have many more keys than typewriters or require you to use combinations of keys to interact with your computer and computer programs.

Let us begin by using the sample Fig. 5-5 to illustrate a sample letter. Entering the text was not difficult at all. If an incorrect key was accidentally typed, all we had to do was press the BACK ARROW key on an IBM keyboard, or <Del>ete of the Apple II system and the mistake was removed. If we didn't notice a mistake until we were well past it, the cursor could be moved by use of the arrow keys until it was positioned over the character or characters to be corrected. The Del key on the IBM and CTRL and R keys on Apple delete the character that the cursor is on and if used several times delete the characters immediately following the cursor. On the other hand, the destructive BACK ARROW key on the IBM and the <Del>ete key on the Apple delete the letters immediately preceding the current position of the cursor.

There are several other simple editing features, and cursor controls to provide quick and easy ways for you to get around within your document. The cursor control keys allow you to move around

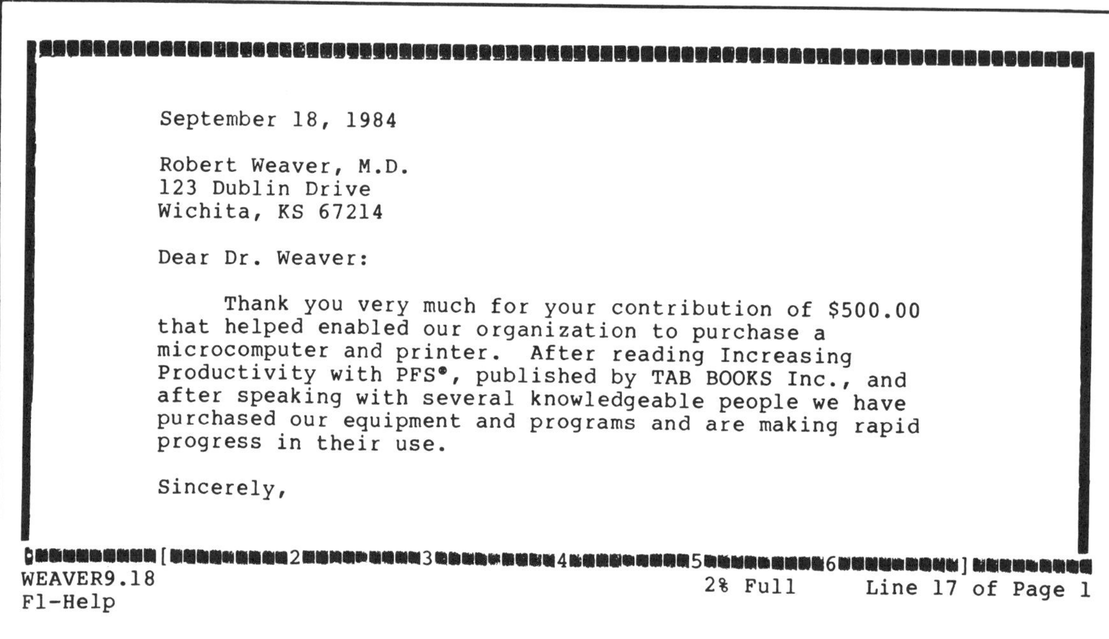

September 18, 1984

Robert Weaver, M.D.
123 Dublin Drive
Wichita, KS 67214

Dear Dr. Weaver:

Thank you very much for your contribution of $500.00 that helped enabled our organization to purchase a microcomputer and printer. After reading Increasing Productivity with PFS®, published by TAB BOOKS Inc., and after speaking with several knowledgeable people we have purchased our equipment and programs and are making rapid progress in their use.

Sincerely,

[2 3 4 5 6]
WEAVER9.18
F1-Help 2% Full Line 17 of Page 1

Fig. 5-5. A sample "Thank You" letter in progress.

on the document without altering any of the existing words already created.

CURSOR CONTROL

The IBM-type numeric keypad has a Num Lock key (number lock) above it. Upon starting *PFS:Write* the numbers are locked out, and the keys in this pad with the small arrows provide cursor control. If the Num Lock key is toggled, numbers will be typed upon striking the keypad keys. Apple *II*e/c users will use the four directional arrow keys to move the cursor to the desired location. Apple Macintosh users will use the mouse to position the cursor.

Home. The Home key, located on the 7 key on the IBM's numeric keypad, brings the cursor to the first available position in the left-most position of the very first line of the document. Pressing CTRL, G (go to) and B (beginning) achieves the same result on the Apple *II*e/c.

End. The End key, located on the 1 key of the numeric keypad, positions the cursor in the next available position following the last typed character of the document. If you have positioned the cursor below the last typed character, the End key will actually bring the cursor up to the end position. CTRL, G (go to), and E (end) does the same on an Apple.

Up. The cursor can be moved in an upward direction by using the UP ARROW key. The cursor will move directly up from its current locale, and will not move to the left-most position on the line as is the case with some word processors. The UP ARROW will automatically repeat itself if it is held down, as will all of the cursor movement keys.

Down. The cursor can be moved downward in a straight path below the position of the cursor by pressing the DOWN ARROW.

Left and **Right**. The cursor can be moved to the left or to the right without affecting the existing text by using the LEFT and RIGHT ARROW keys on the numeric keypad.

PgUp and **PgDn.** Since the screen displays only 22 lines at a time, PgUp, located on the 9 key and PgDn, located on the 3 key, provide an easy way to move from page to page of text. It is faster than moving line by line with the arrows. For the sake of continuity, one line of the previous page remains on screen when you select PgUp or PgDn. CTRL and N (for next screen) and CTRL and P for previous screen are the commands used on Apple systems.

Start of Line. Pressing the SHIFT key and the F3 key simultaneously will cause the cursor to jump to the first character of the line it is currently on. If the line is blank, the cursor will return to the left margin. The CLOSED APPLE - LEFT ARROW brings the cursor to the left-most position of the line on an Apple.

End of Line. SHIFT and F4 will cause the cursor to jump past the final character of the line that the cursor is on. If the line is blank, it will skip to the right margin. If the final character is a period, the cursor will position itself two characters to the right of the period so that you will be ready to begin a new sentence. Otherwise, the cursor will position itself one space to the right of the last character on the right. CLOSED APPLE and RIGHT ARROW will bring the Apple cursor to the end of the line that it is positioned on.

Previous Word. F3 moves the cursor to the first character of the word immediately preceding the present position of the cursor. The OPEN APPLE and LEFT ARROW keys on the Apple command move the cursor to the beginning of the previous word.

Next Word. F4 moves the cursor to the first character of the word that follows the cursor's present position. If there are several blanks beyond the cursor's present position, it moves one space beyond the last character on the line, unless the last character is a period, in which case it moves two characters beyond the last character. Pressing OPEN APPLE and RIGHT ARROW works equivalently on the Apple *II*e/c.

Tabs. F2 or CTRL will set or clear tabs. Tabs can be the typewriter kind or decimal tabs. Decimal tabs automatically align decimals, such as those separating dollars and cents. To set a tab, press F2 or CTRL-T when you have positioned the cursor at the desired tab location. On the status line you will see this message: TYPE IN TABS (T or D); THEN PRESS F10 (or CTRL-C). Type "T"ypewriter tab or "D"ecimal tab and the continue key. Pressing continue without typing a "T" or "D" does not set any tabs.

When typing in the Type/Edit mode, the TAB key positions the cursor at the next tab setting. Pressing SHIFT and TAB or OPEN APPLE and TAB positions the cursor at the previous tab setting. In order to remove a tab setting, simply position the cursor at the tab stop that is to be removed and press F2 or CTRL-T. When TYPE IN TABS (T or D) appears, press the Space Bar to erase that tab stop.

PRINTING YOUR WRITING

Now, we want to see our friendly little letter. Besides, it can serve as documentation for the Internal Revenue Service at tax time since our organization is, of course, an officially approved 501 (c) 3 (tax exempt) organization. To serve as proof, it will have to be printed and signed. So let's print it. To do so, simply press the ESC key to return to the Main Menu, select function 3 PRINT, and then press the continue key to see the Print Menu shown in Fig. 5-6.

The IBM and Apple versions of the program have identical Print Menus except the IBM version includes the extra PRINT TO prompt with a default value of LPT1. Instead, the Apple version has an OUTPUT TO prompt. The Apple program simply assumes that the printer output will be to a parallel card in slot # 1, and offers no prompt. Also, of course, the help screens are accessed and noted by either F1 or OPEN APPLE-H.

The value shown after each colon is the default value. Simply pressing the control key will indicate you accept the default values given. To change one of the values, move the cursor from item to item using the TAB key. If you mistakenly tab past the prompt you want to change, press the SHIFT and TAB keys or the OPEN APPLE and TAB keys together to move to the previous prompt. Or you could keep pressing the TAB key and the cursor will keep jumping from prompt to prompt and eventually back to the first prompt. To change any of the values, position the cursor in the desired location and type the value or the name of the *PFS:File* that is going to be used.

FROM PAGE: 1 TO PAGE: 1. By answering this prompt, you indicate the range of pages you want to have printed. It is sometimes convenient to print only a segment of a total document, such as in the case of revising the final page of a 10-page document. In that case, you would just type "10" after the colon following FROM PAGE. The default values for the range of printed pages are page 1 to the final page. The TO PAGE, for the last page, is automatically updated to correspond to the number of the final page in your document. If you want to print only one page of a multiple page document, use the same number for the FROM and TO values.

Page numbers refer to *absolute* page values in accordance with the defined page length (usually 66 lines per page), which can cause confusion when double spacing is used. Footers can automatically number pages appropriately. However, those numbers will not correspond to the "absolute" page numbers used for the purpose of printing a range of pages.

PRINT TO: LPT1 (not applicable for Apple systems). This prompt allows you to select the printing device. Because a significant number of IBM systems are equipped with serial printers, the value can be adjusted for those systems.

OUTPUT TO (P/L) (not applicable for IBM system). This prompt allows you to tell the system the type of printers you have—one that automatically supplies a line feed (moves the paper up) after each printed line or one that does not.

PAUSE BETWEEN PAGES (Y/N): N. This prompt supplies a convenient way of allowing you to deal with your printer paper. Some printers have tractor feed devices that use sprockets to fit into holes along the sides of paper and continuously feed paper through the printer. Other printers depend upon friction to roll the paper up around the platen. Some printers can handle paper in either manner. It is quicker for tractor feed printers to print continuously, which they will do when you leave the

```
                         PRINT MENU

                 FROM PAGE: 1   TO PAGE: 1

                 PRINT TO: LPT1:

                 PAUSE BETWEEN PAGES (Y/N): N

                 NUMBER OF COPIES: 1

                 SINGLE/DOUBLE/ENVELOPE (S/D/E): S

                 INDENT: 0

                 JOINING PFS:GRAPH (Y/N): N

                 PFS FILE NAME:


 F1-Help                                          F10-Continue
```

Fig. 5-6. PFS:Write PRINT MENU with default values.

```
POSITION THE PAPER IN YOUR PRINTER

Press F10 to continue
```

Fig. 5-7. Insert paper prompt that appears before printing.

PAUSE value "N." If, however, you are using a friction feed printer that is processing single sheets of paper, change the value to "Y," and you will be prompted to insert paper at the proper times. (See Fig. 5-7.)

NUMBER OF COPIES: 1. By typing the appropriate number, you can conveniently print multiple copies of the same document. The default value is for a single copy. If you request multiple copies of a document that is longer than one page, *PFS:Write* will print each document completely through, and then print the next copy, and so on until the number of copies specified have been printed.

SINGLE/DOUBLE/ENVELOPE (S/D/E): S. This prompt allows you to select single spacing, double spacing, or envelopes to be printed. Without making any changes, the default value of "S" will be used and print single spaced documents. Pressing the letter D to replace S will obviously result in double spaced letters and documents. Single and double spacing cannot be used within the same document. To have both, it would be necessary to create two or more documents and use the *JOIN* command to merge the differently formatted documents into one document. The *JOIN* command will be discussed in more detail.

The ENVELOPE option is one of the handiest options that I have ever used on any word processor. Its convenience and ease of use makes the *PFS:Write* worth its price, particularly if you write a large number of letters. After a letter has been printed, it is possible to "lift" the address off of the letter and print it directly onto an envelope without changing any of the letter and without changing any of the margins. Using this handy feature is simplicity itself. At the Main Menu, press 3 to select the Print Option, press the TAB key until the cursor is positioned over the "S," press E, and then press the continue key. The screen will display a message to insert your envelope into the printer as seen in Fig. 5-8.

PFS:Write finds the address in the following manner. It first "looks" at the first line of text. If that line ends with at least two digits, it interprets that line as being the date, and then skips over blank lines until it finds the next line of text (the address). It then prints all of the next few lines of text until it hits another blank line. If you position the envelope properly with the print head at the top of the envelope and the left corner in the normal position that is used for your paper, the program will automatically skip down 10 lines and indent 35 spaces. That is the proper position for business envelopes. If you are using an oversized envelope, it is possible to make an adjustment by inputting the proper number of spaces to indent in the blank just below Single/Double/Envelope. Presto! Instant envelope addressing.

The envelope addressing function also works when you are using *PFS:File* to supply names and addresses for your letters (to be discussed later). If you indicate you want a pause between each page, you will be repeatedly prompted to insert each envelope until your mailing is completed.

Most of the other top-rated word processors do not have an automatic envelope addressing method. With those other packages it may be

```
POSITION THE ENVELOPE IN YOUR PRINTER

Press F10 to continue
```

Fig. 5-8. Insert envelope prompt provides for easy envelope printing.

necessary to first save your letter onto the disk, delete everything above the address (usually the date), delete everything below the address (the text), and change the top and side margins before printing the address. You would then be faced with an interesting choice of whether to save the address, which you might never use individually again, taking up additional disk space, or repeat the whole process from the beginning if you later want to print another envelope.

INDENT: 0. This allows the user to make allowances for special circumstances, such as oversized envelopes mentioned before, or for printers that begin printing extremely close to the left-hand margin of the paper. Use the TAB key to move the cursor to the INDENT prompt and then type in the number of spaces to indent the starting point to correct any strange looking centering in a letter or envelope. It is a handy feature of *PFS:Write* that it is "smart" enough to remember that you want it indented if you save your letter to disk after printing it. When printing the same letter again, the number of spaces you specified will become the new default value for indentation.

JOINING PFS:GRAPH (Y/N): N. This prompt asks if you plan to insert a graph into the body of your document. Normally, we do not, so the default value is N. If you do have a *PFS:Graph* you want to insert, answer Y. When it "finds" the spot in your text where the graph is to be inserted, you will be presented with prompts asking about the type of printer you are using. If you have a graph to insert, leave at least 18 lines in the body of the text for its insertion, since a joined graph will be about 3½ × 4½ inches. It must have been saved as a picture. (See Chapter 4.)

PFS FILE NAME: This prompt is used when you want to merge information from the database manager *PFS:File* into the body of a letter or document. MS-DOS systems such as the IBM PC require that B: precede the name of the *PFS:File* name in order for it to be found in the second drive. Other systems just require the filename and automatically search both drives until the file is located.

When this option is used, the user first supplies retrieve specs such as, for example, people who have Tuesday nights free. Next identifier specs are requested that match the ***blank*** items in the body of your letter that you want filled in, such as *Name* and *Address*. This function will be discussed in detail in the final chapter. In this example of writing a simple letter, we will leave the space blank.

Now that all of the prompts have been explained, we are finally ready to proceed with printing the letter we have written. Let us assume that we have a parallel printer that uses the default values. We press the continue key to accept those values. Because we have forgotten to attach our printer to the computer or to turn it on, the PRINTER NOT READY message appears below the final field, as in Fig. 5-9. If we are all hooked up and all systems are "go," we are then presented with a screen message reminding us that we must have paper in the printer, before we can print.

It is still not too late to back out. Pressing the ESC key will once again return us to the Main Menu with no damage done. The text will still be there and accessible by pressing 1 TYPE/EDIT and the continue key.

When, however, we are ready to see the fruits of our labor faithfully recorded on paper, we simply press the continue key. In a matter of seconds, we can see our completed letter as shown in Fig. 5-10.

Great, huh? What? It looks kind of skimpy? Well, it is a short, one paragraph letter, and there is a lot of empty space on the top and on the bottom of the letter. Perhaps it would be better to have shorter margins to "stretch" it out a little. Let's give it a try. We have printed the letter, but it hasn't gone anywhere.

We are, once again, presented with the familiar Main Menu. Just to reassure ourselves, let's press 1 TYPE/EDIT and the continue key to see the letter again. Yes. There it is. Now press ESC to get back to the Main Menu.

DEFINE PAGE

Now to change the margins, press 2 DEFINE

```
                         PRINT MENU

                 FROM PAGE: 1   TO PAGE: 10

                 PRINT TO: LPT1:

                 PAUSE BETWEEN PAGES (Y/N): N

                 NUMBER OF COPIES: 1

                 SINGLE/DOUBLE/ENVELOPE (S/D/E): S

                 INDENT: 0

                 JOINING PFS:GRAPH (Y/N): N

                 PFS FILE NAME:

                   PRINTER ISN'T READY

F1-Help                                              F10-Continue
```

Fig. 5-9. "Printer isn't ready" message reminds you to turn on the printer.

```
September 18, 1984

Robert Weaver, M.D.
123 Dublin Drive
Wichita, KS 67214

Dear Dr. Weaver:

     Thank you very much for your contribution of $500.00
that helped enabled our organization to purchase a
microcomputer and printer.  After reading Increasing
Productivity with PFS®, published by TAB BOOKS Inc., and
after speaking with several knowledgeable people we have
purchased our equipment and programs and are making rapid
progress in their use.

Sincerely,



Kathryn R. Burton
Executive Director
```

Fig. 5-10. "Thank You" letter output in 60 column format.

```
                    DEFINE PAGE MENU



           LEFT MARGIN: 10       RIGHT MARGIN: 70

           TOP  MARGIN: 6        BOTTOM MARGIN: 6

           PAGE LENGTH: 66



 HEADING:

 FOOTING:


F1-Help                                        F10-Continue
```

Fig. 5-11. DEFINE PAGE MENU w/default values.

PAGE and the continue key. Look at the inner menu for Define Page shown in Fig. 5-11.

In case you're feeling unsure of yourself, note the help message in the bottom left corner. If you press the help key, and you have your *PFS:Write* program disk in the drive, you will see the following explanations. (See Fig. 5-12 for the complete explanation.)

On the Define Page Menu, the blinking cursor will be positioned for the LEFT MARGIN prompt.

```
                    DEFINE PAGE Options

   Option             What to Enter

   LEFT MARGIN:       Column number of the left edge of the document.

   RIGHT MARGIN:      Column number of the right edge of the document.

   TOP MARGIN:        Number of lines for the top margin.

   BOTTOM MARGIN:     Number of lines for the bottom margin.

   PAGE LENGTH:       Number of lines on each sheet of paper.  A typical
                      8 1/2 by 11 inch page is 66 lines long.
   HEADING:           Up to two lines of text to appear as the heading
                      on each page of the document.
   FOOTING:           Up to two lines of text that will appear on the
                      bottom of each page.  The right most number in
                      the footing is assumed to be a page number and
                      will increase by one for each new page.

                     Press F10 to continue
```

Fig. 5-12. DEFINE PAGE help screen.

We can see that there is currently a 60 space line being used since the margins are 10 and 70. Our letter will look better if we had a 50 space line, so we will change the margins accordingly. First we type 15 for the LEFT MARGIN, replacing the original value of 10. Next we press the TAB key to move the cursor to the next prompt, RIGHT MARGIN. We want to move the right margin in five spaces, so we type 65 in the space where 70 was. Now, we have a 50 space line (65 minus 15).

The TOP MARGIN and BOTTOM MARGIN each have a value of 6 lines, a one-inch margin. In this example we will leave those values. They could be changed if we needed more margin on the top of our letterhead, or if we wanted, to change the bottom margin for whatever reason.

The PAGE LENGTH prompt allows you to print on any size paper. Normal 8½ × 11-inch paper has 66 lines. Fourteen-inch legal paper, for example, has 84 standard lines per page. Headers and footers can be defined in the spaces following HEADING and FOOTING; they are constant messages that appear on each page of a document at either the top (heading) or bottom (footing). If you define the footer in a manner similar to Page 1, or Chapter 1, Page 1," the program will automatically assume that the right-most number is a page number and increase it by one at every page—the easiest page numbering system of any word processor.

You may notice that there are no provisions made for vertical centering of your letter, that is, to automatically provide equal amounts of white space at the top and bottom of your letter. Vertical centering is a feature normally used infrequently, such as for preparing title pages. People who need that option are frequently the same people who would need frequent text justification of the right margin such as people who prepare newsletters. Those people will need a different word processor, or will need to make some human adjustments, because neither of those features is to be found in *PFS:Write*.

Since we are working on a single page letter at this point, we are happy to modify only the left and right margins. With the screen appearing as seen in Fig. 5-13, we press the continue key.

Very briefly, beneath the Define Page Menu, we see the CHANGING MARGINS message. If we press 1 TYPE/EDIT we see that the margins have

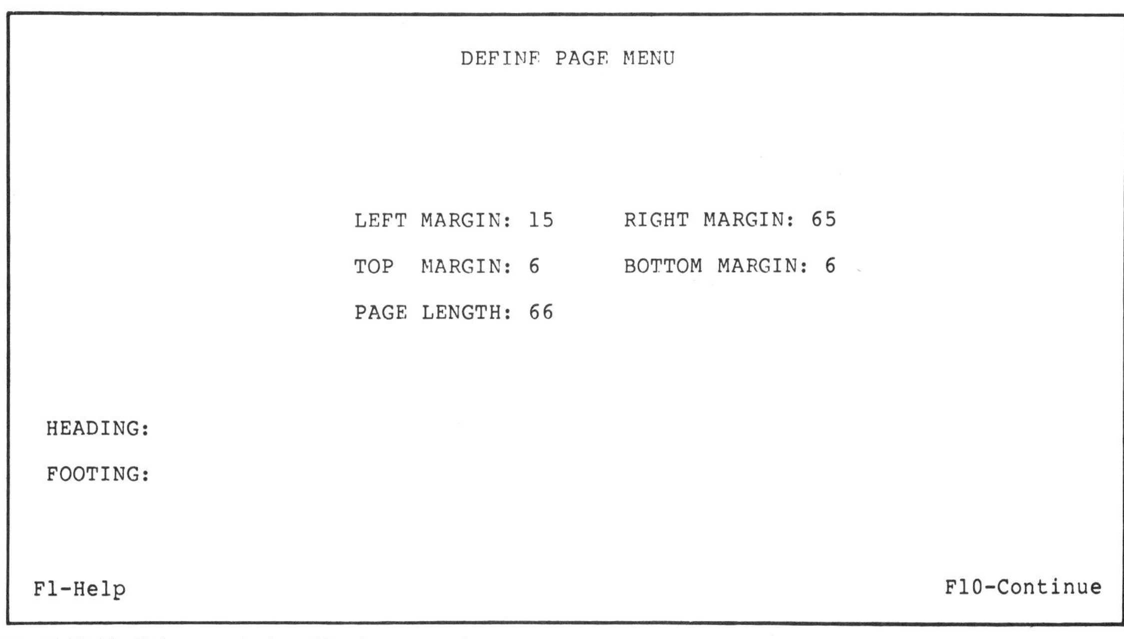

Fig. 5-13. Modifying margin to a 50 column margin.

```
September 18, 1984

Robert Weaver, M.D.
123 Dublin Drive
Wichita, KS 67214

Dear Dr. Weaver:

     Thank you very much for your contribution of
$500.00 that helped enabled our organization to
purchase a microcomputer and printer.  After
reading Increasing Productivity with PFS®,
published by TAB BOOKS Inc. and after speaking with
several knowledgeable people we have purchased our
equipment and programs and are making rapid
progress in their use.

Sincerely,



Kathryn R. Burton
Executive Director
```

Fig. 5-14. "Thank you" letter in 50 column format.

been realigned. Pressing 3 PRINT and the continue key, gives us another printout of the letter, this time with a 50 space margin shown in Fig. 5-14.

There. That's better, right? Still skimpy? There's no getting around it. The letter is just a one paragraph letter and no amount of fancy word processing is going to make it look like too much more than it is. Word processing will, however, let us make modifications painlessly.

EDITING

Again, after printing, the Main Menu appears. Press 1 TYPE/EDIT, and the letter reappears with the cursor blinking in the top left corner. Since we will be fully proficient in the use of this software within a short time, let's offer to supply a demonstration of the ways the system will enhance our effectiveness. The process is as easy as typing the initial information. Position the cursor at the end of the letter, and begin to type as follows:

P.S. There will be a demonstration of our new equipment and software for all interested parties on October 18, 1984, at 3:00 P.M. at our office. Please plan to attend.

Now, printing it again, we have a letter that is more pleasantly spaced as seen in Fig. 5-15.

The letter is beginning to look a little better. However, a word processor makes the necessity of a post script obsolete. (We may want to use it for effect, but only by choice, not necessity.) From the normal TYPE/EDIT mode, move the cursor to the beginning of the P.S. and press the Label key F5 on IBM keyboards, and CTRL-L on Apple keybaord. Use the arrow keys to mark the entire section. It is not necessary to use the RIGHT ARROW to mark each and every letter. The down arrow marks entire lines of text at a time. Figure 5-16 illustrates the appearance of labeled text.

Now press the Del key or the CTRL-R key. The lines disappear, but are stored in the buffer memory. Move the cursor to where you want the labeled text to begin being inserted, in this case in the area between the first paragraph and the closing. When the cursor is properly positioned, press the duplicate keys (F6 or CTRL-D). Now, the letter looks almost right. We again have the opportunity to dress it up a little by adding information that we think is pertinent. By using the insert mode (be sure that you are in the insert mode by checking the status line beneath the ruler), additions are painless. Any extra line spaces between the final paragraph and closing can be quickly eliminated by pressing the Del key or CTRL and R when the cursor is on that empty line and the remaining Post Script. There! That looks better. Let's print it one last time and examine our masterpiece in Fig. 5-17.

Oh no! October 18th will cause a conflict in my schedule. Let's postpone the demonstration a few days. From the Main Menu select 1 TYPE/EDIT. Next, press the Search key F7 on the IBM, CTRL-S on Apple. You will see the following prompts: SEARCH FOR, REPLACE WITH, and MANUAL OR AUTOMATIC (M/A). In the highlighted block

```
September 18, 1984

Robert Weaver, M.D.
123 Dublin Drive
Wichita, KS 67214

Dear Dr. Weaver:

     Thank you very much for your contribution of
$500.00 that helped enabled our organization to
purchase a microcomputer and printer.  After
reading Increasing Productivity with PFS®,
published by TAB BOOKS Inc., and after speaking
with several knowledgeable people we have purchased
our equipment and programs and are making rapid
progress in their use.

Sincerely,



Kathryn R. Burton
Executive Director


P.S. There will be a demonstration of our new
equipment and software for all interested parties
on October 18, 1984, at 3:00 p.m. at our office.
Please plan to attend.
```

Fig. 5-15. Short letter with postscript.

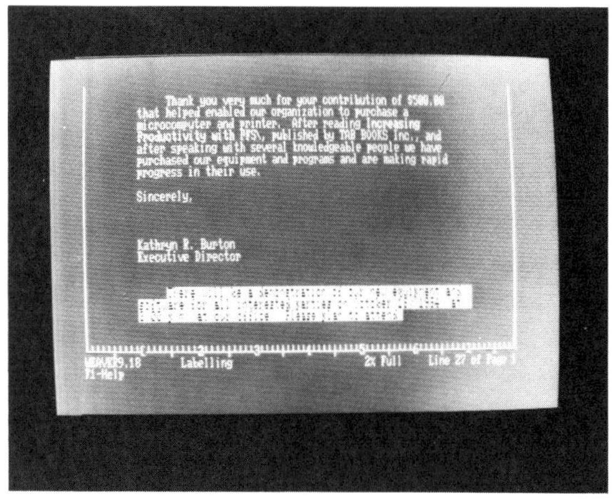

Fig. 5-16. Letter with postscript labeled so that it can be moved into text.

next to SEARCH FOR, type 18. Press the TAB key to move the cursor to the REPLACE WITH field. Place 31 in that highlighted block. The final block is MANUAL OR AUTOMATIC (M/A). In this case, as in most cases, it is prudent to make the changes manually by confirming the change with a REPLACE YES/NO/QUIT (Y/N/Q) response rather than making changes automatically. If you chose to make the replacements automatically, the program would automatically change the date of the letter as well as the date of the demonstration, because they are both the eighteenth. At the first REPLACE YES/NO/QUIT (Y/N/Q), press N because you don't want to change the date of the letter. Press Y the second time, because that is the date you do want to change.

September 18, 1984

Robert Weaver, M.D.
123 Dublin Drive
Wichita, KS 67214

Dear Dr. Weaver:

Thank you very much for your contribution of $500.00 that helped enabled our organization to purchase a microcomputer and printer. After reading Increasing Productivity with PFS®, published by TAB BOOKS Inc., and after speaking with several knowledgeable people we have purchased our equipment and programs and are making rapid progress in their use.

There will be a demonstration of our new equipment and software for all interested parties on October 18, 1984, at 3:00 p.m. at our office. Please plan to attend.

Sincerely,

Kathryn R. Burton
Executive Director

Fig. 5-17. Letter with postscript moved into body of letter.

Anytime you use the search and replace function of *PFS:Write*, the search begins at the current position of the cursor. If you want to search and replace throughout the entire document, you should first bring the cursor to the beginning of the document. As you may remember, that is most easily accomplished by pressing the Home key on the numeric keypad.

Now we could print it again, but I will save you from another printing. This time it is suitable for mailing. This example illustrates that word processing does not always save time. Hopefully, at least, it will help produce superior output. Later, we shall see examples of labor saving features of word processing. Now, we will want to save our letter for future use and reference.

SAVING DOCUMENTS

Saving the document to disk is a convenient means of storage. Those of us who use word processing frequently have almost given up on paper files. Now all we have to worry about is finding the right disk.

In order to save our document, we will press ESC to return to the Main Menu. We select 4 GET/SAVE/REMOVE and then press the continue key. We will then be presented with the Get/Save/Remove Menu (an inner menu shown in Fig. 5-18). If you ever forget the ways in which these commands work, that's what the help feature displayed in Fig. 5-19 is for.

To save, naturally, we select 2. Use the TAB key to move the cursor to the DIRECTORY OR FILE NAME prompt, and then give the document a name. Try to give it a name that makes sense, because that is all that you will have to go on when you want to retrieve it in the future. There is a limit to the number of characters you may use to name a document. Eight characters is the maximum in the "main" part of the name. Additionally, there may be a three-characters extension following a period. For example, in naming the letter of thanks for the contribution these are some of the options that come to mind:

CONTRIB.TKS
GIFT.THK
THANKS.GFT
WEAVER9.18

```
                    GET/SAVE/REMOVE MENU


                     1  GET DOCUMENT

                     2  SAVE DOCUMENT

                     3  REMOVE FILE


                    SELECTION NUMBER:

                    DIRECTORY OR FILE NAME:


F1-Help                                              F10-Continue
```

Fig. 5-18. PFS:Write GET/SAVE/REMOVE MENU.

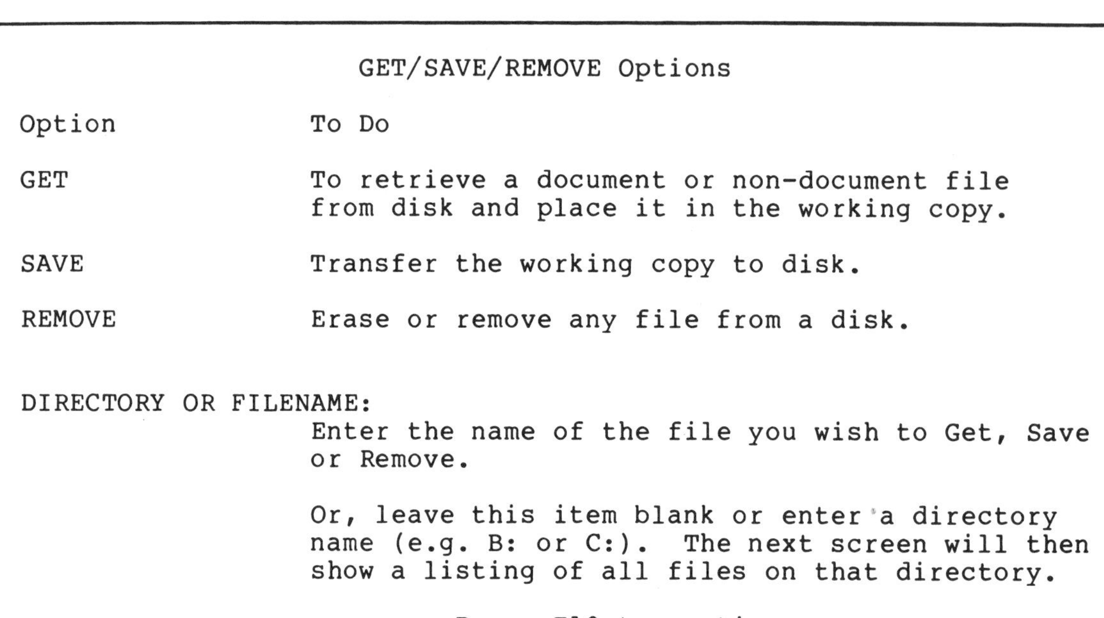
GET/SAVE/REMOVE Options

Option	To Do
GET	To retrieve a document or non-document file from disk and place it in the working copy.
SAVE	Transfer the working copy to disk.
REMOVE	Erase or remove any file from a disk.

DIRECTORY OR FILENAME:
Enter the name of the file you wish to Get, Save or Remove.

Or, leave this item blank or enter a directory name (e.g. B: or C:). The next screen will then show a listing of all files on that directory.

Press F10 to continue

Fig. 5-19. GET/SAVE/REMOVE Help Screen.

The final selection illustrates one way to imbed the date right into the filename. If you want to see the other filenames on the disk before naming the new one, you may press the continue key before naming the document. With MS-DOS systems, you may specify the drive that the document will be saved to. It is a good idea to put the data disk in drive A and its backup in drive B. That way, you may constantly be saving first to a data disk and then to its backup.

The filename that strikes me as being the clearest, and probably the easiest to recall at a later date, is WEAVER9.18. So that is how it will be saved onto the disk. After the correct menu options have been selected, and after the continue key has been pressed, the document will be saved onto the disk in standard file format. Once you have supplied a document a name, the word processor will continue to use that name as a default value on all future saving procedures. There is no need to continually provide the name of the document. Simply pressing the continue key will cause the name of the document to be supplied as the default value for a SAVE WORKING COPY AS prompt. Pressing the continue key causes the default value to be accepted. Also, the most recently designated drive becomes the default drive to which all documents will be saved unless otherwise designated. If no drive has been designated, the first drive, A or 1, will be used.

PFS:Write messages ensure that you are constantly kept aware of the status of your most recent saving procedures. If you choose to exit from the program or clear the document without saving your most recent changes, a message similar to the one shown in Fig. 5-20 will appear.

In a similar manner, the program makes sure that you are aware of when a saving procedure involves saving the document over a document with the same name. Most often, this is the case when you are periodically saving and updating documents. However, it is possible that you would accidentally give two documents the same name, such as "Memo." The message in Fig. 5-21 prevents accidental erasure of a previously saved document.

Even if you decide to retrieve another letter without first saving the latest changes to your document, you will be warned by the message of Fig. 5-22.

```
WARNING
-------

WORKING COPY ABOUT TO BE CLEARED

LATEST CHANGES NOT SAVED

Press ESC to abandon this operation

Press F10 to continue
```

Fig. 5-20. Warning that the working copy is about to be cleared before it has been saved.

```
WARNING
-------

DOCUMENT ABOUT TO BE OVERWRITTEN


Press ESC to abandon this operation

Press F10 to continue
```

Fig. 5-21. Warning that a letter is being overwritten on top of another file.

```
WARNING
-------

WORKING COPY ABOUT TO BE OVERWRITTEN

LATEST CHANGES NOT SAVED

Press ESC to abandon this operation

Press F10 to continue
```

Fig. 5-22. Warning that the letter is about to be replaced without being saved.

In short, *PFS:Write* is a very conscientious helper. It wants to help remind you to save your work. What is really user-friendly about this system, as you can see from all of the messages, is that none of the procedures creates an irreversable situation—you cannot lose a file by pressing a single key or series of keys. The PRESS ESC TO ABANDON THIS OPERATION is a tremendous safety valve.

RETRIEVING DOCUMENTS

Option 1 GET DOCUMENT works essentially the same way the SAVE DOCUMENT selection does. When you want to retrieve a document, you do not have to know its name ahead of time. It is possible to select 1 without supplying a filename. In that case, when you press the continue key, a full directory of the disk will be displayed, and the program will ask NAME OF DOCUMENT TO GET? If you do not supply an exact match of the document's name, including the letters or numbers following the period, you will receive a FILE NOT FOUND message. If the disk has more files on it than can be viewed at one time, the PgDn or CTRL-N (next page) key moves the view of additional documents onto successive screens.

It is also possible to retrieve documents that were not created by *PFS:Write*, *if* the documents are standard ASCII text files. Word processor files created with WordStar or EasyWriter, for example, may be retrieved and displayed on *PFS:Write*. The loading procedure may take considerably longer than the nearly instantaneous loading of a standard *PFS:Write* document. *PFS:Write* will preserve the margins of the originals if at all possible, but replaces any nonprintable characters, such as printer control codes or special formatting instructions, with spaces. Once loaded, you may edit the document from another word processor using all of the commands and features of *PFS:Write*. One obvious limitation is the size of document that can be loaded in this manner. It naturally cannot exceed the limitations of the *PFS:Write* capacity. Many of the other word processors have considerably more capacity then 24-page limit of this system. *PFS:Write* depends upon its ability to append files for long documents. Most other word processors depend more on sheer "horsepower" for handling very large files.

As more and more documents are stored onto a disk, the storage process slows down from an average five second procedure to four or five times that amount. In its use, it seems as if you expect to see a DISK FULL message with each successive save. If you exit the program and ask for a directory you may see that you have used only about half of the available disk space. I generally find it most convenient to store certain kinds of letters on one set of disks, and then file sets of disks at the end of a month of normal business correpondence. With the IBM PC the capacity of the disk is 112 documents. That limitation seems to be due to the fact that there are two screens of letters that can be shown, each with four columns of 14 items.

As you can see, there is no security at all regarding the ability to access document files that you have created. The next generation's scandal sheets will tell of finding disks full of love letters from important personages. Unlike *PFS:Access*, *PFS:Write* has no way to encrypt messages—not even a way to hide the files on the disk. Because some of our correspondence is best forgotten, there is another item in the GET/SAVE/REMOVE section to discuss—REMOVE.

REMOVING DOCUMENTS

It is possible to remove documents by choosing 4 GET/SAVE/REMOVE from the Main Menu and then selecting 3 REMOVE FILE from the inner menu. The exact document name must be supplied. If you do not know the name, it is possible to get a complete listing of the documents on file. As is the case with all irreversible procedures in PFS, there is the display of an appropriate warning of the seriousness of this procedure as well as an opportunity to back out of it. WARNING FILE ABOUT TO BE REMOVED. PRESS ESC TO ABANDON OR F10 TO CONTINUE.

This is one area of possible disaster in the use of this word processor. I have recognized that it is sometimes necessary to remove documents, and I understand that this command logically belongs exactly where it is. However, I am a little nervous about REMOVE being only one iddy-biddy key away from SAVE in a four-key procedure. True, there is a warning message. But be careful to read the warning messages! It is possible to become quite used to seeing the message, WARNING DOCUMENT ABOUT TO BE OVERWRITTEN, in the normal process of saving and quickly press the continue key to get past it. If it actually said WARNING FILE ABOUT TO BE REMOVED, there could be great wailing and gnashing of teeth.

The possibility of this kind of electronic disaster is what keeps many people from taking the leap into word processing. This hypothetical disaster, of course, would be no disaster if backups were kept conscientiously. Most people, though, learn the hard way. If a calamity of this type ever strikes, don't give up. Immediately get to the Main Menu and remove the data disk that has the "disappeared" file. Call up a computer "techie" and beg for help. He will come with a utility disk and probably be able to reconstruct the file. Norton Utilities, for example, has a handy utility for the IBM PC called Unerase. The Beagle Brothers have similar utilities for the Apple. Under no circumstances should you save another document on the disk from which you want to recover a removed file. If another file uses some of the space that was previously allocated for the removed file, there will be no hope for it.

SAVING LABOR

Let us assume that there have been several other contributors to our organization's computer fund. We shall just select the TYPE/EDIT function to make the necessary modifications to our "thank you" letter, most notably, by changing the addressee and amount of the contribution. Retaining the body of the letter will be the most efficient way of sending a similar letter to another person. If we had written other documents, or used the computer for other purposes, we would first have to retrieve the document according to the procedures detailed above.

A shifted F6 or CTRL-E (for erase) on Apple systems erases an entire line at a time. To remove the old addressee, simply move the cursor to any position on the line that is to be removed and press the designated key. Now there will be blanks where once there was an address. Make sure the *PFS:-Write* is toggled into the insert mode, move the cursor to the starting position for the new address, and type it in. Next, the amount of contribution can be changed if necessary. It could be changed by positioning the cursor in the proper position, using the Del key and then inserting the correct amount. Or, the search key, F7 or equivalent could be used to search for $500 and replace it with $100.

The result is another letter—and in a fraction of the time that it took to create the first letter! The "spin off" letter is displayed in Fig. 5-23.

When it is time to save the new letter, we must remember to give it a new filename, let us say MOHR9.18. If we did not give the new letter a new filename, it would save the new letter "on top of" the original letter, which would be lost forever. Of course, there would be warning before that irrevocable procedure took place.

As you can see, the word processor is beginning to pay dividends. By the time we type similar letters to the fifteen contributors, *PFS:Write* will have paid substantially greater dividends. The last chapter of this book, Bringing It All Together—Creatively, details ways you can optimize peak efficiency through the use of "personalized form letters."

CLEARING THE WAY FOR NEW DOCUMENTS

The CLEAR selection in the Main Menu is a way of clearing the document in memory to prepare to begin another one. As mentioned previously, there will be an appropriate warning if the previous document has not been saved prior to using 5 CLEAR. This command is used to produce a "clean slate."

MERGING CHARTS FROM *PFS:GRAPH*

In the previous chapter, we learned that we could save any graph as a picture. Now we shall use one of those graph pictures in the body of a letter to illustrate how a picture can indeed be worth a

September 18, 1984

RoseMary Mohr, Ph.D.
MHA in Sedgwick County
2708 E. Central, Suite A
Wichita, KS 67214

Dear Dr. Mohr:

Thank you very much for your contribution of $100.00 that helped enabled our organization to purchase a microcomputer and printer. After reading Increasing Productivity with PFS®, published by TAB BOOKS Inc., and after speaking with several knowledgeable people we have purchased our equipment and programs and are making rapid progress in their use.

There will be a demonstration of our new equipment and software for all interested parties on October 31, 1984 at 3:00 p.m. at our office. Please plan to attend.

Sincerely,

Kathryn R. Burton
Executive Director

Fig. 5-23. A "spin-off" letter where only the addressee and amount have been changed.

thousand words. A picture plus a 500 word explanation can be worth 1500 words.

A *PFS:Graph* picture will be printed in a space approximately 3½ × 4½ inches, and take about 18 lines. It is best to leave 18 blank lines in your document for the picture. If the graph will not fit onto a page, it will automatically begin on another page. To merge a picture graph, at the place where the graph is to be inserted, place an asterisk followed by "GRAPH or G," the name of the graph, and a closing asterisk.

In order to demonstrate this process, let us use the picture on the back cover of this book to illustrate the advantages we foresee in using PFS software and a computer. We will load the contribution letter according to the procedures described above; at the Main Menu, 4 GET/SAVE/REMOVE; at the inner menu, 1 GET DOCUMENT with the filename WEAVER9.18.

Next, we move the cursor between the two main paragraphs and insert a paragraph explaining that a consultant evaluated our operation and determined that we could save a measurable percentage of administrative time by instituting a computer. At the appropriate position, we place *GRAPH COVER.PIC* and leave 18 spaces.

Following good computing practice, we now save the new document with a filename, "contrib.rev," on our working disk and on a backup disk, and proceed to the print function. This time, after pressing 3 PRINT at the Main Menu, we will place a Y beside the prompt, INCLUDE PFS GRAPH (Y/N) on the Print Options menu.

Following that action, you will be presented with a PRINTER MENU. A sample printer screen for the IBM PC is shown in Fig. 5-24. Any printer can print text, but a printer must have some graphics capabilities in order to print graphics. Each system offers a choice of different printers used in *PFS:Graph*. Apple systems have the choice of Epson, Apple Dot Matrix, NEC/C.ITOH, IDS, Okidata or their compatibles. The Macintosh version is predefined for use with Imagewriter printers.

Answering the prompt and continuing results in a truly effective letter such as the one shown in Fig. 5-25—one that will stand you in good stead when you inform them that next you want to purchase a modem for use with *PFS:Access*.

JOINING OTHER DOCUMENTS, SPREADSHEETS, AND REPORTS

There are two different ways of combining documents produced by *PFS:Write*. During the creation of a document, you may use F9 or CTRL-A. You will then be prompted to provide the name of the file to be appended. This action will cause the materials to be appended to your working document beginning at the location of the cursor. However, it is only the text characters that are appended, and the document's original format margins will be lost as it takes on those of the document being appended.

The only way to maintain a different set of margins is to use the *JOIN* command. If, for example, you want to display a long quote using a format of narrower margins, you would have to save it separately on the disk with a unique filename, such as QUOTE. Then, in the main body of your letter, you would type *JOIN QUOTE* at the proper place to insert the QUOTE. IBM systems would require that the drive that contains the file also be identified, such as *JOIN B:QUOTE*. Apple systems assume that joined documents will be provided from drive 2. Then, to resume the letter, you would have to use the JOIN command again, at the end of the QUOTE file to instruct the program to *JOIN LETTER.PT2*. Joined documents will have their left and right margins preserved, but the rest of the format, such as top and bottom margins, headers and footers, will conform with the original document. Another limitation is that there cannot be single spaced and double spaced lines within the same document unless they are manually entered. Since the line spacing is designated at the PRINT command, and not in the formatting of the docu-

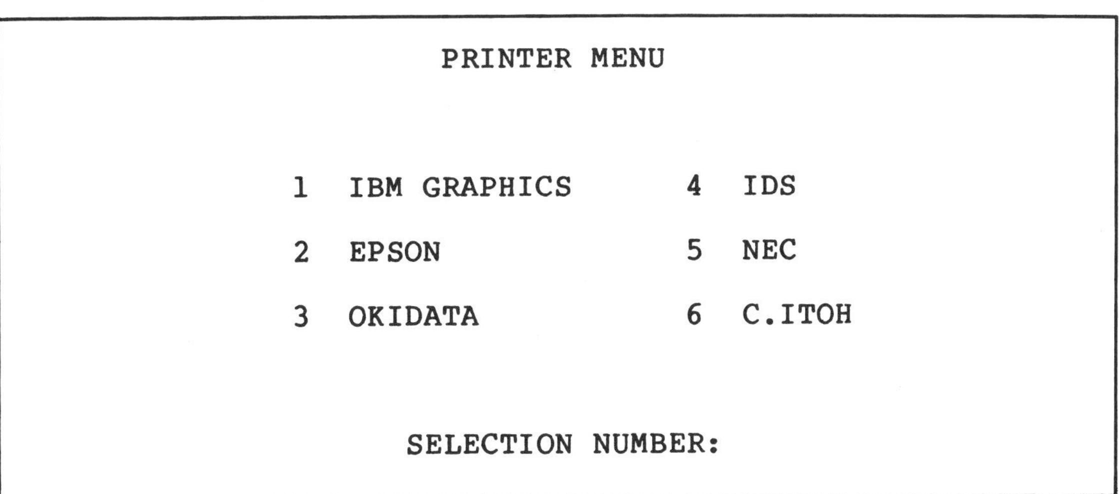

Fig. 5-24. PRINTER MENU that is displayed before a chart is merged into a document.

September 18, 1984

Robert Weaver, M.D.
123 Dublin Drive
Wichita, KS 67214

Dear Dr. Weaver:

Thank you very much for your contribution of $500.00 that helped enabled our organization to purchase a microcomputer and printer. After reading Increasing Productivity with PFS, published by TAB BOOKS Inc. and after speaking with several knowledgeable people we have purchased our equipment and programs and are making rapid progress in their use.

Of course, you are familiar with the consultant's estimation of our growing administration needs. Based on the experiences of one of our sister organizations, I am pleased to say that our administration time should actually decrease after the implementation of our computer system. That will mean more time to provide needed services to our clients.

ADMINISTRATION AFTER COMPUTERIZATION

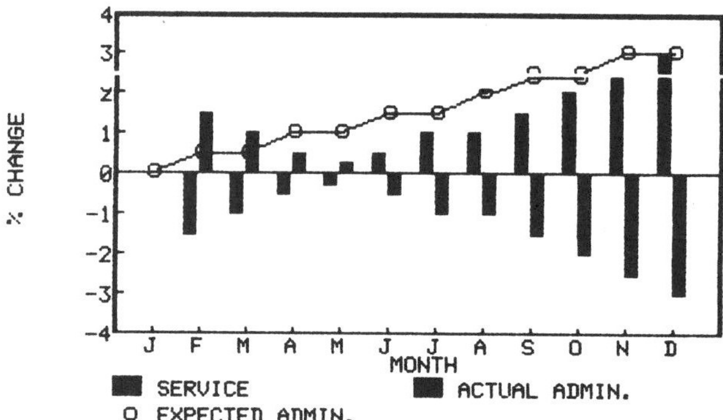

There will be a demonstration of our new equipment and software for all interested parties on October 31, 1984 at 3:00 p.m. at our office. Please plan to attend.

Sincerely,

Kathryn R. Burton
Executive Director

Fig. 5-25. Letter with chart merged into text.

ment, it must do one or the other. One could, of course, manually enter extra blank lines when creating the document.

The JOIN command is also used to join *PFS:Report, PFS:Plan,* or *VisiCalc* information. In order to use it, the report or spreadsheet must have been previously written to a disk file. (See Chapter 8.) If the report or spreadsheet that you want to embed within the document is longer than 80 columns in width, you must make accommodations. One way is to utilize compressed print on printers that support that option. For example, on Epson printers, CHR$(15) sets the printer to a compressed mode. You can send the printer that control code by using the *PRINTER 15* command. Boldface type, underlining, and forced page breaks are supported directly through the program without the need for printer control codes.

SUMMARY

As you can see, word processing can be a labor saving device. When it doesn't save labor, it has the potential to improve the final product. It always has the potential of expanding your capabilities, such as it does by providing the ability to merge graphics with text. Furthermore, it is a springboard for entering the world of telecommunications with the use of *PFS:Access*. Automatic proofreading is available with *PFS:Proof*. Together with *PFS:File*, *PFS:Write* forms the axis around which all of the PFS program modules revolve.

Some of the limitations of *PFS:Write* have been mentioned—no vertical centering, limited document size, inability to undo boldface and underline or to use those features in the search and replace function. Another limitation is the amount of text that can be moved around at one time. For example, if we decide that five pages of a 10-page document need to be in a different place in the document, we will exceed the memory capacity of the buffer (the holding place for text being moved) and will see a message like the one at the bottom of the screen in Fig. 5-26. In order to complete that procedure, you would have to make multiple moves of smaller portions of the block of words. Another minor annoyance is that only one line of text can be removed at a time. Some word processors have the capability of removing paragraphs or complete

```
         which is becomming one of the best in the business.

              Filling out the enclosed enrollment card will get you on
         the mailing list of PFS:NEWS.  PFS:NEWS is a slick little
         newsletter, published quarterly, that will keep you up to
         date with new product releases, such as the new "SOLUTIONS"
         series of templates for PFS:FILE.  It will provide some
         interesting tips and examples of successful applications for
         the entire series of programs.  Most importantly, it will
         make you aware of program updates that will be made available
         at a moderate price to owners of the program.  Some of the
         features that will be listed in this book as "unavailable" or
         missing" will surely be added with subsequent updates and
         releases.  Software Publishing Corpuration is not in
         business to make a quick sale, take your money, and run.
         They know that by keeping in touch and servicing their
         customers they will generate an after-market of sales.  The
         point is that that will benefit the user as well as the
         publisher.


                              Getting Ready To Go
[    T    2         3         4         5         6          ]
BLOCK TOO LARGE TO SAVE.  REMOVE ANYWAY? (Y/N):
F1-Help
```

Fig. 5-26. A message that informs that a labeled block is too large to move.

blocks above or below the cursor position.

We know that *PFS:Write* is not a word processor that will be used to interface with professional typesetting equipment. It will probably not be used by many professional writers. It is aimed at the broadest market, people whose main interest is the timely output of quality letters, memos, and short documents. For those purposes, *PFS:Write* is excellent. *PFS:Write* is an elegantly simple, yet fairly powerful and sophisticated word processor.

PFS:Proof—Avoiding Mistakes

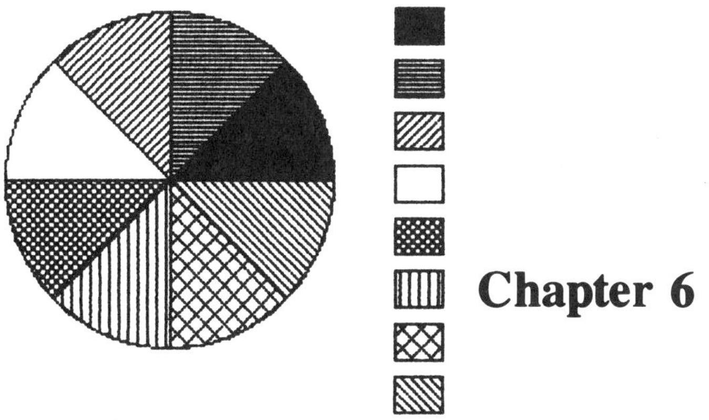

Chapter 6

Those of us who are less than excellent spellers are writers with a kind of quiet desperation. Some of us can blame it on learning to read by the "sight word" method. Some of us just blame it on the English language. All of us can use some help. We may spell a given word correctly half a dozen times in a row, and then botch it up on the seventh. Worst of all, both the correct and incorrect versions look all right at a cursory glance. We know that a misspelling in the middle of a letter can have a devastating effect on the impact of a letter. We know that we should carefully proofread all of our work. However, where do we draw the line? A pretty high overhead results if we check each questionable word. And then, some will ask, how can you find a word in the dictionary if you don't know how to spell it?

Well, *PFS:Proof* is the answer. It is the greatest advance in getting words to the printed page since the advent of word processing. *PFS: Proof* checks for misspelling and allows the user to correct them immediately. It offers "best guesses" of correct spellings, and allows you to cross check its 100,000-word dictionary when you know part of the word you want to spell. Additionally, the program checks for irregular capitalizations and repeated words.

PFS:Proof is the simplest, fastest, easiest to use, and most elegant of the spelling checkers that I have ever used. It proofs and corrects documents in a single pass. Many other spelling checkers require two or more passes of the program—one pass to identify misspelled words, and another to change and insert the corrected words. Its 100,000-word dictionary is one of the most complete on-disk dictionaries available. Speed of operation, though, is not sacrificed because the program utilizes a list of 15,500 most frequently used words for quick comparisons. An average one-page business letter with no errors can be proofed in about seven seconds. In addition to the built-in dictionary, provisions are made for expansion of the list of acceptable words. They may be added instantly when a word is questioned, or added in a group, or even from a list of words supplied on a disk. *PFS:Proof* even "remembers" the types of mistakes that you normally make and makes adjustments in formulating its "best guesses" according to your history of mistakes.

GETTING STARTED WITH PFS: PROOF

To use *PFS: Proof.* you must have a two-drive system, or a system with a floppy disk drive and a hard (permanent) disk drive. Furthermore, at least one of those drives must be a double sided disk drive. In its original release (May, 1984), it was made available only for MS-DOS computers such as the IBM PC and compatible computers.

PFS:Proof does not supply a second (backup) disk in the *PFS:Proof* package. Instead, there are instructions for making a backup disk. There is an embedded counter in the backup program that allows only one copy to be made. The sample document that comes on the original must be transferred onto a second disk that is placed in Drive B in order to follow the demonstration provided in the documentation. Even with the additional inconvenience of that arrangement, a thorough working knowledge of the program can be accomplished within 60 to 90 minutes. That could be the wisest investment of an hour and $95 (suggested retail price), that you will make for some time.

USING PFS: PROOF

Unlike other PFS program modules, there are no provisions for making *PFS:Proof* self-booting by transferring the operating system onto the disk. The program may be started by inserting the program disk in drive A and the document to be proofed in drive B, and then typing PROOF at the DOS Ready prompt. Normally, the document will be a disk that has files created with *PFS:Write*; however, *Proof* also works with any standard ASCII files or with WordStar files. Typing PROOF at the DOS Ready prompt brings the appearance of the *PFS:Proof* Main Menu shown in Fig. 6-1.

A shortcut method allows the user to begin proofing a document automatically. For example, if we have created a letter using *PFS:Write* and named it TEST we could achieve immediate proofing of that document by typing, PROOF B:TEST. Keep the *PFS:Proof* program disk resident in the drive at all times.

Another variation from the norm in this program is that the Enter key as well as the F10 key can be used to designate "continue." Typing 1 PROOF DOCUMENT and pressing a continue key will automatically provide a directory of the disk on drive B similar to that seen in Fig. 6-2. Below the direc-

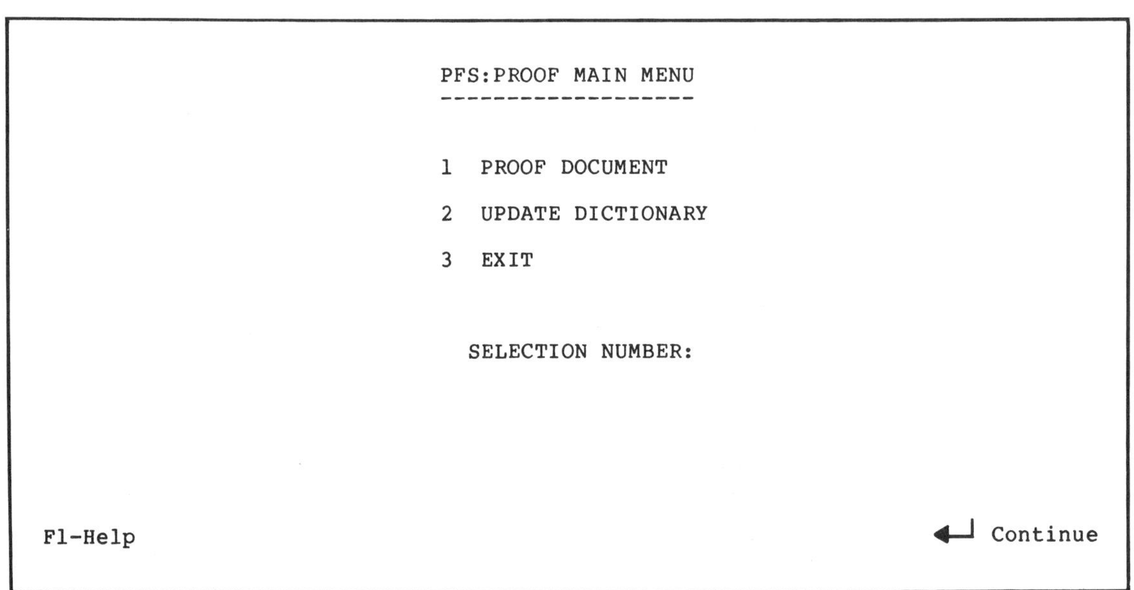

Fig. 6-1. PFS:PROOF Main Menu.

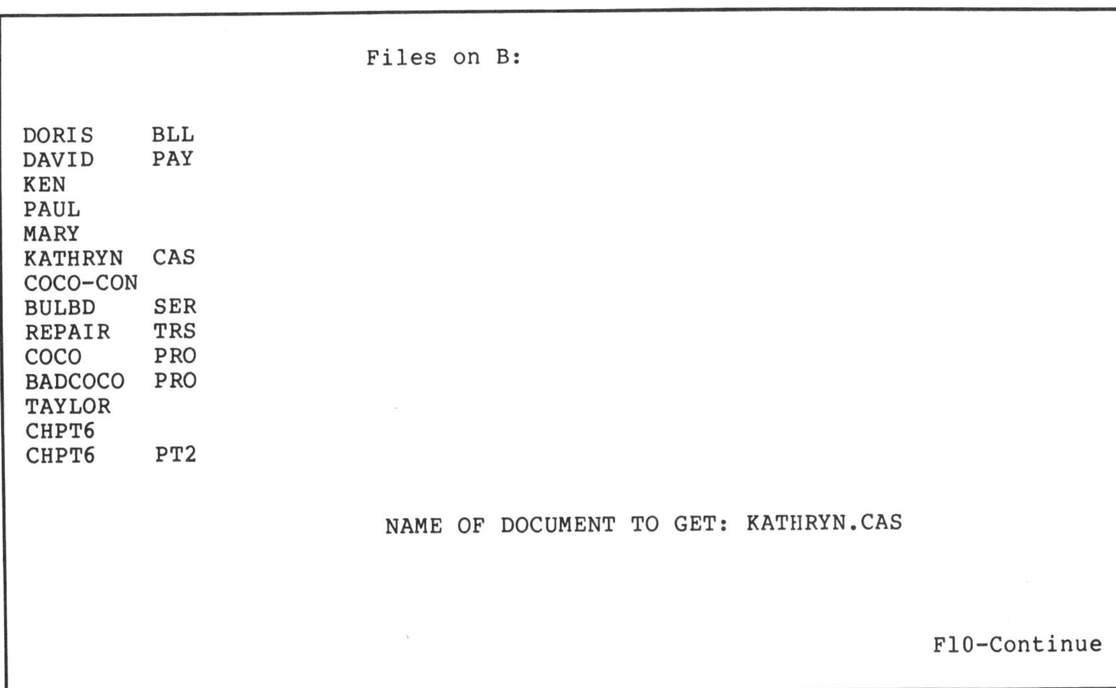

```
Files on B:

DORIS     BLL
DAVID     PAY
KEN
PAUL
MARY
KATHRYN   CAS
COCO-CON
BULBD     SER
REPAIR    TRS
COCO      PRO
BADCOCO   PRO
TAYLOR
CHPT6
CHPT6     PT2

NAME OF DOCUMENT TO GET: KATHRYN.CAS

F10-Continue
```

Fig. 6-2. A directory listing of document files on drive B.

tory of files is a prompt, DIRECTORY OR DOCUMENT NAME:". Typing the proper filename and a continue key will begin the proofing procedure. If the filename is typed incorrectly, a CAN'T FIND FILE message will appear, and you will have another opportunity to input the proper name. The Escape key may be used at any time to terminate a procedure and return to the main menu.

When the proofing operation begins, a message PROOFING PAGE 1 OF Filename appears at the top of a window. The window will display the text of the document that is being proofed when there is a pause to question the spelling of a word, an irregular capitalization, or repeated word. Immediately below the window is the prompt GUESS: that will contain the program's "best guess" of the word to be substituted for the incorrect word. On the bottom of the screen are references for the uses of the function keys. Figure 6-3 shows the appearance of the screen in the proofing process.

F1-HELP is an on-screen help message (Fig. 6-4). It can be a handy reference before the use of the program has become perfectly clear.

F8-GUESS AGAIN is a means of indicating to the program that its "best guess" is not correct, and it should try again. Sometimes the program cannot provide a "best guess." It then informs you with the message NO GUESSES. There are ways of directing the program that will be explained in more detail in the "Correcting Spelling" section. The user may

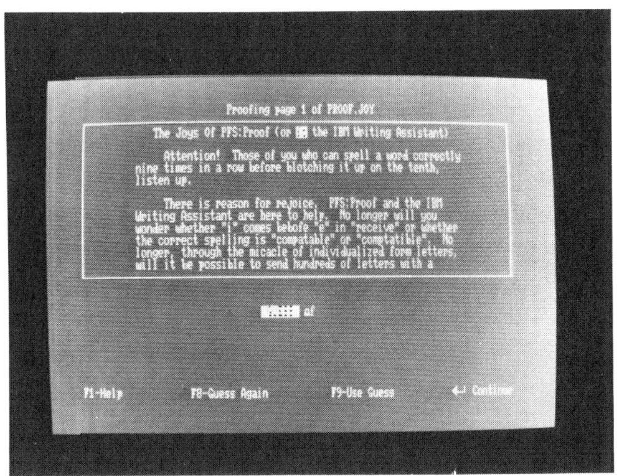

Fig. 6-3. A display of *PFS:Proof* in action, with misspelled word highlighted.

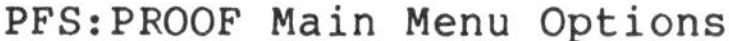

```
                    PFS:PROOF Main Menu Options

Option                To Do

PROOF DOCUMENT        Check a document file for misspellings, irregular
                      capitalization, and repeated words.

UPDATE DICTIONARY     Add or remove words in the copy of the Personal Dictionary
                      that is now in memory.

EXIT                  Leave PFS:PROOF.

     To return to the Main Menu from any part of PFS:PROOF, press the Esc key.
     If you press Esc while proofing a document, you may resume proofing the
     same document by selecting Option 1 again.

                         Press ↵ to continue
```

Fig. 6-4. Help screen for *PFS:Proof* explains each of the main menu options.

insert his/her own correction at any time in the space following the GUESS prompt and is not limited only to the guesses of the computer program.

F9-USE GUESS indicates that the word following the GUESS prompt is acceptable and should be inserted in the text of the document in place of the highlighted word in the window.

F10 or Enter indicates that the program should continue with its proofing operation. If the word that has appeared in the highlighted block in the window is correct and you want no change, the continue key should be pressed. At that time, the use of F9 changes to F9-ADD TO DICTIONARY. Pressing F9 will then cause the word to be added permanently to your dictionary. Pressing the continue key without pressing F9 causes the program to simply ignore the occurrence of the questionable word and proceed to check the rest of the words in the document.

CORRECTING SPELLING ERRORS

When a word is identified by the *PFS:Proof* program as being questionable, it is highlighted by a white box in the window of the proofing display screen (Fig. 6-3). As an example, the program could identify a word in question, "resourses," and guesses that the word should be "resources." We agree and press F9-Use Guess. Now the proper word has been inserted in the block. Pressing Enter or F10 causes the program to search through the rest of the document looking for words that do not match its dictionary. *PFS:Proof* also recognizes words that have been run together, without a space between, and is "smart" enough to make a guess that the words should be separated. For example, "spacebetween" will be highlighted as questionable, and the "Guess" will be "space between."

Later in the document, the program finds a typographical error, "Corpration." It searches and searches but comes up with no "Guess" as to the proper spelling and informes us, "NO GUESSES." We have several options. First, we could simply type in the correct spelling of "Corporation" and press F9 to effect the substitution of the correct word for the incorrect one.

There are two other ways to find a word that utilize the power of the "on disk dictionary" to our advantage. A question mark (?) may be inserted in the position of the character that is in doubt. If we didn't know whether the word that is often abbreviated "Corp." is really "corporation" or "corparation," we could type "Corp?ration" after the Guess prompt and press F8-Guess Again. *PFS:Proof* will search its dictionary and quickly insert "Corporation" in the "Guess" space. Pressing F9-Use Guess will insert the correct spelling of the word in the highlighted position of the document. Furthermore, *PFS:Proof* will have "learned" of our tendency to misspell that word. The next time it occurs, it will not supply "NO GUESS," but will guess that the correct word is "Corporation." This "learning" is of a fairly permanent variety. It will supply the learned word even after the computer has been turned off and the program has rebooted.

Another way to query the dictionary to supply the correct spelling of a questionable is to use the familiar ".." wildcard. For example, suppose the program highlights a word as questionable and responds with the NO GUESS message. If we know the beginning and ending of the word, the program will search for words in its dictionary that match the pattern of letters that you supply. For example, if we enter "alc..ism" in the Guess prompt area, and press F8-Guess Again, the dictionary will supply the word, "alcoholism." Pressing F9-Use Guess inserts the proper word in the proper space.

Using the ".." wildcard search can take up to several minutes to find a match. For example, typing "cond..ding" to find the word "condescending" will take a while because it will start searching for one letter in the wild card spaces, then two, and so on until there is a match with the new four letters supplied. The search may be terminated at any time by typing a period (.) during the search of letters.

FINDING REPEATED WORDS

PFS:Proof identifies repeated words and gives the user a chance to eliminate one of the repeated words. Repeated words, such as "the the" and "is is," are very difficult for human proofers to find, especially if the human proofer is also the writer. When repeated words are identified, the second occurrence of the word is highlighted, and the space under the window that usually has the Guess prompt will have a REPEATED WORD prompt. The function F9 changes to F9-Delete Repeated Word. Pressing F9 eliminates the offending second word. If a repeated word was accidentally removed, it may be replaced by pressing F9 again before pressing the continue key. Repeated words do not necessarily have to be changed. If they should not be changed, pressing the F10 or Enter keys will cause the repeated words to be ignored. The program will go on looking for other questionable words or capitalizations in your document.

FINDING IRREGULAR CAPITALIZATION

Sometimes the shift key is accidentally depressed for an extra keystroke after the intended capitalization. *PFS:Proof* will identify questionable capitalizations. The program assumes that the capitalization is correct if only the first letter of the word is capitalized, or if it is in all uppercase or lowercase letters. Any other combination is questionable. When the program finds an irregular capitalization, it is highlighted in a white box in the window. The prompt IRREGULAR CAPITALIZATION followed by its "best guess" appears beneath the window. F8-Guess Again allows guesses to be made; F9-Use Guess inserts the guess into the document, and the continue key causes the program to move on to the rest of the document.

SAVING THE CORRECTED DOCUMENT ON DISK

If no changes have been made in your document, the message PROOFING COMPLETED NO CHANGES MADE TO THE DOCUMENT appears. Pressing the continue key returns the user to the Main Menu. If any changes have been made on the document, however, the directory of the documents on file on the B drive will be displayed with the notice PROOFING COMPLETED immediately below the directory (Fig. 6-5). Also appearing is a prompt SAVE PROOFED DOCUMENT AS, with the space following it supplying the original name of the document. Pressing the continue key will cause the altered document to be saved directly over the original document on the disk. If you want to recall the original document as it appeared before the document was proofed, you may type in a unique filename for the revised document.

Only the proofed version of the document has been changed. If you have followed good computing practices and kept a backup version, one version will be corrected, and one version will be incorrect.

Since you will have to reload *PFS:Write* to print the document anyway, it is probably easier to load the revised document and save it to the backup disk than it is to reproof the backup version a second time. It is fun, though, to proof backup versions of documents to see what the *PFS:Proof* program has learned about your errors.

You should recognize the limitations of *PFS:Proof.* It will not find errors of syntax, convoluted sentence structure, or dangling participles. If a word is spelled correctly but used incorrectly, it will not be highlighted. For example, "their," "there," and "they're" will all pass the spelling check, but may fail a grammar usage test.

UPDATING YOUR DICTIONARY

Even with 100,000 words, the program's dictionary is not complete. Proper names are not included. Vocabularies of special words from special disciplines are not included. I was surprised that the two-letter abbreviations of the 50 states are not included. *PFS:Proof* makes it as convenient as possible to update your word list.

The first opportunity you will probably have to add a word to your personal dictionary is in the proofing process itself. *PFS:Proof* will highlight a questionable word that is perfectly all right. It may even be your name. You don't want the program to stop every time it encounters your name, so adding the word to a permanent dictionary is a very useful option. When my disk encountered "Burton," it was highlighted. I pressed Enter to continue, and the message 'BURTON' IS NOT IN THE DICTIONARY appeared. When the highlighted word is acceptable, pressing the continue key once causes the prompt beside F9 to change to F9-Add to Dictionary. Pressing F9 will add the word permanently to your dictionary. That's all there is to it. From that point on, the word will match the computer program's dictionary and no longer be questionable. If the word is unlikely to be used often, it is probably not worth using the room on the disk to store it. In that case, simply pressing the continue key again causes the program to temporarily accept that word and continue with its proofing task.

Another way to add words to the dictionary is a direct approach by using the second option on the Main Menu, 2 UPDATE DICTIONARY. That ac-

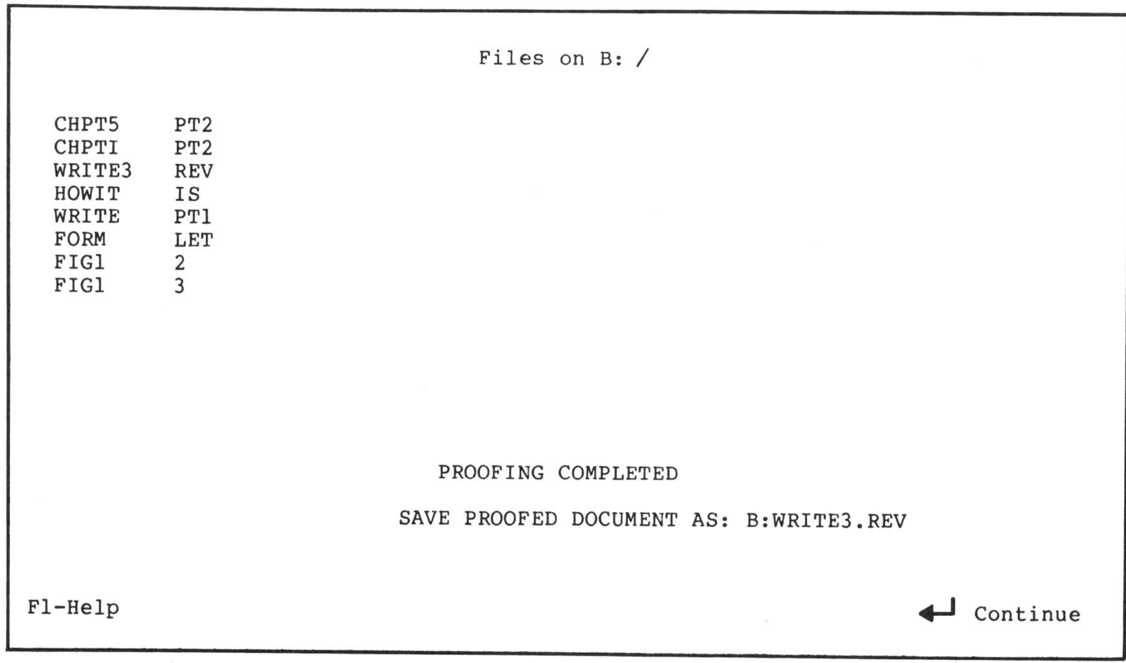

Fig. 6-5. Proofing completed message with prompt of document name supplied for saving corrected version.

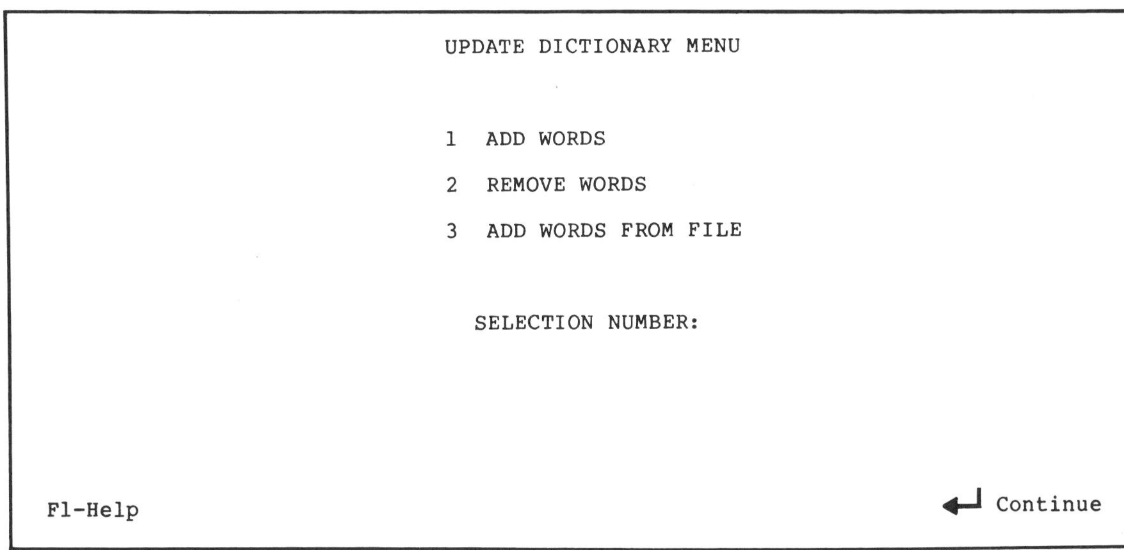

Fig. 6-6. UPDATE DICTIONARY MENU.

tion will bring the UPDATE DICTIONARY MENU to the screen as seen in Fig. 6-6. Choosing 1 ADD WORDS and pressing the continue key will cause your PERSONAL DICTIONARY LIST that has been saved on your disk to be displayed. A sample personal dictionary is shown in Fig. 6-7. Near the bottom of the screen is a prompt "WORD TO ADD." The cursor blinks in expectation of you entering a new word. You may Escape back to the main menu without entering a new word. Any newly

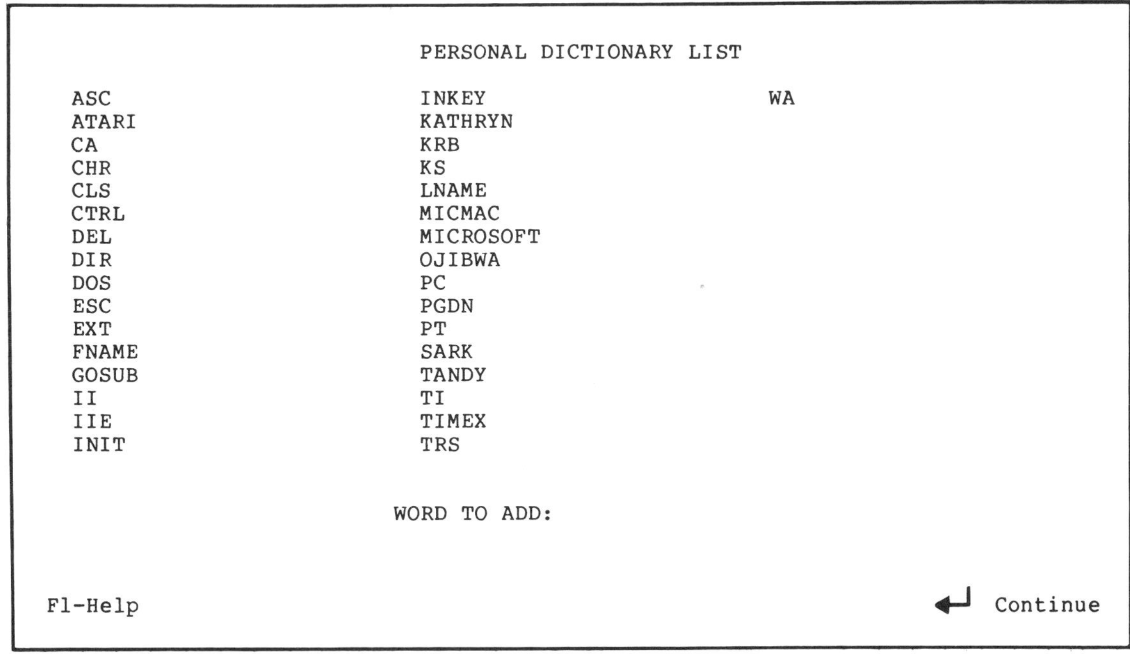

Fig. 6-7. A sample personal dictionary showing words that have been added to the dictionary provided.

entered words will be instantly alphabetized while the program waits for the next WORD TO ADD. When the process of adding words has been completed, press Escape and you will be returned to the main menu.

The second option on the UPDATE DICTIONARY MENU, 2 REMOVE WORDS, works in exactly the same manner, except words are removed from rather than added to the dictionary. If lots of new words have been added to your personal dictionary, the PgUp and PgDn keys allow successive screens of words to be viewed. A shortcut method is available to take you directly to the area you want to view before deleting a word. Typing "T.." at the WORD TO REMOVE prompt, for example, will show you a screen of words beginning with the first word that begins with T.

The creation of some specialized dictionaries would be quite a typing task. The third option on the inner UPDATE DICTIONARY MENU, 3 ADD WORDS FROM FILE, allows for a convenient alternative to hours of typing. Specialized vocabularies are available on disk for legal, medical, and computer terms. These specially prepared disk files can be read directly into the program. Only those words that do not already exist on the program disk will be added to the dictionary. When the task has been completed, the program automatically returns to the Main Menu.

EXITING THE PROGRAM AND SAVING NEW WORDS

In previous program modules, I have stated that it is good operating procedure to use the EXIT option of the programs to ensure that all operations have been properly terminated and all files closed. With *PFS:Proof* it is both good operating procedure and also necessary in order to permanently store the words you have added to your dictionary. If the computer were to be turned off before the 3 EXIT option of the Main Menu were utilized, the program disk would not be updated. If you accidentally remove your program disk before pressing the 3 EXIT selection, there will be an error message prompting you to correct the situation PUT PFS:PROOF PROGRAM DISK IN DRIVE A.

PFS:Access— Talking with the World

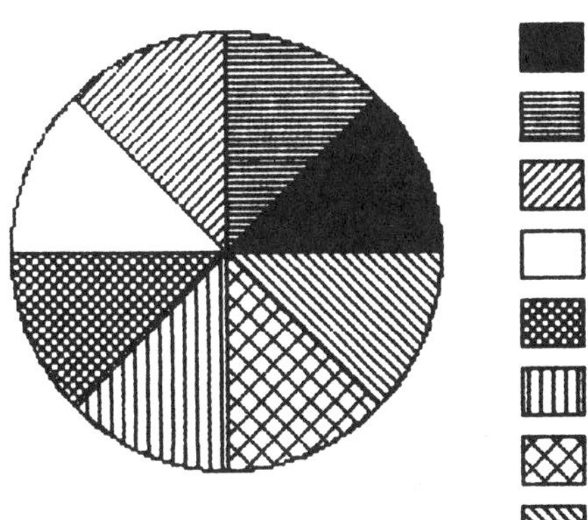

Chapter 7

With all due respect to the post office, who has not had personal experience with a lost letter? Who has not experienced an instance when an important letter or check has taken a week or more to arrive? On the other hand, how often have you spoken on the telephone and assumed everything was wrapped up only to wish you had it in black and white? How often have you been unable to reach the person to whom you would like to speak? Telecommunications using a microcomputer combines the timeliness of a telephone with the security of a letter. Telecommunications also allows possibilities of accessing large databases, of electronic shopping and banking, and more.

PFS:Access is communications software that simplifies communications with electronic services. It is not a terminal program for communicating directly with other computers. In order to use it, you need a modem that allows your computer to send and receive messages over telephone wires. At the time this book was written, it was only available for the IBM PC and IBM PCjr and selected MS-DOS microcomputers. A similar program for the Apple *II*e and other computers is in development. As part of Software Publishing Corporation's integrated concept, *Access* allows you to send *PFS:Write* and *PFS:Report* documents and letters.

GETTING STARTED WITH *PFS:ACCESS*

PFS:Access, like *PFS:Proof*, requires that you make your own backup using the BACKUP program included on the program disk. There is an internal counter that allows for only one backup. After the backup copy is made and the DOS Ready > prompt appears, typing ACCESS and ENTER will cause the program to begin execution and bring the user to the *PFS:Access* Main Menu of Fig. 7-1. There are five preselected services on disk with provisions for adding three of your own. A help screen is available by pressing F1-help (Fig. 7-2). Different help screens are available throughout all of the program's operations.

The first time you use *PFS:Access*, you must tell the program the type of modem you will be using. Do so by pressing 9 CHOOSE MODEM and F10 to continue. The CHOOSE MODEM Menu will

```
                PFS:ACCESS Main Menu
                --------------------

        1.  CompuServe          6.  Other Service

        2.  Dow Jones           7.  Other Service

        3.  EasyLink            8.  Other Service

        4.  MCI Mail            9.  Choose Modem

        5.  THE SOURCE          E.  Exit

                    Selection:


F1-Help                                       F10-Continue
```

Fig. 7-1. PFS:ACCESS Main Menu.

appear (Fig. 7-3). Twelve of the most popular modems are listed as well as accommodations for using any other modem (you will have to specify technical information for the use of other modems).

The selection prompt requires the input of the number corresponding to the modem that you will be using. MODEM CONNECTS TO COM1 OR COM2 supplies a default value of COM1. That value will probably be correct unless you are using a serial printer. The ROTARY OR TOUCH TONE

```
                PFS:ACCESS Main Menu

Before using ACCESS for the first time, you must indicate which modem
your computer is using.  To do this, select option 9.

To access one of the displayed services, enter its number and
press F10 at the Selection: item.

To define a new service, select one of the Other Service options
and then answer the questions on the Service Information form.

Select E to leave ACCESS and return to DOS.



                Press F10 to continue
```

Fig. 7-2. PFS:ACCESS Help screen explains startup procedures.

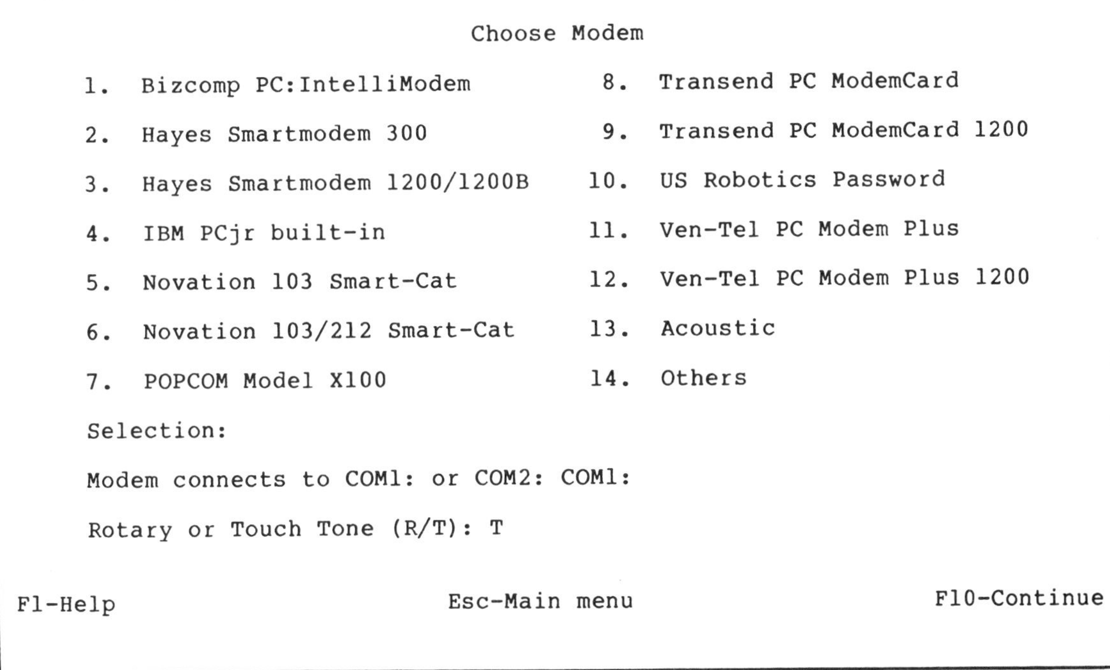

Fig. 7-3. Choose Modem Menu provides choice of most popular modems or of supplying information for not-so popular ones.

(R/T) prompt allows you to specify the type of telephone being used. This is necessary because the clicking of a rotary telephone will be interpreted incorrectly in today's touch-tone world. Once you have specified the type of system that you are using, pressing F10 will record that information on disk, and it will not have to be specified again unless your equipment changes. That action will also return the program to the Main Menu.

USING THE SERVICES

The first step in being able to use the available electronic services is to make arrangement to subscribe and pay for them. Included with the program package are coupons worth a total of more than $200 from each of the services that want your business. Listed are summaries of the services supplied by each of the five services in the PFS:Access Main Menu.

CompuServe—(An H&R Block Company). The CompuServe Information Service is currently the largest commercially operated Videotex service. It features news from electronic newspapers and international newswires, an electronic encyclopedia, family information, national electronic bulletin boards, electronic mail, securities information, personal finance services, travel information, and entertainment.

Dow Jones—(Dow Jones News/Retrievel®. Dow Jones Quotes provides current market quotes with only a 15-minute delay during market hours. Dow Jones Business and Economic News provides highlights from the *Wall Street Journal* and weekly economic updates, as well as freetext searches that enable the finding of information about specific topics dating back to June 1979. Financial and investment services are available from Forbes Directory, Merril Lynch Research Service, Japan Economical Daily, and others. General news and information services include an encyclopedia, news, sports, and weather information retrieval, and cinema reviews. An official airline guide can provide schedules and fares for flights throughout the world. MCI Mail is also available to members of Dow Jones News/Retrieval.

EasyLink—(Western Union EasyLink).

With EasyLink, you can send and receive messages to electronic mail boxes, send mail to people without computers, and access Western Union's WorldWide Telex network. Mail to people without computers or Telex is received at Western Union offices and delivered as quickly as you want to pay for it. EasyLink users also have access to FYI News, sports, and weather. Selected categories of information may be accessed.

MCI Mail. MCI Mail offers computer to electronic post office box and computer to end user service. For an additional fee, MCI can even print your letters on replicas of your own stationery through the use of laser printers. Costs for these express services are typically 30-50% less than traditional express services. The current cost for sending mail to an electronic mail box is $1. An MCI letter, printed and usually delivered within the next day, is $2. Guaranteed overnight delivery (by noon) is $6. A four-hour letter is hand-delivered for a cost of $25. MCI Mail customers also receive a complimentary subscription to Dow Jones News/Retrieval.

The SOURCE-(A Subsidiary of The Reader's Digest Association Inc.) The SOURCE is similar in its scope to the CompuServe service. SourceMail uses electronic mail boxes. Western Union Mailgrams and first class U.S. Mail (usually local, quick delivery) can also be used for communication with people without computers. Live conversations, teleconferencing options, news from UPI wire service, financial news, quotes, and histories are available. Employment services, electronic shopping, member publishing, games, bulletin boards, and research aids round out its substantial list of offerings.

Three other frequently used services may be set up and used in a similar manner. Also, protocols for the various services may be deleted from the Main Menu when they are no longer needed. An increasing number of data bases are being established. They range from MEDLINE from the National Library of Medicine, which enables professional searches of topics from more than 3000 medical journals, to BRS After Dark by Bibliographic Retrieval Service, a collection of over 80

```
                      Service Information

    Service name: MCI Mail

    Telephone number:

    Create automatic sign-on (Y/N): N


                    Communications Settings


    Modem speed (300 or 1200): 300
    Data bits (7 or 8): 8
    Stop bits (1 or 2): 1
    Parity (none,odd,even,mark,space): NONE
    Half of full duplex (H/F): F


F1-Help                    Esc-Main menu                   F10-Continue
```

Fig. 7-4. Service information screen in which all of the technical information needed to connect with MCI Mail has been provided by the program.

different data bases. The information explosion can become manageable if you can effectively use the tools available to you.

All of the technical information required to access the services listed, such as baud rates, data bits, stop bits, and parity, are provided. Only the telephone number to access the service in your area is omitted. Figure 7-4 illustrates the manner in which the information is already provided. The number, including any digits that have to be dialed in order to get an outside or WATTS line, may be entered and permanently stored in the program's protocol. Commas may be entered to signify waiting periods that are usually required to connect to outside lines. If your modem has autodialing capabilities, the complete sequence of accessing a service—including dialing, confirming connection, and entering passwords—can be done by the *PFS:Access* program. Technical information to any of the other services you need will be provided by the service you pay for, and it will need to be entered into the computer only once.

OPTIMIZING THE USE OF *PFS:ACCESS*

Most services charge according to the amount of time that you have spent on the system. Also, the cost of telephone time must be considered. Therefore, it is most efficient to create your document ahead of time using *PFS:Write* or *PFS:Report*. In using MCI Mail, for example, two prompts appear, "name of text file to send" and "privacy code." By entering the filename of the document to be sent, the document can be retrieved in a matter of a couple of seconds. "Privacy Code" enables you to encrypt a document so that the output appears as a garbled group of random characters, unless the receiver is able to supply the same code as you have used.

In receiving information, either from an electronic mail box or from other services such as bulletin boards, the same principles apply. When receiving information, use the F6, Save key to save all of the information, including your commands, on your disk. That way you can scroll back and forth through materials received or even print them out at your convenience. If someone has sent you an encrypted message, it should be returned to normal text format before saving.

CONSIDERATIONS FOR IMPLEMENTING *PFS:ACCESS*

"Time is money" is a well-known saying, but many organizations balk at investing $500 in a modem and additional charges for connecting to a service. There is tendency to take the attitude: "The mails have worked for all of these years. Why change?" That may be true for many organizations, and I am certainly not one to recommend solutions when there are no problems; however, a thorough assessment of your needs should be made. How much time is spent waiting for the arrival of some information before work can continue? What is the potential loss if materials are delayed or not delivered? How much premium is there on timely exchange of information. What is the quantity of information exchanged?

Some nonprofit agencies, for example, undertake an advocacy role for the people they represent. Often that advocacy translates itself into legislative lobbying efforts and support or opposition to legislative bills. We know that telegrams carry more clout than letters, which in turn carry more clout than telephone messages. If that activity occurs a few times a year, individual telegrams would be considerably more cost effective. If, however, your effort requires coordinating grass roots support, informing lots of people quickly, and communicating that concern to your legislators, nothing could be more effective than judicious use of telecommunications. A four-hour letter may be the difference between winning and losing an important vote. That service may not be available through any other means.

Bringing It All Together—Creatively

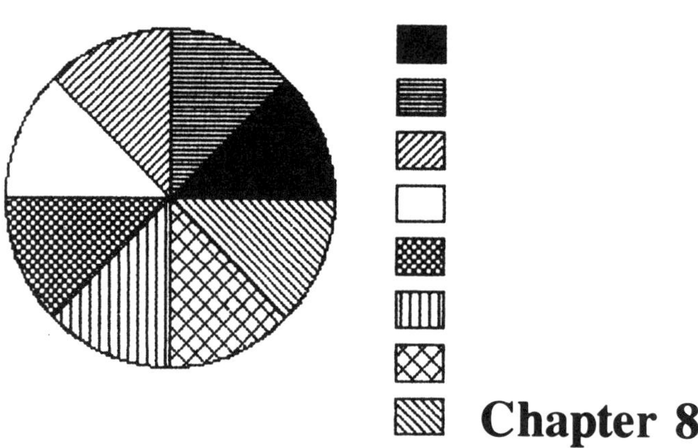

Chapter 8

All of the PFS program modules are handy tools. Each one is potentially helpful in solving a particular business need. Each one can help your operation to become more efficient and productive. Each program can be conceptionalized as a tool. It is great to be able to use a tool such as a screwdriver. Sometimes, though, it is necessary to use a wrench to make the screwdriver of any value. Spinning around and around will not get the job done. Likewise, your most effective use of PFS software occurs when you become a master craftsman in using all of the program modules.

Figure 8-1 illustrates the ways in which all of the PFS program modules interact. As can be plainly seen, *PFS:Write* is the most central program to the system of interaction. It interacts with each of the other program modules. The processing of words, with the support of tables and charts, is central to the communication process. Gathering data, displaying it, or transmitting it is not the final purpose; the goal in using computer technology is to be able to more effectively communicate information.

Second to *PFS:Write* in the amount of interaction with other program modules is *PFS:File*. Again, this seems logical as it is the organizational tool of the series. Communications structured through an organized system makes the system efficient. The ability to communicate is good. The ability to route that information to the proper channels and to properly record and follow up on those communications is critical to success.

Another of the tools frequently used with others in the series is *PFS:Graph*. It is partially a function of today's limited technology that graphics are not an even more critical aspect of communications. Certainly, information is transmitted more clearly and concisely through graphics, or a combination of letters and graphics, than by words alone. Letters of the alphabet are easily transmitted between computers, whether from Apple to IBM or from TI to Tandy and onto a Telex machine. This free exchange has been made possible due to the acceptance of a standard that maintains a consistent format. ASCII standards allow CHR$(1) to be interpreted as an "A" all across the United States and the

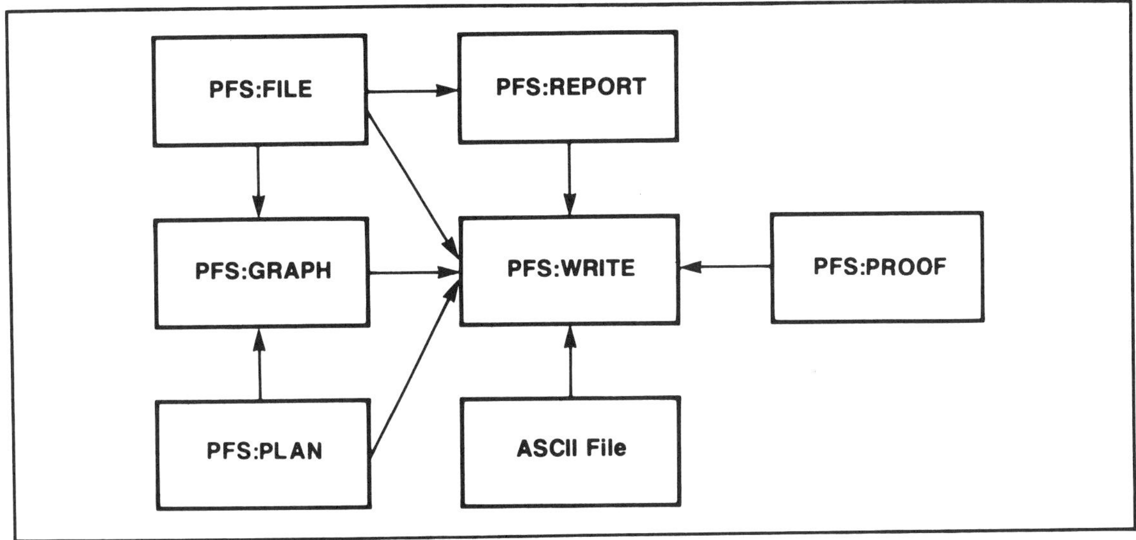

Fig. 8-1. Diagram showing the channels of program interaction.

world. There has been no such standardization of graphics. Each computer has vastly different graphics capabilities, and there is no standard to adhere to. Therefore, telecommunications, at least between different kinds of computers, must currently rely on words and numbers to effect communications.

Another limitation involves the current state-of-the-art for printers. Usually a decision has to be made as to whether to buy a letter quality printer or a printer that does graphics. Some printers are now beginning to offer both capabilities. Some people are opting to buy a reasonably priced letter quality printer and a plotter or dot matrix printer for their graphics needs. That is an expense many of us cannot afford.

The more interaction that you have between program modules, the more convenient it is to have a system with a hard disk drive (see Chapter 1). Systems such as the IBM PC/XT have the advantage of switching between programs almost instantaneously, and without the necessity of swapping disks.

USING *PFS:WRITE* AND *PFS:GRAPH* TOGETHER

Let's leave the theoretical and return to practical examples to illustrate the ways in which utilizing PFS programs in combination can enhance the clarity of communication. After all, I do not want to be accused of describing the perfect "skyhook," a tool that does not exist. PFS brings modern technology within the grasp of nonprogrammers and "nontechies"—those of us who may not care about stacks, registers, and pointers, but who want to use their power.

The letter of thanks in Chapter 5 can be used to illustrate the effectiveness of merging a graph into the body of the letter. Figure 8-2 shows the chart "in black and white," while Figs. 8-3 through 8-6 show how the chart was defined and the data values used to create the chart. The chart merged with the letter effectively communicates the idea that the new computer and software will decrease administration time and increase services, and it also transmits a sense of excitement about the demonstration. "Wow! We can do that? I want to see it."

A photograph of the resulting chart can be seen on the back cover for this book. In order to use this chart within our letter, it must first be saved onto the disk in the form of a "picture." To do so, get to the PFS:Graph Main Menu (it may first be necessary to press ESC). Press 4 GET/SAVE/REMOVE, supply the filename of the graph, and press

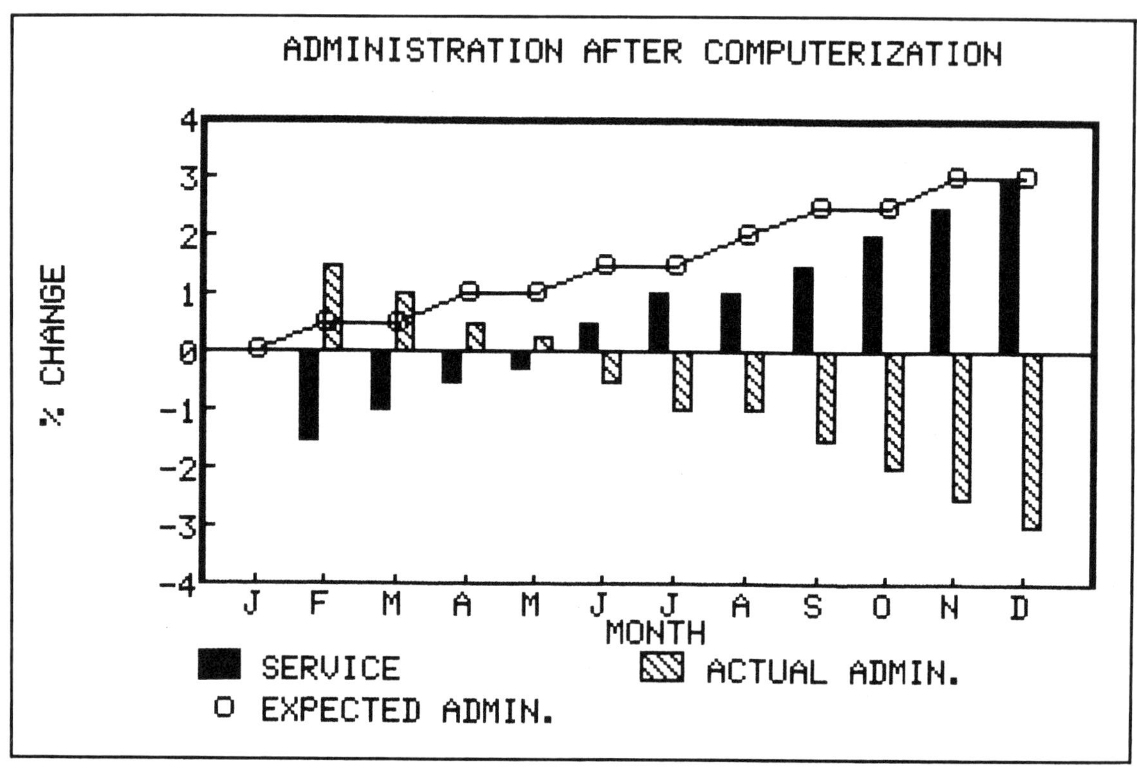

Fig. 8-2. Chart illustrating the way in which administration rises slightly after computerization and then continues to fall.

```
                              DEFINE CHART MENU

                    TYPE                          LEGEND                  CUM
     GRAPH
*      A         BAR                       SERVICE                        N
*      B         BAR                       ACTUAL ADMIN.                  N
*      C         LINE                      EXPECTED ADMIN.                N
       D                                   GRAPH D                        N

  CHART  TITLE: ADMINISTRATION AFTER COMPUTERIZATION
  X-AXIS TITLE:
  Y-AXIS TITLE: % CHANGE

  STACK  (Y/N): N                        Y MIN:
  GRID   (Y/N): N                        Y MAX:
  COLOR  (Y/N): Y                        Y DIV:

                                                                  F10-Continue
```

Fig. 8-3. Chart defined to show contrast of bar and line graphs.

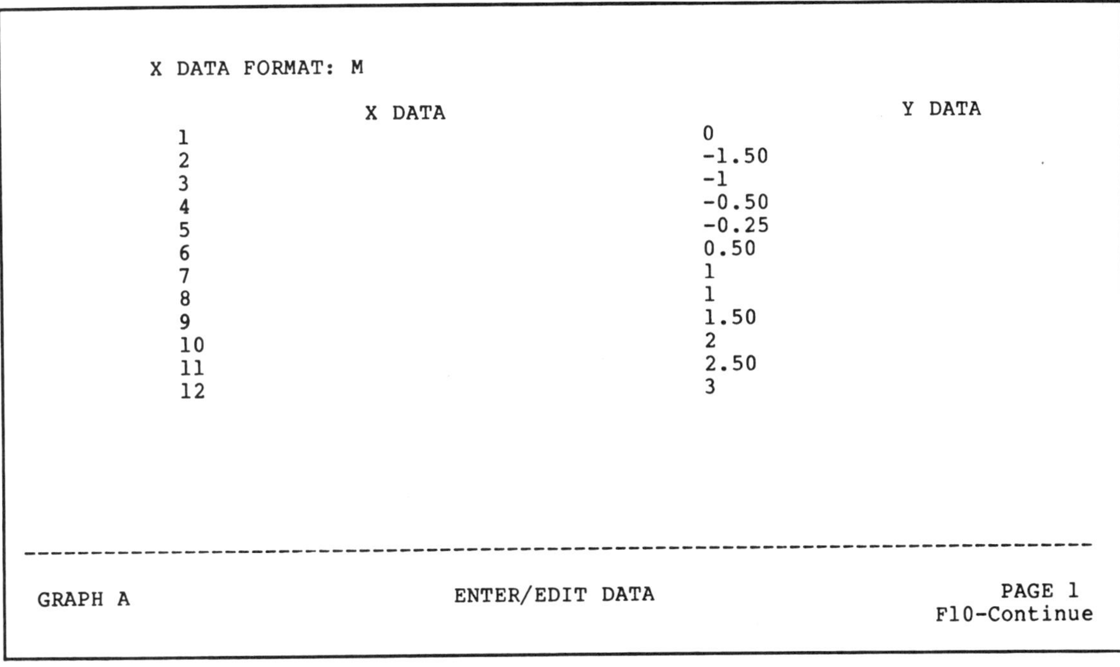

```
X DATA FORMAT: M

                X DATA                          Y DATA
 1                                  0
 2                                  -1.50
 3                                  -1
 4                                  -0.50
 5                                  -0.25
 6                                  0.50
 7                                  1
 8                                  1
 9                                  1.50
 10                                 2
 11                                 2.50
 12                                 3

--------------------------------------------------------------------------------

GRAPH A              ENTER/EDIT DATA                PAGE 1
                                               F10-Continue
```

Fig. 8-4. Data used to determine the points of Graph A.

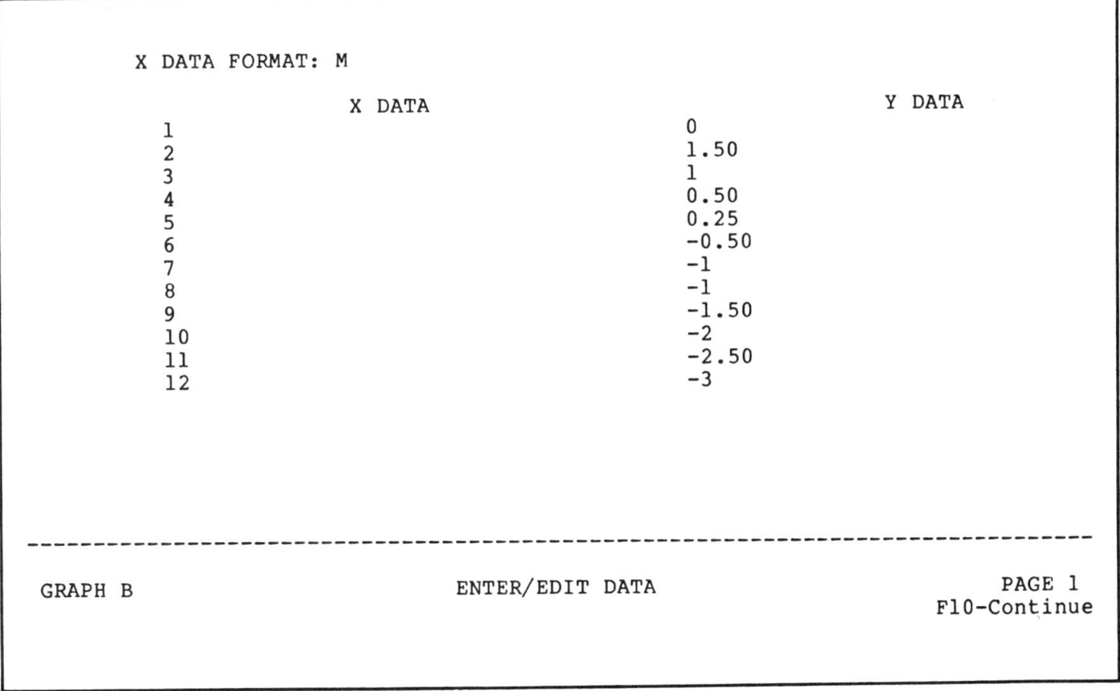

```
X DATA FORMAT: M

                X DATA                          Y DATA
 1                                  0
 2                                  1.50
 3                                  1
 4                                  0.50
 5                                  0.25
 6                                  -0.50
 7                                  -1
 8                                  -1
 9                                  -1.50
 10                                 -2
 11                                 -2.50
 12                                 -3

--------------------------------------------------------------------------------

GRAPH B              ENTER/EDIT DATA                PAGE 1
                                               F10-Continue
```

Fig. 8-5. Data used for Graph B.

```
X DATA FORMAT: M

              X DATA                              Y DATA
1                                        0
2                                        0.50
3                                        0.50
4                                        1
5                                        1
6                                        1.50
7                                        1.50
8                                        2
9                                        2.50
10                                       2.50
11                                       3
12                                       3

---------------------------------------------------------------------
GRAPH C                 ENTER/EDIT DATA                       PAGE 1
                                                         F10-Continue
```

Fig. 8-6. Graph C data.

press the continue key. After its retrieval, press ESC and select 4 GET/SAVE/REMOVE again. This time, select 3 SAVE PICTURE. We will give the chart the filename COVER.PIC. It is not required to give a picture the PIC extension. It is a good practice, though, so that the chart may be easily identified in the list of charts on the disk's directory. The picture of the chart can now be retrieved for inclusion in the body of the letter. Pictures merged directly into a letter take about 18 lines and are about 3½ × 4½ inches large. Exit the *PFS:Graph* program and boot *PFS:Write*. Place the data disk containing the picture of the chart in the second or "B" drive.

After the *PFS:Write* program has booted, select 4 GET/SAVE/REMOVE from the Main Menu. At the inner menu, select 1 GET DOCUMENT and supply WEAVER9.18 for the DIRECTORY OR FILE NAME prompt. That letter, in the form that it was last saved, will be displayed. Move the cursor to the proper location and add a little text to explain the chart that will be included. At the position where the graph should be included, type:

GRAPH B:COVER.PIC (for MS-DOS systems)
or
GRAPH COVER.PIC (for Apple *II*e/c systems)

The use of asterisks in combination with the proper PRINT MENU prompt usage keys the insertion and search and replace features for all of the modules that can supply information to *PFS:Write*. Asterisks, such as those used above, can be printed within a document as long as the PRINT MENU has not indicated Y to the JOINING PFS:Graph (Y/N) prompt. That is a consistent convention used with *PFS:File* as well.

After finishing the letter, press Esc to return to the Main Menu. The PFS:Write Main Menu will appear again. It is time to select 3 PRINT. At the PRINT MENU, use the TAB key to position the cursor beside the prompt that asks, JOINING PFS:Graph (Y/N). Type an uppercase or lowercase Y beside the prompt. In the printing process, the asterisks will instruct the program to "look" for the graph. After pressing the continue key, a PRINTER MENU will appear, prompting you to select the printer. A pie chart should be printed with the same printer that was used when the chart was saved as a picture. Otherwise, the pie chart might not be perfectly round when it is printed. During printing, the program will begin a new page if there are not the 18 lines required for insertion of the graph. I have found that it is most convenient to insert 18 blank lines into the body of the letter so as to maintain the "what you see is what you get" display. That way, it is immediately apparent if there has to be any adjustments in the margins or spacing to make an attractive letter. The program will allow you to insert as many graphs into a document as you wish. Reports or spreadsheets may also be added into the same documents that include graphs.

Next, save the document. Make sure to give the document a unique filename, such as Contrib.pic (contributions, picture). Save letters that began with another letter as a "shell" with a unique filename so as not to lose the original letter from your disk files. During the saving process, the prompt specifying to JOINING PFS:Graph (Y/N): Y will be saved, too.

The end result of a letter modified to include a graph within the body of a letter can only help the process of communication if the graph is germane to the subject. It has that certain amount of pizzazz necessary to attract attention. I bet that the response to the demonstration will be better to this letter than to the "text only" letter. Maybe it will even make the contributors more receptive when they are informed that you need another $600 to install telecommunications capabilities.

USING *PFS:WRITE* AND *PFS:FILE* TOGETHER

One of the greatest time-saving features of computerization is the ability to send individualized form letters. Individualized form letters seem like a contradiction in terms. We are used to form letters that tell us we may have won a contest, and letters from individuals intended for only us.

Form letters are usually thought of as a "Dear Customer" mass mailing. They are usually printed in bulk with offset printing techniques. As technology has become more advanced, they can be printed individually and can include names in the address, salutation, and even in the body of the letter. *PFS:Write* brings that capability and more to your organization. Any field in any of your data bases can be merged into any of your letters. You will select the people to whom the letter is sent by specifying the "retrieve specs" for the data base you are working with.

For example, let's write a letter soliciting contributions for our annual membership drive (Fig. 8-7). Use the mailing list established through the Pierre file to solicit new members. You can see that the recipient's name and title will appear directly in the body of the letter and in the address. The (T) following a field name tells the program to treat the name as Text and adjust the spacing of the line accordingly. That is not necessary in fields such as L3 where the field comprises the entire line.

To produce the desired letters, press ESC to return to the PFS:Write Main Menu and select 3 PRINT. Tab to the last prompt PFS FILE NAME. MS-DOS systems such as the IBM PC require that you identify the drive containing the *PFS:File* data disk, so that you would need to enter B:PIERRE as is shown in Fig. 8-8. Apple *II*e/c users would just answer PIERRE in that prompt while placing the file data disk in the second drive. If you are using individual pieces of stationery for your letters, make sure that the PAUSE BETWEEN PAGES (Y/N) prompt has been answered with a Y so that each page may be inserted.

After pressing the continue key, the program will look to find the *PFS:File* data file Pierre. If the file is not there, the program will inform you with a CAN'T FIND FILE message. If the file is found in the designated drive, you will see your data file form with the status line RETRIEVE SPECS on the status line. We only want to send the letter to people who are not members yet (members will be contacted with a different letter), so we specify "/Y" (Not Yes) beside the field that indicates membership status (Fig. 8-9).

Having specified the retrieve specifications, we press the continue key. We will then be presented with the form, this time with the status line

```
May 1, 1985

*Fname* *Lname**Ext(, Jr.)*
*L2 (T)*
*L3*
*L4 (T)* *Zip*

Dear *Title (Dr.,Ms.)* *Lname (T)*:

     As one who has utilized the services provided by our
agency, you may want to consider supporting our agency by
becoming a member.  This support will allow us to be involved
in more projects, thereby helping even more people.

     Our organization is a certified 501 (c) 3, non-
profit organization and all contributions are tax deductible.
Please take a moment to consider this important opportunity.
A membership form is attached to the back of our
informational brochure.  A check may be enclosed, or
convenient credit information may be supplied in payment.

     We hope that you will decide to join.  Membership, of
course, is not necessary in order to receive the services of
our organization.  We hope that you will continue to utilize
our services.

Sincerely,


Kathryn R. Burton
Membership Chair
```

Fig. 8-7. Form contribution letter designed to reach recipients of organization's services.

```
                              PRINT MENU

                   FROM PAGE: 1   TO PAGE: 1

                   PRINT TO: LPT1:

                   PAUSE BETWEEN PAGES (Y/N): Y

                   NUMBER OF COPIES: 1

                   SINGLE/DOUBLE/ENVELOPE (S/D/E): S

                   INDENT: 0

                   JOINING PFS:GRAPH (Y/N): N

                   PFS FILE NAME: B:PIERRE


F1-Help                                              F10-Continue
```

Fig. 8-8. Completed PRINT MENU for merging with *PFS:File*.

```
Child's d.o.b.(yy/mm/dd):
Title(Dr.,Ms.):
Fname:
Lname:
Ext(, Jr.):
L2:
L3:
L4:                          Zip:
Telephone:
6mo.verify (y/n):            lyr.verify (y/n):
2yr.verity (y/n):            3yr.verify (y/n):      4yr.verify (y/n):

Membership (y/n): /Y
Date Joined:
Amount:




--------------------------------------------------------------------------------
File: B:PIERRE                      RETRIEVE SPEC                        Page  1

                                                                   F10-Continue
```

Fig. 8-9. Retrieve specs for identifying Pierre recipients who are not organization members.

indicating INDENTIFIER SPEC. This allows you to specify any field names that appear differently in the body of the letter than on the *PFS:File* data form. Occasionally we may have placed something like "Membership" as a field to retrieve in the body of the letter when the actual field is "Membership (Y/N)." By typing, "Membership," as the identifier, you may proceed immediately without the need to go back and edit the letter. Most often, there should be no changes necessary, and you will simply press the continue key past the IDENTIFIER SPEC screen. The program will find each form that matches the retrieve criteria that you have designated and prompt you to insert a new piece of paper for every letter. Figure 8-10 shows a completed letter. As you can see, there is no difference between this and a "real" letter.

Envelopes can be conveniently printed that will match each of the printed letters. That can be accomplished by providing the same letter and exactly the same RETRIEVE SPECS. The only change to be made is to indicate Envelope in the PRINT MENU. Envelopes will be printed in the same order as the letters were.

Using a computer generated mailing like this has the ability of paying large dividends. It also has the potential of causing confusion. I would recommend in this instance that the membership form included with this letter be coded in some way so that the Membership (Y/N) field can be updated appropriately. During the next year's membership drive, it could be embarrassing sending the same type of letter if the family has already joined the organization, but did not receive a Y in the proper field of their database file.

CONSIDERATIONS FOR ADVANCED USE OF INDIVIDUALIZED FORM LETTERS

PFS:Write and *PFS:File* can utilize any of the fields found on a form—not only the standards of names and addresses. For example, let's use a letter of thanks to all contributors (Fig. 8-11). The amount of contribution, treated as text, will be inserted in the appropriate place by using the "Amount" field in our MEMBERS database.

Let's assume that we will process a batch of letters once a week during the membership drive

May 1, 1985

Liz Akers
10 Bundle of Joy Lane
Munkinland, MD 14256

Dear Ms. Akers:

As one who has utilized the services provided by our agency, you may want to consider supporting our agency by becoming a member. This support will allow us to be involved in more projects, thereby helping even more people.

Our organization is a certified 501 (c) 3, non-profit organization and all contributions are tax deductible. Please take a moment to consider this important opportunity. A membership form is attached to the back of our informational brochure. A check may be enclosed, or convenient credit information may be supplied in payment.

We hope that you will decide to join. Membership, of course, is not necessary in order to receive the services of our organization. We hope that you will continue to utilize our services.

Sincerely,

Kathryn R. Burton
Membership Chair

Fig. 8-10. Completed letter from form shell.

month. It will be necessary to differentiate the proper letters to send according to the time that their contributions arrived. Avoid sending people two or more letters of thanks for the same contribution. The easiest way to keep track of each of these mailings is through conscientious saving of the form letter each time you change the date and process some letters. Suppose that we last sent the ACK-FM.LET on May 5, 1985. When we recall the letter from our disk on May 12, we change the date of the letter. After pressing 3 PRINT and designating the *PFS:File* as MEMBERS, we are presented with the RETRIEVE SPECS screen. We will search for contribution dates > 85/05/05 (greater than May 5, 1985). After the letters have been sent to contributors whose money was recently received, we will save our ACK-FM.LET again. When we save it, it will include today's date of May 12. We will be warned that the DOCUMENT IS ABOUT TO BE OVERWRITTEN, but we will proceed to save it because in a week or so when it is time to write about some more acknowledgments of contributions, we will have a built-in prompt for the date to use as the basis of our search. Next time, our search criteria will be > 85/05/12.

Individualized form letters do not have to be

form letters at all. There can be information communicated on a unique basis to certain people on the mailing list. Part of the letter will be similar to that being sent to others, or there would be no advantage in processing it along with others. That is one of the reasons I always suggest space on the form for free-form fields, such as "Text". As an example, this form letter to someone borrowing a film and projector allows us to remind him of the necessity of returning the projector by noon because another person has it scheduled after noon (Figs. 8-12 and 8-13).

Free-form text fields work best for forms that are going to be used once, and then stored for records. The major disadvantage in using such fields is that the information inserted in the open field must later be deleted, or it will show up again the next time there is the inclusion of a search and replace field "Text" in another letter.

In the most extreme case, individualized form letters can have only the name and address fields in a "form" format. The rest of the letter can be completely individualized. In that case, it is like having an automatic rolodex to supply the name address and salutation. The major disadvantage of that method is that there will be no record on disk of the

```
May 30, 1985

*Fname* *Lname**Ext(, Jr.)*
*L2 (T)*
*L3*
*L4 (T)* *Zip*

Dear *Title (Dr.,Ms.)* *Lname (T)*:

     Thank you very much for your contribution of *Amount
(T)* to our organization.  It is only through your generosity
that the goals and objectives of our organization are able to
be implemented.  Truely, we are "People helping people".

     Your name will, of course, be on our mailing list to
receive our newsletter and information about all events
related to our area of interest.  Please contact the office
any time that you have any questions or news that we should
know about.

     Please keep this acknowledgement of your contribution
for tax records.  Your contribution is tax deductible.

Sincerely,



Marc J. Wagner
Membership Chair
```

Fig. 8-11. Shell of letter that will thank members for contributions and also provide tax records.

```
May 30, 1984

*Fname* *Lname**Ext(, Jr.)*
*L2*
*L3*
*L4 (T)* *Zip*

Dear *Title (Dr.,Ms.)* *Lname (T)*:

     This letter is to confirm your reservation to use the
film *Film name(T)* on *Date(T)* at *Time(T)*.  You are
scheduled to return the film *Ret.Date(T)* by *Ret.Time(T)*.

     If you are unable to meet this commitment, please notify
us at the earliest possible time.  *Text (T)*

Sincerely,

Steve Bolt
Communications Director
```

Fig. 8-12. Shell of letter for confirmation of film reservations with open text field.

```
May 30, 1984

Bob Ostrander
628 Monterey Avenue
Pinola, CA 94531

Dear Mr. Ostrander:

     This letter is to confirm your reservation to use the
film ONLY HUMAN on June 27, 1984 at 4:00 p.m.  You are
scheduled to return the film June 28 by 12:00 noon.

     If you are unable to meet this commitment, please notify
us at the earliest possible time.  Bob, please remember to
return the film promptly by noon as it is scheduled to be
loaned again at that time.

Sincerely,

Steve Bolt
Communications Director
```

Fig. 8-13. A completed letter confirming the reservation to borrow a film.

complete letter, including the person to whom it was sent, since that information was supplied in the RETRIEVE SPEC prompt.

USING *PFS:WRITE* AND *PFS:REPORT* TOGETHER

At times it will be advantageous to merge information summarized by *PFS:Report* into the body of a letter or memo. In those cases, it will be necessary to run the Report program and "write" the information onto a disk file. *PFS:Write* will then be able to retrieve the report from the disk and insert it into the letter at the proper point.

Suppose that once a month we send a list of outstanding bills to the organization's treasurer for approval for payment. The information we need for the expenditures column has already been collected in *PFS:File*. That is the basis for the greatest part of the report, so why not minimize our efforts and construct a financial report from that information? Normally, however, some of the bills will require an explanation or recommendation. Rather than a straight report, this will call for a combination of a report and a document. This is a task for *PFS:Write* and *PFS:Report*.

First, let's begin with *PFS:Report*. After booting the program, we place the *PFS:File* data disk PAYABLES in the first drive, and a formatted working disk, or "Sortwork" disk into the second drive. Naturally, we would want to pre-define the report in order to use it repeatedly, but for demonstration purposes we will begin by selecting PRINT A REPORT. As is normal, the design of the form will be displayed with the status line reporting that it is in the RETRIEVE SPECS phase of operation.

The forms that we want reported are the ones that were received in June 1984—that is, Date received = 84/06/01 . . 84/06/30 as shown in Fig. 8-14. After pressing the continue key, the REPORT OPTIONS screen will appear. We do not want it printed on paper in the normal fashion, but instead want it stored on a disk file. On IBM and MS-DOS systems, that simply involves changing the default value of "1pt1" for the OUTPUT TO prompt to B:PAY684.RPT or some equally suitable

```
        Invoice no:                 Date received: =84/06/01..84/06/30
        Description:
        Amount:
        Pay to:
        L2:
        L3:
        L4:

        Amount paid:                Date paid:

        Check number:

        Account category:






 --------------------------------------------------------------------------
 File: payables                  RETRIEVE SPEC                      Page 1

                                                              F10-continue
```

Fig. 8-14. Retrieve specifications for identifying only bills received in June of 1984.

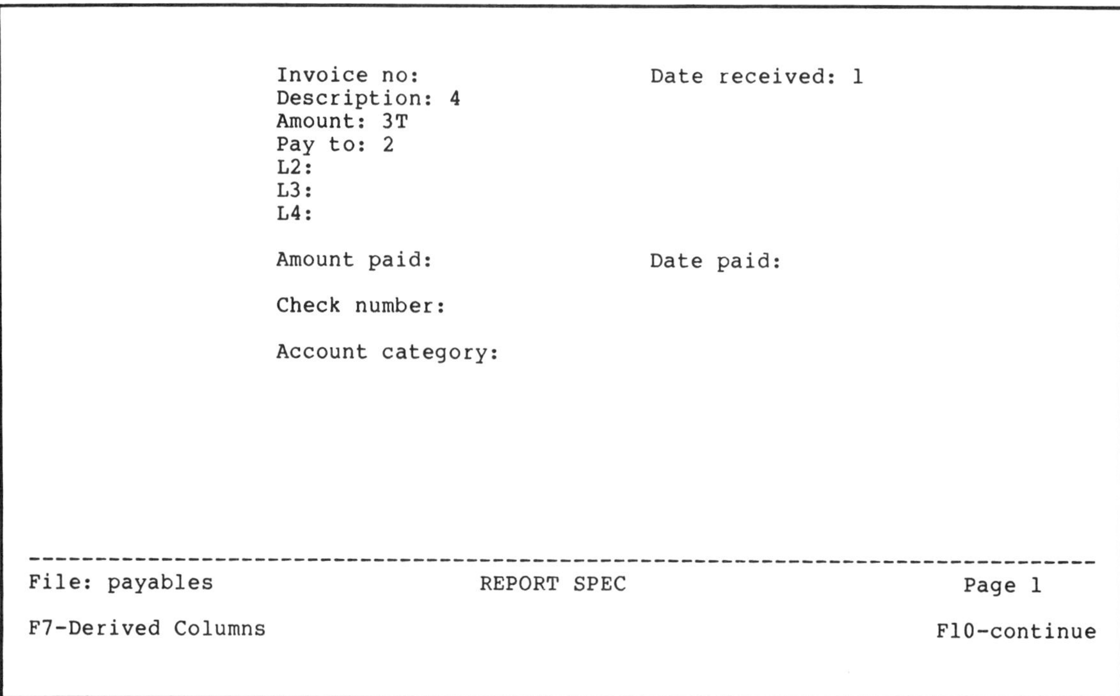

```
Invoice no:                         Date received: 1
Description: 4
Amount: 3T
Pay to: 2
L2:
L3:
L4:

Amount paid:                        Date paid:

Check number:

Account category:

-----------------------------------------------------------------------
File: payables              REPORT SPEC                         Page 1

F7-Derived Columns                                         F10-continue
```

Fig. 8-15. Report specifications for creating a June bills report.

filename. Apple *II*e/c users do not have the opportunity of storing reports on disk. This will mean that reports cannot be merged into *PFS:Write* documents; nor can reports be sent directly with the use of *PFS:Access*.

Pressing on, we see the form design with REPORT SPEC in the status line. We will designate Date received as the first field, since it will make sense to sort the report on an aging basis. The rest of the report specifications will be completed according to Fig. 8-15. Pressing the continue key will cause the report to proceed, and then save the information onto the disk.

Following the creation of the report, we will exit from the report program. Normally it is not too critical to make a backup of such a report. All of the information that created the report is retrievable from the *PFS:File* data disks that are properly backed up. If you choose to create a backup of the report, you may do so by either running the report a second time, or by using the COPY command of your DOS to copy the file onto another disk.

PFS:Write should be booted next. You probably will have stored the introductory message of "Here's the bills" beginning of the letter. All that will have to be changed on each mailing is the date. At the point that you would like to merge the *PFS:Report* into the letter, type:

JOIN B:PAY684.RPT

The report will automatically be inserted at that point during the print phase (Fig. 8-16). The rest of the letter may be dedicated to an explanation of any of the bills, an overview of expected income or expenses, or any other relevant information.

At times it may be necessary to send printer control codes to the printer when the report is wider than 80 columns. That is accomplished by typing *PRINTER control code* where control code is the CHR$ that changes the setting of your printer. For example, *PRINTER 15* will set an Epson MX80 printer into the compressed print mode. Sending another printer control code will return the setting to normal.

```
July 2, 1984

Jodi L. Tyler
2 Doberman Lane
Mystic, CT 05821

Dear Ms. Tyler:

     Here is a listing of the bills received by our
organization during the last month.  I do not believe that
any of the bills requires special explanation.  If you do
have any questions, please do not hesitate to call.


                     June, 1984 Bills

Date received          Pay to                        Amount      Description
-------------   ---------------------------      --------    ----------------
84/06/03        AB Dick                             37.50    Printing supplies
                R & J Properties                   325.00    Rent

84/06/05        Bell telephone                      98.12    Telephone
84/06/08        Professional Administrator          25.00    Subscription
84/06/13        The Learning Co.                   275.00    Film

                                          ----------------
                                          Total:    760.62
                                          ----------------



                          Page 1


     Please do not forget our next Board Meeting on July 10th
at 7:00 p.m.

Sincerely,


Sandy Shatzer
Financial Director
```

Fig. 8-16. A letter that has a *PFS:Report* merged into the body of the text.

USING *PFS:WRITE* AND "CALC" PROGRAMS TOGETHER

VisiCalc, *PFS:Plan*, and other Calc programs may be merged into a *PFS:Write* document in exactly the same manner as *PFS:Reports* are merged. As long as the spreadsheet has been "printed" to a disk, it may be merged with the use of the *JOIN filename* command. Also, printer control codes may be sent to the printer through the use of the *PRINTER* command.

USING *PFS:ACCESS* WITH *PFS:REPORT*

Chapter 7 describes the way in which documents can be created with *PFS:Write*, stored on disk, and then transmitted for maximum on-line efficiency. The same principle applies for transmitting reports created with *PFS:Report* and *PFS:Plan*. Answering the OUTPUT TO prompt with the designation of a disk drive and a filename will store the report to the disk. It can then be retrieved from within *PFS:Access*. All of the normal features of *PFS:Access* are applicable, including the ability to encrypt the data so that the receiver must have the proper password to actually read the report.

Index